AF394369

DEPRAVED

DEPRAVED

the story of

DANGEROUS ART

daisy dixon

faber

First published in 2026
by Faber & Faber Ltd
The Bindery, 51 Hatton Garden
London EC1N 8HN

Typeset by Faber & Faber Ltd
Printed and bound by CPI Group (UK) Ltd, Croydon CR0 4YY

All rights reserved
© Daisy Dixon, 2026

The right of Daisy Dixon to be identified as author
of this work has been asserted in accordance with Section 77
of the Copyright, Designs and Patents Act 1988

A CIP record for this book
is available from the British Library

ISBN 978–0–571–38322–1

Printed and bound in the UK on FSC® certified paper in line with our continuing
commitment to ethical business practices, sustainability and the environment.
For further information see faber.co.uk/environmental-policy

Our authorised representative in the EU for product safety is
Easy Access System Europe, Mustamäe tee 50, 10621 Tallinn, Estonia
gpsr.requests@easproject.com

2 4 6 8 10 9 7 5 3 1

For my mother,
who gave me the freedom and
courage to be myself.

CONTENTS

PREFACE

When I was a teenager, I hated the painter Paul Gauguin. I hated him because I felt deeply protective of my favourite artist, Vincent van Gogh. I'd read about how he and Gauguin lived together for a couple of months in Arles in 1888, and how their friendship quickly became strained and difficult. After weeks of clashing over their artistic visions, one altercation between them on 23 December apparently led to van Gogh severing his own ear with a razor. I always blamed Gauguin for contributing to poor Vincent's mental breakdown.

But later, during my postgraduate studies at Cambridge, I learned details about Gauguin's life that made his treatment of van Gogh pale in comparison. Although an important figure in post-impressionism, Gauguin was a prolific sexual abuser – in his forties he abandoned his own family and then took several child brides in French Polynesia, and it is his portraits of those dark-skinned girls that made him famous; their images that have for centuries adorned the walls of galleries across the world.

So, how should we respond to these paintings? Should we still display them? Should Gauguin be 'cancelled'? Just before the Covid-19 pandemic, I attended a public debate at the London National Gallery about how art-lovers and curators might answer these questions. Once the floor opened to the audience, things got heated. To the idea that we should even discuss this topic, some attendees responded with raised voices, tuts, and sighs; their impatience with so-called 'woke culture' trying to destroy their beloved art and tarnish their favourite artists was palpable. Others, myself included, were concerned that dismissing this philosophical and emotional issue is tantamount to giving Gauguin a moral pass; a wilful avoidance of the horrors that lie beneath his vibrant renderings of French Polynesia – the place he called 'Eden'.

————

A work of art is a strange thing. A single art object can carry us to the soaring peaks of beauty or drag us all the way down to the burning depths of depravity. We often treat artworks as sacred, almost ethereal. But they are an intimate piece of this world – born from the hands of geniuses, and from the hands of monsters. Far from being innocuous and safely contained in museums and white cube galleries, artworks deeply affect our moral compass. Through the ages, paintings, sculptures, novels, films, and music have tested our appetite for wickedness. The atrocities embedded in, and surrounding, so much of art demonstrate the power that these unique human creations exert, and the effects they can have on our daily lives and our treatment of others.

Although it can feel like we live in an era where dangerous art is prevalent to an unprecedented degree, in fact, humans have been making art for at least 73,000 years – and it has not always been innocent or pretty. Art has forever had the power to enchant and delight. But it has also had the capacity to shock, repulse, and harm. In this book I'm going to take you on a journey through the history of immoral art, exploring some of the most controversial and volatile works humanity has ever produced. We will cover art from our prehistoric ancestors and ancient civilisations up to the strange post-modern artworld of today: from cave paintings to videogames and from classical sculpture to extreme metal music. We will learn about erotic literature that has inspired murderers, figurative sculptures that express toxic messages, beautiful paintings created by paedophiles, and enticing performances that use the body – both human and non-human – in troubling ways.

But we're going to do more than that. This is no ordinary art history book. I am a philosopher, and in my day job as a lecturer at Cardiff University, I think, write, and teach about the philosophy of art. How does an artist's own character influence their creations? Can an artwork speak? How does it connect to, or shape, the wider world? So, as well as charting depraved art through history, I will ask (and hopefully answer) some vexing but crucial questions: *how* and *why* is this artwork depraved? *Should* it be considered so? And what should we *do* about it?

At a time when art burns under the spotlight of cultural and political critique, we need more than ever to approach it carefully. We have a responsibility to scrutinise the immoral art in our lives, to take seriously its harmful potential, but also to re-examine what we think is morally bad in the first place. Depravity, as we'll see, can be found in surprising places. Only by understanding the long history of depraved art can we begin to bring our own age into focus, refining the questions we ask ourselves about what is right and wrong, and the role that art plays in our societies. In doing this, we will learn more about ourselves as human beings, and so work towards building a future where we can all flourish.

INTRODUCTION

'I Pass for the Werewolf of these Parts'

The prisoner's hand ached. He sat hunched over his desk in a cold tower of the Bastille jail in Paris, writing in tiny letters on a very long roll of paper – nearly 40 feet in total, made from smaller scraps he had glued together. These were not ideal working conditions. But they would do.

The prisoner was not treated badly in jail. He was a nobleman, which meant he was allowed luxuries in his cell: a wardrobe and tapestries, books and perfume, and his very own housekeeper. Yet he was aware that what he was writing might jeopardise these comforts. So, each night he would roll up his scroll, put it in a copper cylinder, and hide it in a gap in his cell wall. He did not want to risk the guards finding it. And with good cause. For his story was a record of his most debauched thoughts and desires.

Over thirty-seven evenings in the autumn of 1785, the prisoner, Donatien Alphonse François, better known to history as the Marquis de Sade, crafted in secret what he called 'the most impure tale that has ever been told since the world began'.[1]

Set in a remote medieval castle nestled in the Black Forest in southwest Germany – but based on Sade's own castle, Château de Lacoste – the narrative tells of four wealthy male libertines indulging in a savage 120-day orgy, inspired by the vile tales of middle-aged female brothel keepers. Organised by a strict timetable, the procuresses weave stories of their degeneracy, each one illustrating perversions or 'passions' ranging from the simple to the murderous. The exploits they arouse in the libertines involve sexually abusing thirty-six abducted victims, mostly children (some the libertines' own daughters). The children are dismembered and penetrated, flayed alive, disembowelled, and their intestines set alight. There is incest and rape – some victims are as young as three years old. Faeces and vomit and human flesh are eagerly consumed. As these atrocities become increasingly extreme, they ultimately result in the victims' violent deaths, and necrophilia.

This is all narrated in stark, dry detail. Sade presents it to us with wry humour, describing it as a sensuous 'banquet'. The story is known today as *The 120 Days of Sodom*.

———

The Marquis de Sade was abandoned by his parents at an early age. Raised by servants and educated by an uncle, Sade was a spoiled child with a temper and a taste for rebellion. He attended the Lycée Louis-le-Grand, one of the most prestigious schools in Paris. There he was routinely beaten, an experience which instilled in him a lifelong fascination with flagellation and pain.[2] After school he fought in the Seven Years War as colonel of a Dragoon regiment. On his return, Sade married Renée-Pélagie de Montreuil in 1763, a marriage arranged by his father.

For some people, marriage is a settling experience. But for Sade it was the opposite. His notorious sexual indiscretions in Paris led to him being exiled to his castle at Lacoste in 1768 – a place that would become a theatre for his wildest fantasies. Together there, Sade and his wife – ever the loyal spouse – pursued an extreme libertine existence. There were orgies, including one during which Sade poisoned two sex workers with the aphrodisiac Spanish Fly. There was also illegal homosexuality: Sade and his manservant Latour were sentenced to death in absentia for sodomy.

Most notorious was the so-called 'Little Girls' scandal, where Sade abducted five fifteen-year-old girls and sexually abused them in his castle. The abominable crime became a public sensation in Provence, which Sade seemed to relish: 'I pass for the werewolf of these parts,' he said. 'Poor little chicks with their words of terror!'[3] Sade evaded French law by taking refuge in Italy. But a few years later, after committing similar crimes there, he was arrested and imprisoned at the Château de Vincennes at the king's orders, under a *lettre de cachet* (signet letter). After Vincennes closed in 1784, Sade was transferred to the Bastille at the age of forty-five.

Four years after Sade began his debauched novel on the long scroll of parchment, he incited a riot among other prisoners at the Bastille by shouting to a gathering outside his window that prison guards were slitting the throats of inmates. Once order had been restored to the prison, he was removed from the Bastille – 'naked as a worm' – and transferred to an asylum outside of Paris.[4] This sudden removal meant that Sade could not retrieve his novel, which was still hidden in his cell wall. To make matters worse, ten days later, revolutionaries stormed the Bastille. Hearing of the mass lootings, Sade believed his novel had been lost forever. Overwhelmed with grief for his missing masterpiece, he wept 'tears of blood'.[5]

But remarkably, his secret scroll was not lost. It had been

found and saved just before the storming, by a man called Arnoux de Saint-Maximin. After making its way through the hands of a Provençal aristocrat and then a German collector of erotica, the novel was eventually published in 1904 by Iwan Bloch, a Berlin sexologist.[6] Although Bloch was careful to use a pseudonym when he published Sade's work, he did not regard its wild sexual and violent excess to be inappropriate for public consumption. In fact, Bloch considered *The 120 Days of Sodom* to have great scientific and anthropological importance in its categorisation of the most shocking sexual fetishes: 'a similar work will not be found either among the ancients or among the moderns', he later wrote.[7]

Bloch was not alone in his admiration of Sade's art. Throughout the twentieth century the novel was made available via private publications for wealthy patrons, produced pseudonymously or anonymously to evade the authorities. At mid-century a publisher called Jean-Jacques Pauvert put his name on a large print run of a collection of Sade's works, including *The 120 Days of Sodom*. Like Bloch, Pauvert saw Sade's novel as a valuable medico-legal document; while his was the first commercial French edition of the text, he claimed that most of his sales were to the medical community.

Artists, philosophers, and historians began to identify aesthetic, cognitive, and political value in Sade's work. Simone de Beauvoir disagreed with Sade's cruel ethics, but in 1955 she defended the publication of his literature on the grounds that it explored atheistic existentialist themes and therefore had philosophical importance. In 1957, Georges Bataille praised Sade's work in its shameless presentation of man's deepest desires, although he added: 'Nobody, unless he is totally deaf to it, can finish *Les Cent Vingt Journées de Sodome* without feeling sick.'[8]

Around this time, avant-garde artists and writers were harnessing what art historian Alyce Mahon calls the 'Sadean imagination' to critique socio-political issues from fascism to terrorism, and to subvert traditional gender roles by placing the sexual body at the centre of art-making as a form of political resistance.

Eventually, the dam cracked. In a landmark British legal case in 1960, Penguin Books were cleared of any crime for publishing an uncensored version of D. H. Lawrence's *Lady Chatterley's Lover*, a novel condemned for its frequent use of the words 'fuck' and 'cunt'. While the novel had been published privately in small print runs in Italy and France, the UK trial, bolstered by a similar one in the US a year earlier, resulted in mainstream publishers across the world distributing works that had previously been considered obscene and unpublishable – including those of Sade.

This was hailed by many as an important victory in the struggle for freedom of artistic expression. It heralded a general reassessment of the legitimacy of art with subversive or offensive themes. Today, the original manuscript of *The 120 Days of Sodom* is worth at least €6 million and is deemed a French national treasure. Some critics have even described Sade as France's Shakespeare.[9]

Since the middle of the twentieth century, societies around the globe have undergone a collective revolution in standards and attitudes towards obscenity and immorality. In the realms of art, literature, film, and television, words and images that would once have been considered indecent, offensive, or immoral are now commonplace, especially in the West. Where several generations ago it would have been difficult to incidentally glimpse explicit depictions of vice, sex, blasphemy, and violent death, today it would be more unusual to go through a single day *without* seeing one or more of these.

For those who actively seek out obscenity, there is a limitless supply. With pornography at our fingertips via laptops and smartphones, we can access images and videos that would have made even Sade blush. While some genres of pornography aim to encourage a more egalitarian erotic taste in consumers (one that is free from patriarchal conditioning and respects consent), other genres relish in portraying pure horror, including real sexual violence and death. Many of the acts Sade described in words are now actually performed in high-production videos, streamable for free.

This transformation in values and accessibility has profoundly affected the story of art. From sexualised horror films like Alfred Hithcock's *Psycho* (1960) and art performances of masturbation like Vito Acconci's *Seedbed* (1972), to explicit music videos like Cardi B and Megan Thee Stallion's 'WAP (Wet-Ass Pussy)' (2020) and dark true-crime TV shows like Ryan Murphy and Ian Brennan's *Monster: The Ed Gein Story* (2025), traditionally 'immoral' themes and images are now celebrated in art of all kinds. Where medieval Christian art in England was once under threat from the Lollards, who saw image worship itself as heathen idolatry, we now encounter overtly blasphemous art: the figure of Christ submerged in urine; a crucifix penetrating a demon-possessed child; the Virgin Mary painted with elephant dung; and 'JESUS IS A CUNT' stamped on rock band T-shirts (this piece of merch from metal band Cradle of Filth also features a masturbating nun on the front – throughout the 1990s fans were arrested for wearing it in public).

Some find these works and objects amusing or exciting, but others are deeply troubled by them. Allegedly, so many cinema-goers vomited and fainted during the initial screenings of William Friedkin's *The Exorcist* (1973) that theatre staff had to hand out smelling salts. And a very small minority resort to extreme violence in response, as with the terrorist attacks on the offices of the French magazine *Charlie Hebdo* in 2011, 2015, and 2020, which were motivated by the magazine's mocking depictions of the Prophet Muhammad.

Today, violence is mainstream in many art forms, especially in videogames. The *Grand Theft Auto* series is infamous for its portrayal of drugs, sex, and brutality, with one scene inviting the player to perform waterboard torture. And where in the eighteenth century, shunga – Japanese erotic art showing sex between couples – was banned, in 2006 the videogame *RapeLay* was released in Japan. The game centres on a male character stalking and raping a mother and her two young daughters.

As art and its creators have shed their inhibitions in this post-Sadean world, politicians and cultural commentators have reliably lined up to condemn this total freedom of expression as being dangerous to society. In the 1960s, British campaigner and teacher Mary Whitehouse launched her crusade against this ever-growing 'permissive society'. While Whitehouse – often seen as a Christian prude – should be criticised for her organising against sex education in schools, and condemned for her homophobia, some critics now think she was ahead of her time. Her lobbying resulted in legislation which surely was good for society – for instance, the 1978 Protection of Children Act, which criminalised child pornography.

Whitehouse's views culminated in the so-called 'porn wars' of the 1970s–80s. While radical feminist Andrea Dworkin argued that pornography dehumanised women and caused gender-based violence, others like the novelist Angela Carter considered some pornography – including Sade's literary art – to offer a progressive utopian reality where women have autonomy and sexual freedom.

The debate rages on. People still butt heads over 'WAP' and its accompanying music video. Is it a feminist masterpiece celebrating women's sexual empowerment? A step back in women's progress? Or is it just simply 'really, really, really, vulgar', as right-wing commentator Ben Shapiro puts it?[10] Republican politician James Bradley, who claims to have heard the song by accident, echoes Shapiro's disquiet: according to him, 'WAP' is 'what happens when children are raised without God'.

Often these kinds of criticisms can be dismissed as a matter of taste, not to mention prejudice. But where they carry real weight is when artworks can be linked to harm caused in the real world. Many worry that the free and easy availability of pornography and the sexualisation of popular culture has affected young men and women's expectations of real sex; that the celebration of graphic violence and criminality in videogames, films, and music videos glamorises such behaviour to the extent that it inspires copycats. And many twenty-first-century civil rights activists argue that the celebration and glorification of historical imperialists, slave traders, or racist leaders by public statues and paintings perpetuates inequality in the modern world – causing concrete damage to the oppressed groups implicitly targeted by these artworks.

Then there are more specific cases. In the 1980s and 1990s, several white supremacists cited William Luther Pierce's *Turner Diaries* (1978), a racist and antisemitic novel, as influencing their hate crimes and acts of terrorism. The novel tells the story of a violent revolution in the US which leads to a race war, and it has since been credited with shaping white nationalism in the US, the UK, and Germany. And after the disturbed American James Holmes murdered twelve people in a cinema in Aurora, Colorado, in 2012 during a screening of the Batman film *The Dark Knight Rises*, persistent rumours and newspaper reports suggested he was dressed as (and influenced by) the character of the Joker from the previous *The Dark Knight*. The fact that this was untrue – Holmes had dyed his hair red, but not for that reason – did little to dispel the rumour, which seemed to fit the popular belief that violent, dystopian art has the power to induce some viewers to commit terrible crimes.[11]

Sometimes we've got it wrong. Our views on morality and indecency are rife with inconsistency and hypocrisy. As recently as the 1990s, while sexually explicit images of women were plastered over so-called 'lad mags' targeted at heterosexual boys and men, artists like Robert Mapplethorpe were censored for their explicit homosexual art. Mapplethorpe was called a 'human cockroach' by Republican senator Jesse Helms, who blamed the LGBTQIA+ community for the seeming decay of culture. And while museums are bursting at the seams with paintings of naked women, real women are thrown out of museums for wearing too little (a low-cut dress) or too much (a niqab).[12]

Taken together, these cases and others like them suggest a thorny and complex narrative about the philosophy and history of art. The general movement towards unbounded freedom of expression in liberal societies still meets legal, cultural, or social restrictions on the morality of artworks. Art *can* be dangerous – but the very gatekeepers of supposedly depraved art can also be dangerous. What we deem morally acceptable is itself fraught with issues; depravity does not always appear how we might expect it to. It can hide in plain sight like a wolf in sheep's clothing.

———

Immoral art has captivated philosophers and theorists for millennia. Plato panicked over its power to corrupt citizens because of how it could disrupt a person's emotions and ability to rationalise. Oscar Wilde celebrated the provocative capacity of art, declaring that it should aim to transgress our morals and that it can be great precisely because it is able to challenge conventional beliefs. And today, during a time of so-called cancel culture, statue toppling, and debates over censorship, addressing the significance of immoral art has never been more urgent.

Part of the philosopher's job, as Plato put it in his *Phaedrus* (370 BCE), is to 'carve nature at its joints'.[13] How do we classify, identify, or conceptualise parts of the world? The problem of depraved art speaks to philosophy's *raison d'être*. We've got two big concepts as bedfellows here: art and depravity. So we need to handle this weighty phenomenon carefully.

As a discipline, philosophy is packed full of tools to help us answer difficult questions, or to clarify problems so we are at least clear on what it is we're puzzled about. And one of the most important things we must do at the start of any philosophical enquiry is to sharpen our terms and sketch our concepts. Let's begin.

What do we mean by 'art'? Perhaps an artwork is an object that represents something in the world, and which aims to be aesthetically pleasing or to convey some deep truth. Perhaps art is simply any artefact which has been conferred the status of 'art' by institutions with sufficient authority (think of early readymades like Marcel Duchamp's *Fountain*, a urinal which he boldly plonked into a gallery in 1917).

This book is not the place to choose and defend one of these definitions. Instead I'll follow the example of United States Supreme Court Justice Potter Stewart, who, when pressed to define hard-core pornography during an obscenity trial in 1964, stated: 'I shall not today attempt further to define the kinds of material I understand to be embraced . . . [b]ut I know it when I see it.'[14]

So, of art: *I know it when I see it.*

I hope you don't see this as a cop-out – it's a deliberately broad approach and will include things made in familiar and traditional media like paintings, novels, plays, sculptures, films, and music. But I will also explore more contemporary art forms like videogames, installations, and performance art. To my mind, these are artworks, even if they are tricky to pin down. And given their often-troubling relationship with morality, they will be vital for our study.

What is depravity? Derived from the Latin for 'perverse', or 'crooked', when we think of the depraved, we tend to think of wickedness, debasement, and pure evil. Though we sometimes describe natural disasters which destroy livelihoods or parasites like those that blind the Greenland shark as 'evil', this is technically inaccurate. Hurricanes and copepods don't have moral capacities and so can hardly be accused of wrongdoing. But we can describe people and their actions as evil or depraved. The Protestant theological doctrine of Total Depravity, for example, holds that human nature is essentially sinful: that people are necessarily corrupt because of the original sin. Since the Fall of

Man, so the Bible says, we are fundamentally flawed and predisposed to evil.

Regardless of your views on human nature and religion, it is true that nobody is perfect. And even if there were what the philosopher Susan Wolf called 'moral saints' – people who are entirely morally perfect – they would likely get on our nerves, and be pretty dull company.[15] If moral saints are hard to come by, the world is sadly littered with moral fiends – think of serial rapists, or genocidal dictators. Their actions and beliefs are so awful that they become difficult to understand as human beings, to the point of us describing them as demons or monsters.

The core of depravity, as I understand it in this book, is morality. To be depraved is to be extremely immoral. It might be a little wrong for me to tell you the white lie that I like your outfit before your big job interview, but it's certainly not depraved. To systematically lie and manipulate you as part of a wider pattern of domestic abuse, slowly weakening your sense of reality, as Gregory does to his wife Paula in the film *Gaslight* (1944) – this is a depraved thing to do.

So what does it mean to be immoral? At its base, morality is a set of principles and norms that govern our conduct with each other and the natural world. These rules of conduct tend to be seen as having a special authority and the force of commands. To be immoral is to somehow violate these commands and do something egregiously wrong. But what exactly is it that makes something right or wrong? Perhaps actions are right insofar as they produce good consequences like happiness, and wrong insofar as they produce unhappiness, or pain. Philosophers who believe this think that outcomes solely justify our actions. Others think the opposite: something is wrong insofar as it violates a fundamental moral law regardless of outcomes;

a law given to us via reason or by some divine being. One such law might be that we should treat each other as ends in ourselves and not merely as a means, to respect human autonomy.

There are also more abstract questions about the nature of morality itself: are there moral facts? If so, where the hell are they? Numbers exist, but you don't trip over the number 9 when taking a walk. So, numbers must exist in some abstract realm. Do moral facts exist in this way? Or are they instead reducible to fleeting expressions of human emotion?

While there's much more to say about these positions on morality – what makes something right or wrong, good or bad, and what kind of fact this may involve – again, this book is not the place to settle such disputes. But what I will do is make assumptions throughout about what is terribly wrong, claims that most if not all ethical theories would agree upon, even if they disagree about how exactly we arrive at those conclusions. So: genocide, slavery, rape, abuse, paedophilia, and non-consenting sadistic torture, for instance, are deep wrongs. Then there are those wrongs of structural injustice: racism, sexism, ableism, homophobia, transphobia, and social inequalities like the unfair distribution of wealth and resources. These things may be wrong because of the pain they cause, or because they break moral laws. Whatever the reason, we can rely once again on the intuitive approach outlined above.

Of depravity: *I know it when I see it.*

People do disagree over moral judgements – over whether euthanasia is wrong, or whether extreme menstrual taboos and practices like *chhaupadi* are wrong. Such disagreements lead some to embrace a moral relativism: what is right and wrong is only ever relative to a part of society at a certain point in time, and there's no deeper objective truth of the matter beyond what different cultures happen to think is good or bad.

I am not a fan of moral relativism. Of course, it's vital that some cultural and religious differences and conventions be respected. But moral disagreements themselves don't necessarily undermine the existence of moral facts, which do stay steady – globally, and across time. A remark I come across often when discussing the ethics around public sculptures of slave traders is that slavery 'wasn't seen as wrong back then'. This is a very peculiar response. First, who are the moral judges being referred to here? The 15 million black men, women, and children who were enslaved over at least four hundred years during the transatlantic slave trade surely did not make such a moral judgement.[16] And second, those few who sincerely did believe that slavery was permissible likely did so because they had other interests for which they needed justification, such as financial and territorial gain. This white supremacist elite probably isn't the most reliable source of moral truth.

Of course, *beliefs* about what is right and wrong do change over time and place. It wasn't too long ago that homosexuality was seen by many as immoral (and in some parts of the world it still is). Trans people are now suffering similar treatment in the mainstream to that experienced by homosexual people in the not-too-distant past. But again, changing beliefs don't mean that there aren't *any* objective moral sentiments. Human enslavement and sexual harassment, for instance, are wrong. Those who may have believed 'back in the day' that these were morally permissible, or even good, were simply incorrect; so too are those who did or do believe that gay people and trans people are somehow immoral, or that selling young girls into marriage is permissible. They're mistaken about the facts; they've added 2 and 2 and gotten 5.

So, when it comes to the nature of depravity, I won't endorse a particular moral theory, but I do endorse a broad objectivism: there are moral facts which do not reduce to varying opinions. There are very real wrongs, and these won't be up for discussion. Yet, given all of this, depravity in art isn't always what it seems. What *conventionally* has been considered depraved will be put under the spotlight in this book. But art that positively champions abuse and oppressive systems, like racism and sexism, will be considered genuinely immoral, especially in cases where this wickedness is shrouded in dazzling beauty.

The Hydra

Now that we have some clarity on what we mean by immorality, we can lay out the backbone of this book. Art can be depraved in five ways. First, many artworks explicitly *show* immoral states of affairs such as gratuitous violence or obscene scenarios. We will see, however, that such judgements of obscenity can have a surprisingly sinister underbelly. Second, an artwork may somehow *cause* a person to do something terrible. While this is often difficult to prove in practice, we will see how art can still stoke the coals that already lurk within us. Third, an artwork may *express* dangerous messages in how it invites us to think and feel about something. More specifically, art can be a form of hate speech, which creates and sustains social hierarchies. Fourth, sometimes works of art are created by immoral *artists*. Knowing an artist's biography and their moral character often affects how we interpret and value their work. But *should* it? I'll argue *yes* – when we look at art, we see the world through its creator's eyes. Lastly, the way an artwork has been *created* may be morally suspect, by exploiting humans, non-human animals, and the natural world. Many of us are happy to eat meat, so why draw the line at killing an animal for art – an artefact which, after all, lasts a lot longer than a juicy burger?

These are our five faces of depraved art. I want you to think of this concept as a Hydra, the infamous serpent-monster that dwelled in a lake at the entrance to the Underworld in Greek and Roman myth.[17]* The reason I want you to think of depraved art through this monstrous concept is because the Hydra possessed many heads. For convenience, let's posit five heads, though its exact number varies across ancient sources. Depraved art as a whole has five distinct relationships to morality, and like the Hydra's heads, they all belong to the same creature. They are all connected to one another; they do not work in isolation. To truly understand obscene art, we must acknowledge that such art isn't merely showing us something but is expressing something significant about its subject matter. To truly understand art's capacity to induce criminality, we must factor in the artist's identity but also acknowledge that art can be dangerous even without an artist's fully fledged incitement to violence. And to truly understand how an artist's own depravity leaks into their art, we need to understand how art's ethical and aesthetic value is bound up in its very production.

After unearthing this Hydra, we'll be ready to tackle its stench and toxicity by confronting an urgent political issue: what do we *do* with this monstrous art? Nothing at all? Or do we burn it all down – as Simone de Beauvoir asked: 'must we burn

---

* The earliest narrative where the Hydra appears is in Hesiod's poem *Theogony* from 730–700 BCE, and its earliest image is found engraved on a Boeotian bronze fibula dating from *c.* 700 BCE.

Sade?' We'll see that censorship in general creates more problems than it solves: we can't simply chop off a head of the Hydra, for it'll just grow another one. Instead, I suggest an alternative to traditional iconoclasm; what I call 'metaphysical iconoclasm' through the form of artistic counterspeech. Paul Gauguin's disturbing paintings of his Polynesian child brides, for instance, should not be forever buried in the vaults – there are more creative ways to respond to their malevolence. Effective strategies such as decolonised art education, transparent and progressive curation, and protest art can 'speak back' to hateful art in a less destructive manner. This constructive counterspeech allows us to adequately confront the dark art in our lives and pave the way for a brighter aesthetic world. Depraved art is a many-headed monster, but one that we must tame rather than slaughter.

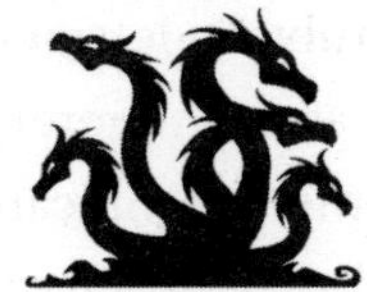

1 | OBSCENITY

An early human carefully carved a piece of woolly mammoth tusk with stone tools. They shaped the ivory into a small, squat adult female body, with large protruding breasts, an accentuated vulva, and broad shoulders. With their sharpened chisel, they forcefully made incisions horizontally across the torso, perhaps to indicate clothing. In place of a head, our artist crafted a small loop, possibly to thread a cord through so the figure could be worn as an amulet.

Millennia passed. Its creator long gone, the small figurine lay in undisturbed fragments under red-brown silt in a large cave in Germany's Swabian Jura. Nearby were bones of reindeer, bear, and horse, a broken flute carved from vulture bone, a substantial phallic object, and a tiny, exquisite water-bird sculpture.[1]

In 2008, the palm-sized female figure and the flute were discovered in the now-named Hohle Fels cave by an archaeological team based at the University of Tübingen, led by Nicholas Conard. The artefacts' estimated age dates them to the Aurignacian culture of the Upper Palaeolithic, about 35,000 years ago.

The discovery radically shifted understandings of prehistoric cultural innovation and just how far back *homo sapiens* and other hominids began creating music and aesthetic objects (there may be earlier figurines: Morocco's Venus of Tan-Tan could be up to 500,000 years old, but its status as an artwork rather than just a naturally weathered rock is still debated). Up until this discovery of the figure now known as the 'Venus of Hohle Fels', human female imagery in Palaeolithic Europe at least was entirely unknown, with previous finds having been dominated by animal and shamanistic imagery.

Nicholas Conard interpreted the Hohle Fels piece as similar to other 'Venus' figurines that have been discovered across Eurasia, and clearly a symbol of fertility, stating that 'there can be no doubt that the depiction of oversized breasts, accentuated buttocks and genitalia results from the deliberate exaggeration of the sexual features of the figurine'.[2] Today, the meaning of these prehistoric figurative artworks is still hotly debated among scholars; even the name 'Venus' seems inappropriate given that this refers to a Roman fertility goddess, which is relatively recent by human history's standards.

But what did follow was a sensational frenzy in the West's media. On release of the discovery in the respected journal *Nature*, the press as well as other scientific researchers branded the figurine as 'smut carved from a mammoth tusk',[3] the 'world's first Page 3 Girl',[4] a 'prehistoric pinup', and a '35,000-year-old sex object'.[5] The magazine *Science* wondered if the small sculpture might be the 'earliest pornography'.[6]

This reception assumes that the world's earliest figurative art is pornographic, and by extension, obscene. But is it? We don't know who made this figurine. We will never fully understand the purpose of prehistoric sculptures. But quickly branding them as 'pornographic' and 'smut' carries connotations of immorality and indecency. Why do so many automatically assume, with little evidence, that any depiction of the naked female body, no matter how many thousands of years ago it was made, must be filth? More generally, is it right to judge artworks which simply show sex and nudity as obscene? And what exactly makes the immoral so captivating anyway?

Temples of Horror

One archaeologist describes the Stone Age as 'sex-mad'.[7] This is a fair judgement. Since the dawn of artistic creation, humans have portrayed sex and the naked body. Evidence of these creations can be found across the globe. Algeria's famous Tassili n'Ajjer rock art from the Neolithic period is filled with wondrous images of cattle and wild animals like giraffes and elephants, depictions of herding, hunting, and dancing, but also obvious scenes of copulation in various sexual positions. In Brazil's National Park of the Serra da Capivara, rock art possibly up to 36,000 years old shows animals like lizards, jaguars, and armadillos, as well as human sexual activity including bestiality and group sex.

San-people rock art in the Southern African Drakensberg, and in Mutoko, Zimbabwe, shows menstrual blood flowing like rivers from between the legs of women and girls, possibly forming part of ancient rituals and ceremonies for menarche rites of passage.[8] The Aboriginal Maliwawa Figures in Arnhem Land, Australia, with their distinctive red pigment, include images of people vomiting, impaled macropods, and sexual intercourse – one picture appears to show a man with dots emerging from his penis (it's not clear which bodily fluid is represented here though).[9]

For a very long time, such themes were considered a central part of life and religion, and not something to be ashamed of. Before European contact, elders in ancient and medieval

depraved

African tribes such as the Baganda in Uganda, for instance, would often teach the young about sex without contempt or condemnation. While pre-colonial beliefs about sex were wide and varied across the continent, sex was generally not considered a shameful act reserved simply for reproduction, but instead was connected to love, pleasure, and spirituality.[10]* Ancient Mesopotamian societies positively revered the naked human body, especially the vulva, and had multiple deities for sex and love. The art of the Sumer people, from around 3000 BCE, which included terracottas, poetry, and sculpture, was brimming with vaginal and anal intercourse.

This art was celebratory. Sumerian poetry described vulvas as tasting like beer and honey, and even as beautiful – something Sigmund Freud would strongly have rejected, as according to him the genitals are exciting but hardly ever beautiful.[11] Consider the royal love song of Shu-Suen from the Ur III period (2100–2000 BCE):

> The beer of my . . ., Il-Ummiya the tapstress
> Is sweet
> And her vulva
> Is sweet like her beer
> And her beer is sweet!
> And her vulva
> Is sweet like her chatter
> And her beer is sweet!
> Her bittersweet beer
> And her beer are sweet![12]

* These teachings and beliefs were of course complicated by the fact that many of these groups were patriarchal, though the Baganda are now challenging oppressive norms around women's sexuality.

Assyriologist Zainab Bahrani notes how the Sumerians did not even have a word for nudity, but did have a large array of terms to describe genitalia – words which did not have negative connotations like they do today (like 'cunt' being used as a biting insult).[13] Sex in ancient Mesopotamia did not have the unfavourable reputation it does in some parts of the contemporary world. It was instead seen fundamentally as an expression of love:[14] the two formed sides of the same sacred coin for this ancient civilisation, which also gave us arithmetic, the wheel, and the earliest written language.

Vulva imagery almost disappeared in the later ancient Greek and Roman world,* but phallic symbols and male nudity remained an important part of cultural expression. The male warrior figure that epitomises ancient Greek art would nearly always be shown naked in public monuments and on 'naughty pottery' like drinking vessels. This nudity extended to portrayals of all sorts of activities, even precarious scenarios like fighting a battle.[15] As classicist Mary Beard writes of the pervasive phallic imagery in Roman Pompeii:

> Power, status and good fortune were expressed in terms of the phallus. Hence the presence of phallic imagery in almost unimaginable varieties all round the town . . . There are phalluses greeting you in doorways, phalluses above bread ovens, phalluses carved into the surface of the street and plenty more phalluses with bells on – and wings.[16]

---

* There were some rare exceptions. Small terracottas of headless vulva-women with their face carved into the abdomen, called *baubo*, were thought to be kept just by women, functioning as protective amulets during pregnancy. Thank you to my Cardiff colleague Rachel Wood for pointing this out to me!

Portrayals of sex, including bestiality, were standard during this time. The first-century Roman erotic art found in Herculaneum and Pompeii ranges from frescoes found in brothels to household objects like phallic oil lamps and mosaics. A notable piece in this collection is a small-scale white marble sculpture of the rustic god Pan having sexual intercourse with a supine female goat, which is thought to have adorned the side of a garden pool in a Herculaneum country villa.[17]

While in fourth-century BCE Greece and Rome there was punishment for blasphemous or heretical expression, *sexual* explicitness was not state-regulated at the time (although Plato did advocate partial censorship of Homer's *Odyssey*, specifically its descriptions of lust, out of concern that it would weaken young readers' self-restraint).[18] Even with the advent and spread of Christianity, which increased censorship on religious grounds to regulate blasphemy, state bans of sexually explicit material were not enforced.

Prevailing views of sex did begin to shift when Christianity became a more dominant religion. A far cry from the heady days of ancient civilisations, fornication was now considered sinful by Christian doctrine. While medieval European literature included genres like the fabliaux – comics full of lusty monks, horny wives, and scatology, which would often criticise the church (Geoffrey Chaucer's *The Canterbury Tales* (1387–1400) being an archetype) – the sexual acts represented there were now seen as subversive and wrong, despite their artistic expression technically being legal.[19]

Christian anxiety around lust did have significant effects on religious imagery, however. Michelangelo's *Last Judgement* (1536–41) in the Sistine Chapel, for instance, faced hostility throughout the sixteenth century from the clerical elite. Falling victim to the Council of Trent's decrees on sacred art for its abundant nudity, it was ordered that drapery to hide genitalia be added to the masterpiece after Michelangelo's death.[20]

It was with the German invention of the modern printing press in 1428 that state censorship began to increase across Europe, for indecent books could now find their way into the hands of the general populace. But again, these state regulations were directed not at sexual obscenity per se but at blasphemous and heretical content. This may have been because of aesthetic tastes at the time: Elizabethan society in England, for instance, had a love of coarse humour and sexual banter.

Eventually, the influential Puritan view of sex, along with the explosion of the novel in the eighteenth century, led to a significant development of the legal concept of obscenity. Diabolically paired with the developing libertine philosophy in France at the time – whose extreme hedonistic doctrine held that pleasure should be the superior aim in life – many novels became increasingly sexual at the cost of moral stability.[21]

The novel offered new and immersive make-believe worlds, so it is unsurprising that those which vividly portrayed copulation and incest would result in legal crackdowns on distribution. John Cleland's *Memoirs of a Woman of Pleasure* (1749) – now notoriously known as *Fanny Hill*, the name of its protagonist – has been characterised by author George Ryley Scott as 'the rankest pornography ever perpetuated by an English author having any claims to literary craftsmanship'.[22] The novel tells the story of a young woman's sexual escapades, including orgies and flagellation, all via outrageous euphemisms. The publishers were charged with corrupting the king's subjects, and Cleland was ordered to withdraw the book.

———

depraved

Christianity around this time, with its shame towards lust and nudity and its rejection of pagan gods as inventions of the devil, became the lens through which much art of the past was understood by the West. One astonishing case of this was how the Hindu and Jain sculpture in India's medieval temples (which involved some nudity and expressions of sexuality) incensed European travellers and colonisers. They were left aghast at what they saw, in part due to the influence of the so-called 'monster stereotype': the medieval Christian perception of Indian, non-Christian gods 'with their many arms' as evil demons. A Friar Odoric of Pordenone, who visited India in the fourteenth century, reportedly witnessed a colossal Buddha figure – possibly one of the Buddha statues of Bamiyan in present-day Afghanistan – and thought the sculpture was the devil himself.[23]

This deep fear of unfamiliar bodily imagery continued well into the early modern period, particularly in relation to India. A sixteenth-century Dutch merchant, J. H. van Linschoten, described the sculpted gods in temples on Salsette Island as: 'so fearefull, horrible and develish formes, . . . that it is [an abomination to see]. The other temple, with so evilled favored and uglie shapes, that to enter therein it would make a mans hayre stand upright.'[24]

Linschoten wasn't alone in his outraged goosebumps. The young seventeenth-century French traveller Jean de Thévenot exclaimed of the temples at Masulipatan that they were 'so full of lascivious Figures of Monsters, that one cannot enter them without horror'.[25] * In 1724, the Scottish merchant Alexander Hamilton, who was also briefly employed by the East India

* 'Masulipatan' was presumably used then to refer to what's now known as Machilipatnam.

Company, declared of a 'Gopasvami' temple in Odisha: 'Around his Temple and on the Coach are carved figures of Gods and Goddesses in such obscene Postures, that it would puzzle the Covent Garden nymphs to imitate.'[26]

This incredulity saturated the colonial mindset, where negative aesthetic judgements were also opportunities to denounce non-Christian religion and culture. The Khajuraho monuments in Madhya Pradesh, India – also known as the 'Kama Sutra Temples' even though only 10 per cent of the structures show erotic sculpture – were re-discovered in 1838 by the British engineer Captain T. S. Burt. Affronted by the explicit carvings of orgies and acrobatic sexual positions, Burt reported his findings in the *Journal of the Asiatic Society of Bengal*:

> some of the sculptures here were extremely indecent and offensive; which I was at first much surprised to find in temples that are professed to be erected for good purposes, and on account of religion. But the religion of the ancient Hindoos could not have been very chaste if it induced people under the cloak of religion, to design the most disgraceful representations to desecrate their ecclesiastical erections.[27]

In the same journal volume, a Lieutenant M. Kittoe described the temples in Sambalpur as having 'few . . . pretensions to elegance, and the generality are covered with most obscene figures badly executed'.[28]* By denouncing these artworks as disgraceful desecrations, these merchants could simultaneously denounce

---

* These views were by no means shared by all scholars. The eighteenth-century pantheist Charles François Dupuis, for instance, attacked the idea that Indian figures were 'monstrous' and made efforts to take Indian art seriously, as part of his universal religion thesis and 'Christ Myth Theory'. See Mitter 1992, pp. 88–104.

non-Christian religions – in their apparent inability to impart true beauty – as treacherous, false belief systems.

Secretum

Due to their enduring shock value, many works of prehistoric and ancient art have been denied entry into countries and hidden from display or destroyed, even though these reactions wouldn't have made sense to earlier societies.

A long way away from Sumerian adoration of the vulva, the medieval stone carvings of mostly older women with exaggerated vulvae – sheela na gigs – which adorn churches in Spain, Britain, and Ireland, have been called 'obscene', 'lewd', 'ugly', 'hags of the castle'.[29]* Despite the myriad interpretations of these sculptures – ranging from fertility symbology and attempts by the church to quell sexual desire, to protection from evil spirits and pagan appropriation by the Catholic Church – sheela na gigs nevertheless became the target of an iconoclastic campaign. Against the backdrop of the so-called 'witch craze', whose mass hysteria had by now spread throughout Europe, priests across Ireland in the seventeenth century were ordered to burn and bury sheela na gigs, fearing them as horrific symbols of women's sexuality.[30]

Art in museums has not been safe from moralising crusades either. The Obscene Publications Act 1857 in the UK, for instance, resulted in the creation of the secretum: a forbidden collection hidden away by museums, considered too

---

* Some scholars suggest that the medieval masons who created these carvings in fact did not see them as obscene at all. Rather, they may have been attempts to calm sexual desire and not ignite it, as part of the church's campaign *against* immorality to castigate sins of the flesh.

corrupting for the public gaze. The British Museum's Secretum concealed, among other things, the *Statue of Tārā* – an almost life-sized Sri Lankan gilt-bronze of the female Buddha from the seventh to the eighth century CE – apparently because of the figure's exposed breasts and hips.

The 8.5-foot-wide Turin Erotic Papyrus from 1150 BCE Egypt was also hidden throughout the nineteenth century. It shows men and women in various sexual positions, exaggerated penises, and even what we'd today call 'dirty talk': in one scene a woman who appears to be masturbating on top of a pot calls to a nearby man, 'Come here you dirty sex criminal.'[31] Although it's now available to the public, this scroll-painting has been cloaked in a familiar rhetoric – described as the 'world's first men's mag'[32] – which again makes significant assumptions about who made the papyrus and why.

The erotic art of Pompeii and Herculaneum, which was fully excavated in the eighteenth century, was also banished to a secret museum by Francis I, future king of the Two Sicilies, in the nineteenth century. Deemed too obscene and therefore classified as 'pornographic', this collection was secured behind a bricked-up doorway and was reportedly only accessible to those 'mature persons whose impeccable morals are well-known'. These decisions indicated a widespread anxiety in the wake of the Industrial Revolution and the dawn of the public museum. Until the nineteenth century, archaeology and art-collecting were a wealthy gentleman's pursuit. Now, art of the past was being made available to the masses, and with this came a panic that women, children, and those of lower social status were prone to being corrupted by its more salacious examples.[33] This is why provocative sculpture and paintings were locked away: to mitigate risk of sexual hysteria and a breakdown of society.[34]

depraved

Meanwhile, Japan's explicit woodblock prints from the Edo period (*c.* 1603–1868), composing the genre of shunga, were suppressed during Japan's Meiji period (1868–1912). This 'sex art' was used for arousal but also for sex education and had an audience of men and women across the class system. Japan's major religions of Shinto and Buddhism did not share the Christian view of lust as being shameful or sinful, so art like shunga was largely tolerated by the authorities. But while these prints were made nominally illegal – an open secret – in Japan in 1722 (due in large part to the Kyōhō Reforms rather than a prevailing negative view of sex), it was with the growing influence of Christianity after Japan's largely isolated existence in its Edo period that shunga met its fate. Some scholars have argued that its suppression was due to the social pressure of foreigners, which led to cultural self-censorship in Japan in a bid for European assimilation. Shunga remains problematic in Japan to this day.[35]

And despite its innovative focus on ordinary people in a morally corrupt society, one of the world's earliest long-form novels, *Jin Ping Mei* (The Plum in the Golden Vase, 1610), was banned in China during the Ming dynasty (1368–1644) for its erotic content about a lusty merchant. The ban continued into the Qing dynasty (1644–1911) and was further exacerbated by the sexual repression of the Cultural Revolution. It was only in 2004 that an unexpurgated edition of the book became widely available.[36]

This censorship of subversive art continued well into the twentieth century. While the ancient Sumerians saw female pubic hair as beautiful, it was the pubic hair of Amedeo Modigliani's nudes which proved so indecent that his paintings were removed by French police from the artist's solo show in 1917. Up until this point, the depiction of body hair, especially on women, wasn't acceptable in Western art.[37]*

Outcries around obscenity were not just targeted at sexually explicit art: the mere idea of subversive love was enough to emit shockwaves. Radclyffe Hall's ground-breaking *The Well of Loneliness*, which tells the story of a lesbian couple during the First World War, was banned in 1928 by the UK courts for its defence of 'unnatural practices between women . . . living in filthy sin'.[38] The novel was reviled for its apparent immorality – not because of any sexually explicit content, but purely because it championed queer love.

Vladimir Nabokov's infamous *Lolita*, which tells the story of a paedophile's obsession with and abuse of a twelve-year-old girl, faced similar hostility, albeit for different reasons. One publisher even said to the author that if he were to print the book, they would both go to jail.[39] The novel was eventually published in Paris in 1955, but there soon followed an uproar. After the *Sunday Express* branded the work as 'sheer unrestrained pornography',[40] the British Home Office ordered for all copies entering the UK to be seized. The book was then banned in France for two years, before its eventual re-publication. In an afterword to his novel, Nabokov expressed his frustration at this furore by, among other things, protesting the

---

* This widespread attitude is epitomised in an infamous anecdote about the nineteenth-century art historian John Ruskin. When Ruskin and his new bride Effie Gray were unable to consummate their marriage, his excuse to her was that 'he had imagined women were quite different to what he saw I was, and that the reason he did not make me his Wife is that he was disgusted with my person the first evening'. While it's not exactly clear why Ruskin was so repulsed by Effie's naked body, an influential theory put forward by British author Mary Lutyens is that Ruskin expected women to look like the sleek, smooth girls in classical paintings and sculptures, and that he was shocked to see that women actually have pubic hair.

depraved

charges of lewdness and pornography, which he said were 'idiotic charge[s] of immorality'.[41]

Watershed

This barricade against the obscene, which had slowly built up over the centuries, eventually reached breaking point. Undoubtedly influenced by the emerging Sexual Revolution, a landmark obscenity trial saw the dawn of a new era for artistic expression.

Before 1959, obscenity in the UK had been a common-law and then statutory offence, where the obscene was defined as material with the tendency to 'deprave and corrupt those whose minds are open to such immoral influences'.[42] However, the amended Obscene Publications Act 1959 introduced a key liberalising element – its Section 4. Now, a conviction could not be carried if the art in question had some kind of merit: 'If it is proved that publication of the article in question is justified as being for the public good on the ground that it is in the interests of science, literature, art or learning, or of other objects of general concern.'[43]

This change in the tide emboldened Sir Allen Lane to have Penguin publish D. H. Lawrence's *Lady Chatterley's Lover*, which tells the story of an aristocratic woman's affair with a working-class gamekeeper. But prosecution swiftly followed. Barrister Mervyn Griffith-Jones infamously opened the trial at the Old Bailey with his angry observation of the book's abundant use of certain Anglo-Saxon words: 'The word "fuck" or "fucking" appears no less than 30 times . . . "Cunt" 14 times; "balls" 13 times; "shit" and "arse" six times apiece; "cock" four times; "piss" three times, and so on.'[44] He'd clearly been keeping tally.

But on grounds of the novel's literary merit, testified by several esteemed authors and critics, and its potential to educate all rungs of the social classes, the jury quickly delivered a unanimous verdict of not guilty. Ecstatic applause erupted from the courtroom, which was instantly shushed by the usher.[45]

As we saw in the Introduction, a tidal wave release of sexy and abominable literature followed. The bricked doorways came down, and the once-forbidden artworks in the secret museums burst free into the public eye. In some ways, we had come back to an almost ancient world of sexual imagery, unshackled by law. But it has not been a full circle return. Obscenity legislation across much of the world holds a similar clause to the UK's Section 4: the art must have some serious value for the public good to be saved from damnation.

Despite this new era of artistic expression, works of art have continued to be forbidden and met with angry backlashes – and it's not always on grounds of sexual content. The infamous photograph showing a plastic crucifix submerged in a glass tank of the artist's urine – Andres Serrano's *Immersion (Piss Christ)* (1987) – has been vandalised several times for its apparent flagrant blasphemy; the artist even received death threats. The piece was denounced as a hideous desecration of Jesus Christ, and an insult to the Christian faith. For many, the artwork and its promotion by the US's National Endowment of the Arts encapsulated the scandal that public money was being used to fund utter filth.

To add further insult to injury, a few years later the Virgin Mary was portrayed in excrement. Chris Ofili's *Holy Virgin Mary* (1996) shows a black woman in the traditional blue robe of the Virgin Mary – the Black Madonna – presented in elephant dung and pornographic collage. Despite the work being highly praised and Ofili becoming the first black artist to win the Turner Prize just two years later, the painting was denounced as 'sick' by the then Mayor of New York City, who brought a court case against the Brooklyn Museum for its display of the work.[46] He failed, though, and was sued by the museum.[47]

Delightful Repulsion

But what is obscenity? We tend to use the word quite liberally. We might use it to describe something simply shocking, something we're just really angry at, or something we consider depraved. We should get to the bottom of what this concept really amounts to.

'The Obscene' conjures up images of moral perversity and terrible vulgarity. While there has been a dearth of helpful legal definitions, we can nevertheless reconstruct the core features of this concept by reflecting on its chequered history. Obscenity concerns apparently sinful and immoral things – often explicit sexual content – from which we derive or are invited to derive peculiar enjoyment or pleasure. Sex becomes obscene when it is injected with moral anxiety.

In fact, the modern term 'pornography' was apparently coined out of embarrassment by the German scholar Karl Otfried Müller, in reaction to the 'obscene' objects unearthed in Pompeii and Herculaneum which, although shocking to nineteenth-century scholars, nonetheless required proper cataloguing. The concept of pornography, derived from the Greek *pornographos* meaning 'whore-writer' (ancient Greek authors who wrote about sex workers), was used to conveniently classify these salacious discoveries.[48]

However, we must be careful not to conflate 'sex' and 'pornography' with the 'obscene'.[49] The former two terms describe, respectively, a familiar human activity that is considered by most to be morally neutral in itself, and sexually explicit material designed to sexually arouse. But 'obscene' is a normative term: it condemns something as being disposed to generate a shocking disgust. Some pornography is obscene; the US Supreme Court, for instance, vaguely defines this as showing 'offensive hardcore' sexual conduct, which is not protected under the First Amendment.[50] But it's not the case that *all* pornography is or should be condemned as such. And while some obscene things happen to be pornographic, they needn't be. Monty Python's sketch of Mr Creosote comes to mind, whose excessive eating and projectile vomiting concludes with his graphic explosion after consuming the infamous wafer-thin mint.[51]

The obscene doesn't just involve brazen vulgarity which makes us feel unpleasant. In fact, vulgarity and the obscene can come apart in some cases, as the philosopher Matthew Kieran notes. Someone boasting about their banker's bonus and new Ferrari at a funeral would be seen as terribly vulgar, and not to mention disrespectful, but not obscene per se. In fact, some historians suggest that the sheela na gig may have been intended by medieval craftsmen to appear vulgar, but not necessarily obscene.[52] The obscene can even be expressed with elegance. For instance, the nineteenth-century Japanese artist Kobayashi Eitaku produced illustrations of bestiality that are actually quite pretty – surreal images of enormous bats, mice, and frogs performing cunnilingus on young women are rendered in delicate and colourful paintwork – but their subversive sexual content is nevertheless considered obscene at the same time.

Obscenity is also a morally loaded concept. When we judge something as obscene, we implicitly 'appeal to some notion of moral violation';[53] we condemn the representation or act for its blatant infringement of moral law. The obscenity of Mr Creosote's demeanour and actions at the dinner table is not found merely in their vulgarity, but in their expression of his flawed moral character trait of extreme gluttony. The obscenity of Eitaku's erotic paintings is not just found in their explicitness, but in their elegant representation of a deep moral transgression between human and non-human animal.

But how exactly can a work of art, including pornographic art, violate a moral law or norm? The key here is what the work is *asking* or *inviting* us to do in response to what we're being shown. Merely showing something shocking or disgusting is not enough. A medical textbook full of explicit images of faeces used for educating doctors might be unpleasant for the layperson to look at, but we wouldn't call this book 'obscene', just highly informative. The very same images, however, could be used in a different book to elicit sexual pleasure among scatology enthusiasts. And many would judge the images to be obscene in this context.

It is the purpose of the representation that matters here, not just what is shown. And this purpose can be determined, at least in the arts, by the intention of the artist, the content of their art, and the context in which it's consumed. It is because Sade in *The 120 Days of Sodom* invites his reader to find humour and arousal in the heinous acts he describes that his story becomes obscene. A mere description of the very same acts of sexual violence as part of a criminal trial, however, would certainly be distressing but not an obscene representation or recounting. It is because Sade *invites* his reader to delight and relish the senseless violence in his art that it violates our ethical codes: he asks us to do something really, really bad.

The fundamental character of the obscene concerns this manner of representation: how are things being shown to us, what is the artist trying to get us to feel? As Kieran shows, art is obscene when it invites us to feel 'morally prohibited' responses to its subject matter.[54] This could involve feeling sexually excited towards sexual torture and rape like we find in Sade's literature. Or it might involve feeling joy and intrigue towards pain and death. The twenty-first-century horror film franchises *Final Destination* and *Saw*, for instance, show wildly violent deaths and torture in such gruesome detail, and with such alarming frequency, that they clearly invite the horror fan to delight in the egregious gore fest.

Now, many artworks, as we'll see later in the book, are morally bankrupt because of what they invite us to feel and think towards their subject matter; because of their *moral perspective*. For instance, fascist propaganda films like Leni Riefenstahl's *Triumph of the Will* (1935) are immoral due to their solicitation of feelings of pride and glory towards a totalitarian regime. But would we call such a film 'obscene'? It is morally depraved for sure, but it *feels* immoral in a different way to an artwork that invites us to derive pleasure from torture and death. This is another distinguishing feature of the obscene. How we experience it – its phenomenology – fundamentally concerns a *pleasurable* repulsion.

We can think of this emotion on two levels. The first is the repulsion or disgust felt by being invited to have a morally bad response. We feel the pull of the wickedness. But the second is the supposed pleasure or attraction that comes from indulging in these prohibited responses. Basically, the joy of breaking the rules. But what would motivate us to have such obscene enjoyment, and get a thrill from such abominations?

It might be that the artwork presents us with an opportunity to safely indulge in our deepest darkest desires, but ones we would never act out in real life. Art can supposedly be a safe space insulated from the real world in which we can imaginatively engage with our base instincts without actually harming anyone. A desire for extreme sexual domination or subordination, for instance, may be satiated by an artwork that calls upon us to find its portrayal of depraved acts exciting.

Of course, many people do not have such desires. But they may enjoy pretending or imagining that they did. This desire for a desire, what Kieran calls a 'meta-desire', involves an appetite to be morally perverse even when such transgression goes against what we ordinarily stand for. People are fascinated by debauchery in part because it involves violating traditional moral and social codes and stepping outside the boring everyday.

Reading Sade's *The 120 Days of Sodom* may be a harrowing experience, but for some there is something intriguing about its stark moral taboos and world of extreme human violation. We'd never dream, *in real life*, of binding a child down on a table and slowly roasting her skin on a grill while penetrating her, or slicing off penises, clitorises, and breasts, or eating amputated buttocks and dead foetuses, or sewing up vaginas and anuses until they burst, or flogging a pregnant woman until she miscarries. And yet, fiction and art like this provide an escapism where we can make-believe such a transgressive world.* It is this complex, dark desire which grounds the thrill of the obscene.[55]

The fact that this pleasurable disgust is being warmly *invited* may be what distinguishes obscene art from straightforwardly

---

* The enjoyment of the obscene is an instance of what philosophers have called the 'paradox of tragedy', or 'paradox of horror': why do we delight in unpleasant emotions invoked by art?

horrific art. Denounced as the most disturbing film of all time (please take this as a content warning), Srdjan Spasojević's *A Serbian Film* (2010) follows retired porn-star Miloš as he unwittingly becomes embroiled in a necrophiliac and paedophilic snuff film. Now, the film does *show* obscene acts, but it's not clear that the film *itself* is obscene as a work of art.

The worst scene (fictional, I should say), which shows a character raping a newborn baby, portrays the rapist as deriving pleasure from his abominable act. This is a portrayal of surely the ultimate obscenity. But the protagonist, Miloš, whose perspective the viewer is invited to adopt, is notably distressed at this incident and flees. The film is therefore not inviting *us*, the viewer, to feel pleasure towards what is probably the most despicable act ever represented. The film shows obscenity while not itself being obscene, just deeply horrific.

Nonetheless, it'd be reasonable to charge that even just showing this heinous act of 'newborn porn' was a step too far – a prohibited image. It's no wonder that the film has been banned or expurgated in New Zealand, Brazil, Spain, Norway, and the UK, to name a few countries. Even as an avid horror fan myself, I confess that I've seen this film and remain scarred for life.

Disonesto

Despite the peculiar pleasure indicative of the obscene, judging an artwork to be depraved in this way has serious consequences for the artwork itself, and its maker. Branding a work of art as obscene carries with it an accusation of immorality, and some philosophers have argued that a work's immorality can pollute its artistic value.

depraved

From the Roman poet Horace's claim that a goal of poetry is to give life lessons, to Tolstoy's declaration that the great work of art morally elevates its audience, this ancient philosophical view holds that art should improve our character. So, when a novel or painting does the opposite, its greatness is compromised.

The philosopher Berys Gaut, for instance, has argued that when a work of art has an immoral perspective – when it invites us to have an unethical response to what it shows us – its artistic and aesthetic value is tarnished. There are many ways to glean what this value amounts to: a work's beauty, elegance, or complexity, but also the knowledge it imparts to us, or simply how well the artist realises their creative aims. One argument Gaut gives centralises the notion of artistic achievement: insofar as an artist fails in their aim for the work, this constitutes an aesthetic *flaw*.[56]

Consider a horror film where the director has clearly set out to create a film that, among other things, is scary. That's the basic point of the genre. But imagine that the director and producers fail to make the film scary – or worthy of being scary. Perhaps the camera shots, narrative, and acting simply don't warrant a fearful reaction from us as viewers. Maybe we even find it funny. For instance, *One Missed Call* (2008), which tells the story of people hearing their own terrifying final moments on mobile phones, was criticised for its bland performances and jaded shock tactics. It scores badly on Rotten Tomatoes because it's just not frightening. Because the film is inviting us to have an inappropriate response (a response the film itself doesn't justify), we'd say that this is a *bad* horror movie. It fails in an aim internal to it – to be frightening – and so is aesthetically and artistically flawed.

The same thought supposedly applies in the moral case. Imagine a film or novel that invites us to have an *unethical* response towards it. Perhaps it invites us to find heartless cruelty funny, or paedophilic sexual violence arousing and exciting. Here, the work of art is inviting us to have an unethical response. But for Gaut, an unethical response is just another type of unwarranted or inappropriate response. Thus, a work of art that is immoral in this way is artistically flawed in its morally inappropriate invitation.[57]

Another tarnishing effect of the obscenity charge comes from its intimate connection with pornography: the two often come together. When an artwork is declared 'obscene', this is oftentimes because the work is extremely pornographic. But some art historians have considered 'art' and 'pornography' to be incompatible categories, there being 'a clear dividing line' between them; a line which tends to be drawn on aesthetic grounds.[58]

The idea goes that pornography is explicit and objectifies what it represents – bodies and sexual organs – as part of its straightforward aim to be arousing. Art, on the other hand, is supposedly concerned with things of a loftier nature: beauty, subjectivity, imagination, and reflective representation. Enjoying a Paul Cézanne landscape painting, for instance, partly involves finding pleasure in the representation itself: the brushstroke gestures, palette, composition, and so on. These aesthetic features draw us in to the piece, while we imaginatively reflect on what we're being shown, and why. Pornography, by contrast, 'is not interested in persons but in organs', as one author puts it.[59] It is devoid of aesthetic experience and aims simply at sexual arousal; two mental or physiological states which some have taken to be irreconcilable.[60]

Of course, much art does deal with sex, but it's called 'erotic art' when this sexual content is handled in a special way. This might be via narrative, like the subjectivity of the sexual relationship presented to us, or expression of moral themes like love and equality.[61] Erotic art is heralded as original aesthetic expression, whereas pornography is rebuked as formulaic and full of clichés. As philosopher Hans Maes characterises this sentiment, 'Art is concerned with beauty, while pornography is non-aesthetic and "smutty".'[62] Erotic art, then, escapes the moral exile faced by pornography and the obscene. But is this really a robust conceptual divide, or does it have an ulterior motive?

Central to many approaches towards the art/porn divide is the assertion that pornography by definition lacks artistic qualities. So, no wonder it can't be art. This reflects legal definitions of obscenity that we saw earlier: something is declared obscene in part when it lacks any literary or artistic value. But definitions of pornography which *assume* an absence of artistic merit beg the question at hand: if used to show that pornography cannot be art, these definitions assume the very thing they're supposed to prove; that the two are incompatible.

In a bid for philosophical transparency, we must use a neutral definition of pornography, something along the lines of: a sexually explicit representation with a central function to sexually arouse its audience. This doesn't make any assumptions about its artistic quality or merit.[63]

Once we have this definition in hand, we can see clearly that art and pornography can in fact be willing bedfellows.[64] Examples of this abound, from shunga art like Hokusai's famous *The Dream of the Fisherman's Wife* (1814), which shows a woman happily receiving cunnilingus from an obliging octopus, to Robert Mapplethorpe's works like *Helmut and Brooks, N.Y.C.* (1978), which shows one man fisting another man's rectum.

These meet at least a neutral definition of pornography, but are also indisputably major works of art.

However, the real contrast between erotic art and pornography may not be found in their visual (or linguistic) differences at all, but rather their external sociological uses. Philosopher A. W. Eaton persuasively shows that the conceptual distinction between erotic art and pornography is somewhat illusory, in the sense that it quietly tracks a social-class divide. Sexually explicit imagery in Renaissance Italy, for instance, would be considered *disonesto* (the opposite of *onesto*, which means 'morally virtuous') if it appeared in widely distributed prints, but *onesto* if it appeared in higher social settings, such as a fresco in a palace or wealthy household.

Italian artist Giulio Romano, for example, made explicit drawings of a couple having sex in a variety of positions – *I Modi*, or *The Sixteen Pleasures* (1524). These were distributed throughout Europe as racy prints but were censored or destroyed by the Vatican. The very same artist, though, created an even more vividly sexual image of Zeus seducing the queen Olympias in the Sala di Amore e Psiche of the Palazzo del Te (1526–28), apparently referencing his earlier drawings. While this latter painting may be read as even more pornographic than the prints, it was considered *onesto* due to its highbrow purpose and its location, which was a mark of social esteem. It was because sexually charged images now reached the lowest ranks of society – and so posed a threat to a privilege that historically only the elite classes had enjoyed – that they were deemed immoral. Eaton claims that this *disonesto/onesto* distinction is an ancestor to the porn/art distinction of today.[65]

The sociological use of sexually explicit representations has varied throughout history. The supposed divide between erotic art and pornography would have been alien to ancient Near East cultures: so-called high art or erotic art and low art or pornography 'were not differentiated genres in ancient Mesopotamia', according to Zainab Bahrani. Rather, images that today we might consider pornographic were 'often pious works associated with a deity's cult'.[66] While many images of women in Sumer were apparently there to titillate the viewer, they were not for this reason considered lowly or debased cultural artefacts.

Despite the conceptual weakness of the line dividing art and pornography, it is a line that nonetheless persists in the public imagination, and functions as a weighty moral declaration. The tabloids and archaeologists who describe the Palaeolithic female figurines as 'paleo-porn', then, effectively reduce the artworks' status as *art*. Branding prehistoric sculpture as smut or obscene subordinates it to a lower cultural class: to *disonesto*.

Raised Without God

Branding a work of art as obscene has an air of objectivity. Calling a Palaeolithic female figurine 'smut' suggests that the piece is inviting us to have a morally prohibited response to it; one that finds the depicted female body arousing. But not only does this promote the worrying view that women's sexuality is fundamentally debased, it also makes wild anthropological assumptions about what the figurine was even designed to do; what it was meant to elicit from its viewers.

Our declarations of obscenity therefore *rank* the art object as inferior. But how is the supposed moral prohibition determined, in both the social and legal realms? Is this or that artwork *really* immoral? And for whom? We must examine whether the moral code we're implicitly deferring to is correct, and whether our judgement slots a bit too conveniently into problematic ideologies as part of wider cultural imperialism or domination.* Finding non-consensual sexual violence pleasurable to watch or read is indeed morally repugnant. But finding vulvas beautiful as encouraged by erotic Sumerian poetry is surely not. Just because ancient Greek society thought so – a society which derided the female body as inherently dangerous – doesn't mean vulvas are actually bad or ugly things.[67]

As we've seen, these judgements have consequences for the art we deem valuable and important, and can perpetuate existing divides between so-called high and low art. It was convenient for those early modern European merchants to banish the medieval Indian art they saw to immoral purgatory, and thereby dismiss its importance to cultural history. Labelling the art 'obscene' effectively hurls it into the trash as not really art at all – a narrative which would have neatly propped up the East India Company's imperialist agenda in the eighteenth and nineteenth centuries.

This aesthetic supremacy wasn't new. Renowned art historian Kenneth Clark wrote in 1956 that the nude 'is an art form invented by the Greeks in the fifth century'.[68] Eurocentric art history has praised ancient Greek culture as 'discovering' the beauty of the body. Their 'invention' of the nude with the fourth-century BCE sculpture *Aphrodite of Knidos* has become the barometer of beauty against which other art across the globe has been measured, and has ultimately fallen short. This judgement derives, Bahrani argues, from frameworks used by the ancient Greeks to legitimate their power: Greek/barbarian, man/beast, male/female.[69] Plato implied this sentiment when

* For more on the concept of cultural imperialism, see Edward Said's *Culture and Imperialism* (London: Chatto & Windus, 1993).

he claimed in his *Epinomis* that whatever the Greeks take from foreigners, they make it better.[70]

According to scholars, the ancient Greeks used the naked body as a site of difference between them and the uncivilised, obscene 'beast'. During Hellenistic colonisation of the Near East in the fourth century BCE, Greek aesthetic expression of the female form met local resistance, in part due to its erasure of the vulva and casting of the female figure as passive and modest, in comparison to the confronting and explicit Near Eastern portrayals of the female body. The ancient Greeks' claim to superior aesthetic sense – one that permeates our art history books today – meant a claim to superior intellect and morality. Aesthetic judgements like these, then, are self-fulfilling acts of rationalisation: a dominant group's suppression of another group is justified if the subordinated group creates inferior art.

As well as propping up these structures of cultural imperialism, where a dominant group's culture others and alienates an oppressed group's aesthetic ways of navigating the world, reckless judgements of obscenity lead to questionable scholarship, scientific enquiry, and curatorial practice. For instance, the prevailing view since the nineteenth century that the Upper Palaeolithic female figurines discovered across Eurasia and Africa are sex objects has been dubbed the 'Venus hypothesis' by anthropologists April Nowell and Melanie Chang. The hypothesis is composed of several myths and assumptions about the significance of these prehistoric artworks, which reflect contemporary society's sexual mores and are not adequately supported by archaeological evidence.

Many of these false assumptions will be familiar: that Upper Palaeolithic artists were only men, that only men enjoy(ed) erotica, that all the figurines have the same body type of a small waist and large hips, and that any portrayal of women's bodies is either erotic or maternal by default. These myths hold fast despite ample counterevidence, and viewing the artefacts through this restrictive lens both obstructs archaeological enquiry and has unwelcome consequences for society's attitudes towards women today. As Nowell and Chang observe:

> By not challenging, and therefore tacitly accepting, questionable interpretations and assumptions about the artifacts and what they meant to Paleolithic people, many paleo-anthropologists embed current constructs of gender and gender relations into the past, possibly with negative social effects.[71]

This attitude towards the female body is also evident in what ancient art scholarship *doesn't* do: in its striking lacuna of detailed discussion of the vulvae imagery found in Near Eastern art – an avoidance likely 'a legacy of the Judeo-Christian taboo'.[72]

Even the way forbidden art has been catalogued, illustrated, and displayed betrays implicit obscenity charges. The Roman art in Francis I's secret museum in Naples, for instance, was sanitised by texts and engravings which 'played down the highly charged sexualized contents of the room' – a form of censorship in itself.[73] This reflected a broadening nineteenth-century prudishness towards sex, which resulted in ancient Greek and Roman art being isolated from its contexts to the point of being fetishised. For instance, rather than being catalogued and displayed according to their original placements and domestic or civic functions, erotic artefacts were grouped together, and instead of finding one such object that might have adorned a single doorway, we'd find a whole drawer of them. Such practices distorted contemporary views of Roman attitudes towards sex; the phallic objects that would guard doorways for instance were not originally seen as simply expressions of indulgent sexual arousal but rather as protection from evil forces.[74]

———

When we approach more contemporary art, we must similarly be wary of bias and double standards tainting our experience. Declarations of the obscene are often inconsistent and applied unfairly to oppressed groups, leading to further marginalisation, withdrawal of funding, and even imprisonment.

For instance, Cincinnati's Contemporary Arts Center (CAC) and its director were charged with obscenity in 1990 for displaying a retrospective of Robert Mapplethorpe's provocative photographs; the first prosecution of its kind in US history. The travelling collection on show – *The Perfect Moment* – held 175 images, including still lifes, two portraits of nude children, and five sexually explicit images of gay S&M culture, and had by this point been exhibited in Philadelphia, Chicago, and Washington DC. (By the time the exhibition reached Cincinnati, the artist had died from AIDS.) The focus of the obscenity charges levelled against CAC was the S&M images, and the two portraits of nude children (the latter were at the time defended on the grounds that they are not sexualising and were taken consensually with the parents' full knowledge).[75]

While the director and the CAC were acquitted on the grounds that the photographs were undoubtedly art, the charges of obscenity revealed an insidious stigma at the centre of the 1980s/90s AIDS epidemic. At the time of the trial, the fear of AIDS had reached hysteria, and Mapplethorpe's unashamed homosexuality became a focal point for Republican senators' wrath against the National Endowment for the Arts for funding work *they* considered obscene.[*]

Jesse Helms of North Carolina was one such senator who decried Mapplethorpe and the LGBTQIA+ community in vitriolic, homophobic speeches at the Senate and the White House – where President George H. W. Bush had earlier blamed AIDS patients for their illness. While Mapplethorpe's groundbreaking photographs have since been praised for their 'beauty', 'honesty' and 'intimacy',[76] Helms would frequently condemn Mapplethorpe's art as not art at all, but 'garbage', all because of its homoerotic content.[77] In 1989, he told the *New York Times*, 'There's a big difference between *The Merchant of Venice* and a photograph of two males of different races in an erotic pose on a marble-top table.'[78] As one critic wrote of this controversy:

> Mapplethorpe was caught up in what seemed like a debate about arts funding and censorship, but this was really a pretext for connecting sex to disease to a general sense of cultural decay — Helms called artists like Mapplethorpe 'human cockroaches' — and blaming it all on LGBT people, a convenient minority scapegoat.[79]

This rejection of queer art as inherently obscene is sadly not a thing of the past. In 2010, South African government minister Lulu Xingwana walked out of a Johannesburg exhibition by the artist Zanele Muholi, which featured striking photographs of naked, black lesbian couples intimately embracing. The minister denounced Muholi's art as 'immoral, offensive and

---

[*] At the time, Cincinnati was considered 'the most anti-gay city in the country'; it blocked enactment or enforcement of gay rights laws until 2004.

going against nation-building'.[80] At a time when gay rights are still not recognised in many African countries and punishment can include 'corrective' rape or even the death penalty, Muholi emphatically refuted the claim that their work is in any way obscene, or that homosexuality is 'un-African'.[81] The artist argued that their photography is a form of visual activism in the ongoing fight for queer liberation.

Bias towards the obscene, then, is at its most entrenched when it comes to the body – specifically, marginalised bodies. In 2014, Megumi Igarashi was the first woman in Japanese history to be charged on grounds of obscenity, for her artwork *Man-Boat* (2014). The work – a yellow kayak in the shape of a vulva – was made in the design of the artist's own genitalia using a 3D printer. Igarashi was arrested for this work because it counted as distributing obscene data, violating Article 175 of the Japanese criminal code. Igarashi told *Glamour* magazine:

> My work is meant to make the female sex organs funny and fun and cute . . . I hadn't thought any of that fell even remotely into the purview of 'obscenity' in the first place. But the judicial courts have this idiosyncratic concept of the vagina as something that will arouse men when they see it no matter what.[82]

Amazingly, while Igarashi was serving jail time and appearing in court for her trial, huge penis sculptures were paraded at the annual Kanamara Matsuri (Festival of the Steel Phallus) – a Shinto Japanese festival during which celebrants pray to gods for marital happiness, easy childbirths, and protection from STIs – which is considered perfectly acceptable by the authorities. According to this double standard, the vulva is a shameful object of arousal to be hidden at all costs, whereas the penis is something to be actively celebrated and represented in enormous shrines and tasty lollipops.

Just a year later, Canadian Indian artist and writer Rupi Kaur was censored on Instagram for posting self-portraits showing her menstruating. Part of her university art project, one of the images shows Kaur lying on a bed fully clothed and facing a wall, with a patch of blood between her legs which has dripped on to the sheets. Kaur's work aimed to demystify ancient stigmas around menstruation, which still cause harm to women across the world today.

The portrait was swarmed with hate: 'come over here and let me make your vagina bleed' and 'fuck your feminism' were among the many comments. Kaur even received death threats. Instagram then deleted the photo, twice, not because of the online abuse and trolling but because Kaur's imagery violated their terms of service. Kaur responded to the censorship on Facebook:

> Thank you Instagram for providing me with the exact response my work was created to critique . . . I will not apologize for not feeding the ego and pride of misogynist society that will have my body in underwear but not be okay with a small leak when your pages are filled with countless photos/accounts where women (so many who are underage) are objectified, pornified and treated less than human.

Kaur's *Period* (2015) deftly exposed society's double standards towards obscenity – blood becomes obscene when it leaks out of a marginalised body. The taboo around menstrual blood is an ancient, almost universal one. While flowing blood itself is often seen positively and even as divine in the case of sacrifice and martyrdom, menstrual blood has been derided as dirty and shameful for thousands of years, despite it being a natural process for so many people.

This damaging perception may arise from a deep-rooted fear of the 'abject' body – one that is deemed repulsive and threatening to the 'natural order' of things. Developed by philosopher Julia Kristeva in her *Powers of Horror* (1980), the concept of the abject – which normally manifests in corpses and exposed bodily functions or fluids – describes the dissolution of meaning into pure physical material, where the self must confront its own corporeality. Abject horror is particularly potent when it comes to menstruating bodies:

> The normal body is not a bleeding body . . . A body threatening to burst its boundaries and give birth . . . leak milk from her breasts . . . and spill blood from between her legs . . . is viewed with horror and fascination (Kristeva 1982, 3). It is this cultural representation of a sticky, messy femininity that places menstruating women at the borders of social legitimacy.[83]

The menstruating body is still considered obscene today – it disturbs the boundaries of what is morally and culturally acceptable.[84] The lack of period representation in popular culture testifies to the contempt that still clings to menstruation. In 2020, I saw a character in Michaela Coel's black comedy-drama *I May Destroy You* simply sit down on the toilet and change a bloodied sanitary pad. I was thirty years old and had never seen this most ordinary of acts depicted on TV or in film.

While I was pleased with this long-awaited representation, I also felt anger. Why had it taken so long for this mundane routine to be shown on our screens? We can easily find images of gruesome abominations and gory cruelty, but rarely do we ever see *period* blood. The disdain for women's monthly blood surely explains the fact that TV advertisements have only just started showing sanitary products with *red* liquid rather than blue, and why period products were not even tested with actual blood until 2023.[85]

Probably the most notorious double standard in an obscenity outcry to emerge in recent years was Cardi B's 'WAP (Wet-Ass Pussy)' storm in 2020. The song, featuring guest rapper Megan Thee Stallion, is a bombastic ode to female pleasure. I must here pause to draw an irresistible similarity between 'WAP' and an ancient Mesopotamian love poem:

> My vulva is wet, [my vulva is wet],
> I, the queen of heaven, [my vulva is wet],
> Let the man on top [put his hand] on my vulva,
> Let the potent man [put his hand] on my vulva.[86]
>
> Yeah, you fuckin' with some wet ass pussy
> Bring a bucket and a mop for this wet ass pussy
> Give me everything you got for this wet ass pussy.

While the track has been hugely successful – it was the first female rap collaboration to reach number one on the Billboard Hot 100 and has been streamed and downloaded millions of times – it was violently condemned by conservative figures.

'[It] made me want to pour holy water in my ears,' exclaimed Republican congressional candidate James P. Bradley. Condemning the song and its video as 'what happens when children are raised without God and without a strong father figure', Bradley and others despaired that Cardi B and Megan Thee Stallion were now role models, and that the 'vile' 'WAP' had set back feminism by a hundred years. Ben Shapiro lamented that the feminist movement today wasn't really about the emancipation of women, but simply about 'wet-ass p-word'. Concerned on medical grounds too, Shapiro reportedly consulted a doctor – his wife – about the very existence of a 'wet-ass p-word' and whether such intense lubrication is even possible.[87] The outrage also became an opportunity for right-wing politicians to admonish the left: 'Bernie Sanders campaigned with Cardi B. Kamala Harris called her a role model . . . The Democrats support this trash and depravity!' wrote former Republican candidate DeAnna Lorraine on X.

The truly astonishing aspect of this crusade is that singing about female sexual pleasure was considered depraved because it's obscene, while at the same time the US President was normalising sexual violence and assault. As *Rolling Stone*'s Charles Holmes writes:

According to conservatives, 'WAP' threatens the very future of women everywhere. In a way it does, if the right wing wants to keep its oppressive vision of the world intact. Contrary to popular belief, Republicans aren't offended by the thought of sex — if they were, Donald Trump's multiple sexual misconduct allegations would have impeded his political aspirations. What they are furious about is the racial and economic make-up of who gets to enjoy and speak about sex.[88]

As Holmes observes, the outcries of obscenity here were not rallied against sex per se, but against *who* was taking ownership of sexualisation. Sexual explicitness is tolerated in the men's locker room, but not when celebrated by a woman of colour. Megan Thee Stallion responded to the 'WAP' outrage by noting how women celebrating their sexual agency simply 'freaks men the hell out'. She told *GQ* magazine that it comes from 'a place of fear and insecurity . . . like why would anyone be mad about my WAP? It belongs to me.'[89]

The music industry today is brimming with explicit material, but accusations of depravity and decaying feminism do not fall upon the creator anywhere near to the same extent when they are a man. Hypersexualised imagery of women is common in hip-hop music. For instance, rapper BRS Kash's 'Throat Baby (Go Baby)' (2021) is an explicit description of fellatio, and has drawn criticism for its derogatory representation of women. Regardless of the misogyny present in the song, it has also been praised as a celebration of male sexual desire and has not received anything like the backlash faced by 'WAP'.

In countless songs like 'Throat Baby (Go Baby)', women are objectified and nobody bats an eyelid. But if a woman self-objectifies or sings about her own sexual pleasure with zeal, she is condemned as obscene – as an affront to God.

————

We have looked in the eye of the first face of depraved art: artworks which explicitly *show* supposed immoral things. When we try to think of what depravity looks like, we might picture 'obscene' images – perhaps perverted sex, blasphemous scenes, or squirting genitalia. Obscene art doesn't just simply show us alleged immorality though; it invites us to respond in a peculiar way, to enjoy and relish its gruesome ethical violation.

But on closer inspection, there is a defectiveness in the very way we think about obscenity. While a robust philosophical concept, it has been misused as an abuse of power – accusing artworks and artists of obscenity can have sinister effects. A woman who sings about being turned on is condemned as obscene, but a man doing the same thing is celebrated. The ancient and medieval nude art of the Near East and South Asia is branded as debased smut, while the nude art of Greek and Roman antiquity is celebrated as lofty beauty. These inconsistent and morally loaded aesthetic judgements are disguised weapons wielded against suppressed groups and civilisations. If we are to get any nearer to a just world, we must learn to judge the obscene better.

As we move on to the second guise of our many-headed monster, I want you to bear this critical stance in mind. People are often quick to castigate art they think is immoral without reflecting on whether it contains true or objective moral perversions. The depravity we fear may not reside in the artwork before us, but rather within ourselves.

2 | CRIMINALITY

While [the bath] is prepared the girl is sitting in a chamber
Looking at a certain painted panel: on it was this picture,
How they say Jupiter once sent a golden shower into the
    lap of Danaë.
I too started looking and because he played a very similar
    game
Once upon a time, all the more my heart rejoiced,
That a god should turn himself into a man and creep
Onto someone else's roof tiles to trick a woman through a
    skylight.
And what a god! 'Who shakes the quadrants of the sky
    with his clap.'
And I, mere mortal, shouldn't do it? You bet I did it, and I
    loved it![1]

(Eunuchus, Act 3: 583–91)

In this scene, the young Athenian man Chaerea describes how he follows a girl, Pamphila, to her house. He enters on false pretences, disguised as a eunuch. As Pamphila prepares a bath, she and Chaerea gaze at a painted panel in her chamber. The painting shows the moment that Jupiter impregnates Danaë with a golden shower from above. While Chaerea does not initially intend to commit assault, he is overcome with lust inflamed by the painting, bolts the door, and rapes Pamphila. He tears her clothes and her hair, and she silently weeps.

depraved

This extract from the comedy play *Eunuchus*, written by the second-century BCE Roman playwright Terence, encapsulates the power of art to seduce us into doing the most abominable things. Captivated by the painting in the chamber, to the point of it sending him reeling from his senses, Chaerea imitates Jupiter – the principal seducer in ancient Greek and Roman mythology – in a bid to feel God-like in that very moment.

While a fictional story, this play speaks to the potentially dangerous impact that artworks can have on our behaviour. Scholars mostly agree that Chaerea's actions are detestable; that his blaming the painting is a 'lame excuse',[2] and that his boastful narration ought to have disturbed ancient audiences.[3] Saint Augustine joined in with this denouncement when he declared that Chaerea accepts the painting as 'authoritative precedent for his own licentiousness'.[4]

But some scholars ask whether the impressionable Chaerea is at all absolved given that he is intoxicated by the painting's beauty. In classical antiquity, rape in art – which was a common motif – was often excused and the rapist's responsibility diminished if accompanied by drunkenness.[5] Perhaps the painting in the chamber is like wine, dulling Chaerea's inhibitions. So is the artwork a culpable catalyst, or simply a scapegoat for the weak will of this young man?

Intoxication

Plato thought that much art was indeed a guilty catalyst for pushing us into depravity. He feared that it could overwhelm the very souls of citizens in his ideal society. For Plato, the soul is divided into three parts: reason, spirit, and desire, and reason above all should be in control. But he worried that poetry, especially in theatre, corrupted the soul by disrupting the balance of its parts. Such art was prone to stirring our base instincts by seducing us into false or irrational sentiments, which Plato believed would hinder our ability to think rationally and control our appetites. Because of this, the rulers of Plato's ideal state – the Philosopher Kings – would have banned this dangerous poetry from society.

It's easy to dismiss the anxious Plato as just being overly dramatic. But maybe he was right to worry. History is littered with cases where art has been accused of tipping people over the edge, igniting terrible passions, and inciting violence. Legend has it that the first Greek sculpture of female nudity – the *Aphrodite of Knidos* from the fourth century BCE – was considered so lifelike and beautiful that one man attempted to have sex with it, ejaculated on to it, and then upon being discovered, in shame threw himself off a cliff.[6] Whether or not this legend from the second century CE is true is beside the point – what it does is highlight the carnal effect sensual depictions of the human form can have. This life-sized sculpture of Aphrodite sent, as Kenneth Clark put it, a 'sensual tremor' across the ancient Mediterranean and beyond.[7]

Supposedly, art does this by harnessing our imaginations and seductively portraying a person or another world. Fictional works of art, which we know are not entirely real, can still inspire us to do good and bad things. Towards the end of Elizabeth I's reign, Shakespeare's *Richard II* – which tells how the king was deposed by Henry IV and murdered – was performed all over London to the rich and poor alike. The play had striking parallels with the reign of the ageing queen, and in a time of political and religious upheaval, an important scene where Richard II resigns his throne was removed.

But on Saturday, 7 February 1601, Shakespeare's Company was asked to perform *Richard II* at the Globe in London – this time showing the censored scene – by supporters of Robert Devereux, Earl of Essex, who was plotting against Elizabeth I and planned to seize her throne the very next day. Supporters paid the Company over the odds to perform the unredacted play, hoping that it would convince the audience of the rebellion and invigorate an uprising. But the rebellion failed, and Essex was captured and beheaded for treason.

While we can't blame Shakespeare for inciting a rebellion (his actors were not arrested and were even ordered to perform the play for the queen herself on the eve of Essex's execution), supporters of the Essex Rebellion clearly believed that Shakespeare's art would be a sure-fire way of getting the public on Essex's side.

And then there are more depraved cases. Between July 1963 and October 1965 in Manchester, England, Ian Brady and Myra Hindley sexually assaulted and murdered five children – Pauline Reade, John Kilbride, Keith Bennett, Lesley Ann Downey, and Edward Evans. Three of the victims were buried on Saddleworth Moor, and possibly a fourth – Bennett – but the whereabouts of his body is still unknown.

At the trial, the killers' personal libraries were inspected and were found to include works by the nineteenth-century German philosopher Friedrich Nietzsche and the Marquis de Sade. It transpired that during their relationship, Brady had indoctrinated his accomplice with Sadean literature and a kind of moral relativism – the belief that what makes something right or wrong is simply a human and cultural creation, and therefore fluid and mutable (this view is in part derived from some interpretations of Nietzsche's philosophy). As for ideas gleaned from Sade's literary art like *The 120 Days of Sodom*, Brady and Hindley relished the notion that pleasure and pain are the only real or natural values, and that morality itself is constructed to control society.

While Brady apparently claimed to hold these Sadean ideas before he read any Sade, it is difficult not to worry that art which glamorises and eroticises such sexual violence, even in an imaginary, fictional world, might have some influence over the people who consume it. Brady saw himself as one of Sade's protagonist heroes – someone who transgresses conventional moral standards in the pursuit of ultimate power and pleasure. The similarity between the lovers Brady and Hindley, and Sade and his wife Renée-Pélagie, is unsettling to say the least. Sade's horror stories were made a reality once again.

The fear of art's virulent influence has sometimes led people to destroy it. In what became known as the 'bonfire of the vanities' in Florence's main public square in 1497, supporters of the Dominican friar Girolamo Savonarola – an ascetic who radically opposed secular art – burned books, sculptures, and paintings that were thought to tempt sin. In the mid-eighteenth century, Louis I, Duke of Orléans – a religious fanatic – attacked with a knife Correggio's famous mythological painting *Leda and the Swan* (*c.* 1532) and ordered more of the painter's works to be cut up into pieces, all because he so strongly disapproved of their pulsating eroticism.[8]

It's not just painting, sculpture, and literature that we should be wary of. Music, arguably the most affective of the arts in its expression of emotion and feeling, has throughout history been used to convey beauty and to foster communal bonding, but it has also been feared for its capacity to induce madness and pandemonium.

In ancient Greek mythology, it was the haunting songs of sirens that were more of a threat to sailors than the swelling ocean. And it was the deadly war chants of the enemy that put the fear of God into medieval warriors, the bugles and drums that sent infantry vigorously over the top in the First World War trenches, and Igor Stravinsky's ballet *The Rite of Spring*, performed in Paris in 1913, that sent its audience into a riot with its dissonant score and unsettling dancing figures. Likewise, who could forget the legendary Pied Piper of Hamelin, Germany – the disgruntled rat-catcher who, in revenge for not being paid, lured 130 children down into a cave with his melodies, never to be seen again. To this very day, music and dancing are not permitted on the street where the children were apparently last seen in the thirteenth century – called 'Bungelosenstrasse' (Street Without Drums).[9]

Music's power to evoke excitable emotion has worried philosophers and theologians for millennia. Plato thought music resembled parts of the soul, and so banished all but two of the musical modes – the Dorian (for courage) and Phrygian (for peace) – from his ideal state. For him, the Ionian and Lydian modes were unbecoming 'drinking songs', and the 'mixed' Lydian and 'extreme' Lydian modes were too dirge-like and sorrowful – completely unacceptable: he wrote, 'even women, if they are respectable, have no use for them, let alone men'.[10] Any music which was pleasurable or overly sensuous was a threat to our rational faculties.

Islamic figures shared a similar view: the Prophet Muhammad held that music could be both halal and haram, and Sufi masters thought that music could evoke feelings of love but also make men murderers.[11] Others felt music should only be reserved for the elite in society for fear of music-induced copulation.* The eighth-century Caliph ibn Walid is quoted as saying,

> O, Umaiyads, avoid singing for it decreases shame, increases desire, and destroys manliness, and verily it takes the place of wine and does what drunkenness does. But if you must engage in it, keep the women and children away from it, for singing is the instigator of fornication.[12]

And while Kǒng Fūzǐ (Confucius) saw moral benefits to music, the philosopher Mozi demanded its eradication due to its distracting listeners from more important duties. Writing during the Warring States period in ancient China, Mozi felt that musical performances were a waste of vital resources, and that the more music develops, the more chaotic society becomes.[13]

There is a nugget of truth to this unease: music can have a huge influence over our lives. We know that lullabies soothe babies, that favourite songs help Alzheimer's sufferers connect with childhood memories, and that listening to music can provide pain relief.[14] Studies show that our limbic system, which regulates emotion and memory, 'lights up' with increased blood flow when we listen to music.[15] Those chills you feel in response to a particular tonal arrangement or a big drop in electronic dance music are supposedly the result of a dopamine dose.[16] It's no wonder, then, that many fear that this remarkable art form can send us to ominous places, too.

---

* This has indeed happened. At Fatboy Slim's set at Woodstock '99, some festival-goers in the rave hangar were reportedly on all fours doing all manner of 'biblical' things.

Total Fucking Darkness

Some of the most provocative genres of modern music – heavy rock and metal – have regularly made headlines in the wake of school shootings and hysteria over Satanic cults.[17] By the 1990s, Marilyn Manson and his band had become one of the most controversial rock acts in history; Manson was a household name and an icon for disillusioned youth. His salacious concerts were often picketed by religious conservatives and parents, who accused his music of corrupting their children by inciting 'rape, murder, blasphemy and suicide'.[18]

The most notorious of these outcries was after Colorado's Columbine High School shooting in 1999, where two high school seniors shot and killed twelve students and a teacher, before committing suicide. After the tragedy, the media alleged that the shooters were fans of Marilyn Manson, and even wore his band T-shirts during the massacre. Despite these allegations being false – the shooters reportedly hated the music – Manson remained a scapegoat whom the media continued to sensationalise, with headlines that read 'Killers Worshipped Rock Freak Manson' and 'Devil-Worshipping Maniac Told Kids To Kill'.[19]

Manson stringently denied that either his music or the goth subculture was to blame for such violence, stating: 'This tragedy was a product of ignorance, hatred and an access to guns.'[20] In subsequent interviews, Manson insisted that his music does not promote violence and hate, but instead encourages youths to challenge widely held societal norms and embrace difference.

Just three months after the Columbine tragedy was the infamous Woodstock Festival '99 in upstate New York. While one of the organisers, Michael Lang, wanted to recapture the peaceful haze of the original Woodstock of 1969 and use the 1999 instalment to send a clear anti-gun message, things instead took a turn for the worse. Due to inadequate infrastructure, extortionate prices for water and food, poor sanitation, and blazing hot weather, festival-goers became increasingly frustrated. So, imagine the disaster that followed when nu-metal band Limp Bizkit took to the stage on the Saturday (following Korn on the Friday), and lead singer Fred Durst shouted to the frenzied crowd of more than 200,000 to 'take all that negative energy and let all that shit out of your system . . . I want you to fucking kick in!!!', right in the middle of their smash hit song 'Break Stuff' (1999).

Well, stuff was indeed broken. Parts of the stage set were dismantled, plywood was torn off towers and used for crowd surfing, and huge mosh pits and rampant trampling resulted in bloody injuries and broken bones. After being pulled off stage by security, Durst simply said: 'Dude it's not our fault.'[21] But this was only the beginning. After Red Hot Chili Peppers closed the festival on the Sunday, a candlelight vigil spiralled into major arson. The entire festival site was eventually burned to the ground in scenes that looked like the last days of Rome.

The metal and rock bands at Woodstock '99 certainly cannot be solely blamed for the bedlam that ensued that weekend. They *especially* cannot be blamed for the rapes, sexual assaults, trench mouth, and 'shit-mud' (open sewage) that came to define the festival and doom the Woodstock brand forever. But their music did arguably offer a seductive channel for releasing a lot of pent-up aggression, even if it was wider societal issues such as toxic masculinity and misogyny, plus the festival's appalling organisation, which arguably put that aggression there in the first place. As one reporter aptly described the festival chaos: 'kerosene, match, BOOM!'[22]

Sometimes there is a tighter connection between music and violence. In the dawn light of Christmas Day in 1992, a young man treading through snow approached a nineteenth-century wooden Methodist church in Sarpsborg, Norway. He set it alight. Sirens were soon whirling as the church quickly went up in flames. One of the firefighters called to the scene died while trying to extinguish the blaze. The suspect, a well-known local Satanist, was never convicted.[23]

This arson attack was one of at least thirty church burnings across Norway directly connected to the early Norwegian black metal scene of the 1990s, a brutal style of heavy metal inspired by British bands such as Venom. Its signature sound – buzzy, trebly guitar and guttural vocals backed by pummelling percussion – lends a stark aesthetic to the exploration of themes ranging from pagan religion and the occult to Nordic folklore and passion for the natural world.

While the genre has been central to the development of extreme metal music, its early core artists and fans – part of the so-called 'Black Metal Inner Circle' – committed many similar acts of arson, as well as assault, murder, and possible animal sacrifice (a decapitated hare was found at the door of another burnt down Norwegian church earlier in 1992).

One figure in this original circle, Bård Guldvik 'Faust' Eithun, killed a gay man in the town of Lillehammer by stabbing him thirty-seven times. Eithun reportedly felt no remorse over the murder, claiming he simply wished to release some aggression. Another central figure, Kristian 'Varg' Vikernes – founder of the band Burzum – stabbed to death Øystein 'Euronymous' Aarseth – founder of the band Mayhem – allegedly over disagreements about record contracts and the state of their emerging genre. Vikernes was sentenced to twenty-one years in prison, and on the day of sentencing, two churches were burnt to the ground in a symbolic show of support.[24]

As well as its core members murdering and assaulting each other, this scene – which was composed largely of young white men – was notorious for its shocking performances, sonic innovations, and espousal of misanthropic and militant Satanist views. One lead singer of Mayhem – Per 'Dead' Ohlin – would slit his wrists on stage, hoard dead birds under his bed to enjoy the stench of death, and adorn himself in 'corpse paint'. He eventually committed suicide aged twenty-two in a house in the woods near Kråkstad, leaving behind a note which read, 'Excuse the blood . . .'. He was found by Euronymous, who photographed the corpse with a disposable camera and used the picture as the cover art for a forthcoming Mayhem album.[25]

Would the original scene have become as popular and influential if it weren't for its shocking past? In early black metal, the art itself was infused with the bloodshed that surrounded it. The genre's sonic characteristics were reinforced by its brutal origins: this music *sounds* violent, aggressive, and angry. Dead's macabre spectacle combined with his fast-paced howling music created a powerful expression of emotional pain and mental illness, among other difficult topics. This demonic theatre is part of the marvel of the genre – I can say this from experience after seeing the Swedish metal band Watain in a little backstreet venue in Reading, England, and being splattered with pigs' blood while the musicians screeched in front of a flaming altar of impaled fish-heads.

At the end of the day, these young men were accountable for their own criminality. Most black metal fans (including myself) have not set fire to churches or stabbed anyone, and the genre today has substantially developed and mostly left behind its literal Satanic leanings to embrace themes of social justice and eco-activism. And yet, some lovers of the music are still vulnerable to its allure. In a 2016 interview, the vocalist of black metal band Carpathian Forest, Roger 'Nattefrost' Rasmussen, alleged that he knew of two or three cases where people had committed suicide because of his music. He admitted that Carpathian Forest may well 'make an impression' on fans, but that ultimately 'people should do whatever they feel like . . . kill each other, whatever, right?'[26]

———

So can we really hold paintings, films, music, or books responsible for our misdeeds? Does it matter more when the artwork itself explicitly invites us to sin? There are at least two types of causation relevant here: arousal and incitement. The former concerns anything from a felt physical chill to a fullblown terrible act committed in reaction to an artwork. But the latter involves the artwork itself calling or urging its audience to engage in particular immoral behaviour – here there is a closer connection between art and criminality, and one that justifies such art's prosecution.

This distinction will be important when exploring causal connections between art and immorality. We will see that it has been difficult to prove that artworks with violent content, like videogames or rap and metal music, have directly aroused or incited people to commit violent acts. But where empirical studies leave the state of things somewhat unclear, philosophy can step in to scrutinise art's causal relation to depravity. Something's being fiction does not prevent its messages leaking out into the real world; doing depraved things in virtual worlds is still problematic.

But we must also be wary of how art is accused in this way: society is often quick to denounce certain art forms over others, and such inconsistencies can betray lurking prejudices. Criminal charges of incitement have a bad habit of sticking like mud to some music genres and not others, which can perpetuate the discrimination of those already marginalised in society.

Imaginary Evil

In the videogame *Rape Day*, players have control of the Boss: a serial killer and rapist whose main aim during a zombie apocalypse is to rape and murder as many innocent people as possible, especially women. The gameplay advertised includes 'violence, sexual assault, non-consensual sex, obscene language, necrophilia, and incest'.[27] Its blurb on an online gaming platform reads:

> Verbally harass, kill, and rape women as you choose to progress the story. It's a dangerous world with no laws. The zombies enjoy eating the flesh off warm humans and brutally raping them but you are the most dangerous rapist in town . . . So skip the foreplay and enjoy your Rape Day; you deserve it.[28]

Denounced as one of the most hideous videogames of all time, this visual novel – an interactive fiction with images and prewritten story choices – went online in March 2019, only to be refused distribution by the service Steam. Amid public outcry and a petition on Change.org, Steam stated that 'after significant fact-finding and discussion, we think "Rape Day" poses unknown costs and risks and therefore won't be on Steam'.[29]

Rape Day's developer, a man named Jake who goes by the alias 'Desk Lamp', defended his game: 'Most people can separate fiction from reality pretty well, and those that can't shouldn't be playing video games.'[30]

Is Jake right? We can fairly judge *Rape Day* as disgusting, but Jake's defence does reflect a common belief about immoral art: it's just fiction. It's designed to be a realm of make-believe far away from the real world. In videogames, the player's actions are virtual; no real harm occurs. When a player sexually assaults a character, no one is in fact sexually assaulted. Other art forms like literature, painting, and music are also often just fictional worlds created for us to enjoy; they have no bearing on the outside world.

This claim has been made to defend the distribution of violent genres of pornography. Amid the 'porn wars' of the 1970s and 1980s, where feminist thinkers such as Andrea Dworkin and Catharine MacKinnon argued that pornography harms real women, there were some dissenters who held that pornography couldn't be harmful because it was fictional.

There is some truth to this. A lot of pornography bears the traditional hallmarks of fiction – such as crafted plots and narrative techniques – as well as formulaic scripts with unrealistic events and characters. Pornography invites us into a world of erotic imagination. We're supposed to take it as mere fantasy, much like innocently watching a Disney film or reading the *Chronicles of Narnia*, and then afterwards returning to the real world supposedly unchanged.[31]

But to claim that the fictionality of pornography, or of a

painting, novel, or videogame, somehow insulates it from the real world ignores how fiction actually works. Most fiction is not entirely false, separated from the world; it frequently merges with it: 'There is truth – literal truth – in fiction, since most fictional stories play out against a background of fact,' observes philosopher Greg Currie (or at least, a background of *purported* fact).[32] Fictions express content that is true inside the fiction, but also content that purports to be true outside of it.[33] Authors frequently set their stories in real locations amid historical events, and often make profound assertions about the actual world.

It is widely agreed that we can learn something substantive from such fiction.[34] We can learn a great deal about Henry VIII's court from Hilary Mantel's *Wolf Hall* (2009), about nineteenth-century Russian bourgeois society from Leo Tolstoy's *The Death of Ivan Ilyich* (1886), and about the ethical use of power from Ursula Le Guin's *Earthsea* (1968–2001). We value art for its unique ability to communicate truths about historical events but also about the human condition. It enriches our ability to make moral judgements in the real world – art enables us to imagine what it would be like to be in a certain situation, and so expands our emotional intellect and cultivates our tools for general moral reflection. We take this art seriously, and many artists and authors wish us to.[35]

But this means we can learn bad, false things from art as well. Some philosophers argue that pornography's being somewhat fictional doesn't mean consumers won't infer dangerous falsehoods about sex and desire from it, in part because so many young people now consume it as a form of sex education rather than as mere entertainment.[36] As philosopher Jeremy Waldron observes:

> The visibly pornographic aspect of our society has a pedagogical function . . . Not only does pornography present itself as undermining society's assurance to women of equal respect and equal citizenship, but it does so effectively by intimating that *this is how men are taught, around here*, on the streets and on the screen, if not in school, about how women are to be treated.[37]

Like pornography, immoral art merges with the real world, so we must be wary of its impact on us. But what kind of impact are we talking about?

As Oscar Wilde put it, 'life imitates art', and ancient audiences took this idea quite literally. Art in antiquity would induce the world to imitate it. Didactic art in ancient Rome was a familiar sight, ranging from pagan, Jewish, and early Christian wall paintings in the catacombs which illustrated polytheistic and biblical teachings, to paintings of sex found in brothels, which were there for sex workers and their clients to copy. Literary works, too, gave instruction and inspiration for the bedroom. Ovid's *Art of Love* (*c.* 2 CE), for instance, was a poetic how-to manual on a variety of sexual positions and acts, including threesomes.[38]

The fine and theatrical arts similarly aimed for verisimilitude, whether in a sculpture of the human form or the performance of a tragic hero. Pliny the Elder tells us that the artist Pythagoras of Rhegium's technique was so realistic that his bronze sculpture of a lame man left viewers with sore feet themselves.[39] And mime in Roman theatre would push realism to the brink by bypassing representation altogether, showing unsimulated sex acts on stage.

It was common to experience art – painting, sculpture, and theatre – not as inert representation, but as very much alive.

Because of art's lifelikeness, its *mimesis* of life, it was thought that people would feel what the depicted subject felt. Aristotle believed that we literally become what we see; that we physically change to conform to what we behold in an artwork – even the jelly of our eyes changes colour to match a perceived object.[40] He wasn't quite right about that detail, but he was certainly correct about our empathetic reactions to art: when a work is executed with astonishing detail and accuracy, we can closely identify with the subject portrayed.

This 'mimetic contagion' – where the artwork 'transcend[s] its presumed frame as a mere fiction and propagate[s] itself in the world of the viewer', as classicist Robert Germany described it – meant that these ancient viewers would supposedly absorb the behaviours and ethical qualities of the artwork. Seeing was the same as becoming.[41]

This contagion troubled ancient thinkers. For Plato, everyone has irrational parts of the soul which delight in shame and unmeasured feeling. When we see a striking performance of vice, we lose ourselves to these unruly desires:

> When we hear Homer or one of the tragic poets representing the sufferings of a hero and making him bewail them at length, perhaps with all the sounds and signs of tragic grief, you know how even the best of us enjoy it and let ourselves be carried away by our feelings . . . Yet in our private griefs we pride ourselves on just the opposite, that is, on our ability to bear them in silence like men, and we regard the behaviour we admired on the stage as womanish.[42]

For Plato, such poetry perverted its audience – apparently making them 'womanish' – because it was *transparent*, as philosopher

Alexander Nehamas observes. In Greek tragedy, the actors on stage with their vivid scripts were so convincing in their vulgar display of unrestrained emotion that audiences felt pleasure in response to what they saw, and so became disposed to react the same way in their own lives.[43] And it wasn't just the audience: Socrates worried that the madness of a fictional character could become the actor's own; that performers themselves were also prone to such contagion.[44]

Mimetic contagion might now seem like an alien concept, lost in the distant land of antiquity. But it's very much alive today, perhaps even more so. Nowhere is this more powerful than in method acting, where actors risk their health and sanity to become their creations. Research shows that actors sometimes feel their own personality getting stuck in a role, or the character bleeding into them.[45] For instance, Robert De Niro prepared for his *Taxi Driver* (1976) role by losing two stone and working many hours as a real cab driver. Lady Gaga essentially lived as her character from *House of Gucci* (2021) for a year and a half. In a *Vogue* interview, she described encountering 'psychological difficulty' as a result: even when the cameras were off her, she still felt like she was on a movie set and spoke in an Italian accent for nine months.[46] And when preparing for his role as the Joker in *The Dark Knight* (2008), Heath Ledger locked himself up in a hotel room for a month and kept a sinister journal. The performance proved mentally and physically draining for Ledger, and while his later accidental overdose was reportedly not connected to the role, his immersion in the villainous character led many to believe that it was his art that eventually killed him.

———

With advances in technology, the boundary between fiction and reality is becoming increasingly porous. Videogames might be fictional, but they differ from canonical fictions like theatre and painting, mainly because of their interactive and 'self-involving' design.[47] The videogame is about *us*, albeit through a game character, with whom we influence what happens in the game-world. It is this self-involved imagination, made even more immersive with Virtual Reality and haptic feedback (players can now feel things like rain or weaponry impacts in a game), that heightens our playing experience to an incredible degree.

This blurring of fiction and reality has been shown to affect our cognition, and possibly our behaviour too. The 'Proteus effect', for example, is where people's actions and attitudes begin to align with their avatar or digital self. Imagining yourself as someone different can affect the attitudes you hold after gameplay. For instance, studies show that players with taller avatars in a virtual world subsequently behave more confidently in a non-virtual task, compared to those with shorter avatars.[48]

We can see how this could become sinister as players take on more troubling attitudes in gameplay, which may leak out into their everyday lives. Consider playing as an immoral character, perhaps as the Boss in *Rape Day*. The concern is that even if you believe that the Boss's attitudes towards women and sex are abhorrent, these attitudes may still seep into your own psyche, in the form of what philosophers have called 'imaginative contagion'.[49] Much as a child may continue to feel frightened that there is a shark in their paddling pool after their make-believe playtime has ceased, this theory suggests that videogame players may not be able to fully detach themselves from the emotions and desires they felt during their imaginative gameplay. Because I am not imagining someone else going on a bloodthirsty rape spree but am, in fact, imagining *myself* doing so by playing as the Boss, the attitudes I hold temporarily during this imaginative process may actually become part of my psychology.

One way imaginative contagion might work is by habituation, according to philosopher Alex Fisher.[50] Habits enable us to do things that we might not ordinarily wish to do, like go for regular runs on cold dark mornings. They can also push us into doing things at odds with our interests: by regularly taking cocaine on the weekends, the routine could leave you addicted.

Similarly, if an actor immerses themselves in a role, and even spends time as that character off-screen like Lady Gaga and Heath Ledger did, their imagined attitudes while pretending to be their character become habituated and can start to affect their own personality and health. As Lady Gaga put it to a *Variety* interviewer: 'I brought the darkness with me home because [my character's] life was dark.'[51]

In much the same way, when we play an immersive videogame, over time and with repetition (as videogames are often played habitually) we can start to form mental habits of responding to situations with certain attitudes and desires outside of the gameplay world, even if those attitudes do not align with our pre-held proclivities. Studies suggest a robust correlation between violent videogames and aggressive mindsets, even if not full-fledged aggressive behaviour. Psychologists Craig Anderson and Karen Dill found that players of a violent videogame had more accessibility to aggressive thoughts when compared with those who had played a non-violent videogame.[52]

It's not just general violence that we should be wary of – videogames can also influence sexist and racist mindsets.

Sexual violence and objectification overwhelmingly target women in videogame design. *Rape Day* isn't the only game that allows the player to sexually assault female characters in the game-world.[53] A rudimentary yet shocking example of this is *Custer's Revenge* (1982). Players have control of a naked cowboy who must navigate his way through a dangerous field towards a Native American woman, who is tied to a post. If he reaches her, he can rape her as a reward. Misogyny, then, can be exacerbated by such videogames. One study found that a videogame containing sexual objectification and violence against women resulted in a statistically significant increase in the acceptance of rape myths – rape-supportive attitudes – for male participants but not for female participants.[54]

Moreover, people of colour – both as playable and non-playable characters – are underrepresented in videogames; women of colour are virtually invisible. And those that do appear are often racially stereotyped: black characters are often portrayed as criminals, or they are exoticised.[55] In general, ethnic minorities – typically male – are often represented as 'sinister, unattractive, untrustworthy, violent, and having a lower work ethic'.[56]

Far-right groups have used such game design to reinforce their racist campaigns. In *Ethnic Cleansing* (2002) – a videogame created by the neo-Nazi organisation National Alliance – players can choose to be a neo-Nazi skinhead or a hooded Ku Klux Klansman, and murder 'sub-humans' – black and Latinx people – and their 'masters', the 'personification of evil': Jewish people. The racism embedded in this depraved fictional world is further entrenched by tropes and caricatures, such as monkey noises and placing the 'Jewish overlords' in the city's sewers.[57]

In these extreme cases, it might be beside the point to test whether these gamers became racist as a result of their gameplay – many of them probably were already. But studies do show that videogames can further entrench and affect our beliefs about race and ethnicity. While the widespread racial stereotypes in videogames involve characters that are not real, studies show that 'they can still provide fodder for negative social judgments and negative reactions to real Black men'.[58] One study of over three hundred white US college students found that frequent gameplay cultivated real-world beliefs about black people, 'such that individuals who spend more time playing video games have less egalitarian views of Blacks'.[59]

Jake's (or Desk Lamp's) defence of *Rape Day* that 'most people can separate fiction from reality pretty well' therefore woefully underplays the dark reality of videogames, and of immoral art in general. The habitual way gamers interact with these digital worlds has led to negative changes in attitudes and thoughts: increased aggression, reinforced racial stereotypes, and misogynistic mindsets. In 2022, the revenue from the global gaming market was approximately 347 billion US dollars, and it's still growing. This art form is here to stay, and it's only going to become more sophisticated, and potentially more sinister.

———

Despite the wealth of psychological research on the adverse effects of videogames, there is currently no clear consensus on the claim that violent art actually makes people more violent. For instance, a recent study of extreme metal music suggests that this broad genre doesn't *make* listeners angrier or more aggressive, but rather that listeners seek it out *because* they are feeling angry, and that it can form a healthy way to process negative emotion (as we saw above with Woodstock '99, though, music is not always a safe channel for such feelings).[60] While these results somewhat differ from the studies of video-games, where evidence does point towards players' cognition negatively changing in response to gameplay, the *behaviour* of gamers has not been proven to change in the same way.[61]

So, if there's currently no strong evidence to suggest that some immoral art does in fact cause people to *do* bad things, are our fears unfounded? Is it irrational to blame art for a person's depravity? As Eminem puts it in his song 'Sing for the Moment' (2002):

> They say music can alter moods and talk to you
> Well, can it load a gun up for you and cock it too?
> Well, if it can, then the next time you assault a dude
> Just tell the judge it was my fault, and *I'll* get sued!

Eminem is right that art doesn't literally load your gun while you commit a crime. In this sense, we can't blame art for *directly* causing any bloodshed.

But we should not rest easy. Immoral art might rarely outright cause people to commit violent acts, but what we know about the effects of videogames on our cognition suggests that art can help mould the overall character of a person, which can in turn eventually lead to violent behaviour. This insidious effect needs to be taken seriously.

Again, we can draw lessons about immoral art from research on the effects of pornography. It is this gradual shaping of our cognition that philosophers have identified as the root of some pornography's toxicity. Much like with videogames, while it is empirically contentious to claim that watching violent pornography *causes* consumers – mainly men – to go out and harm women afterwards, the claim that some pornography affects its consumers' cognition and sexual desire is grimly accurate. The pornographic aspect of our society, as Jeremy Waldron put it above, is today almost inescapable. As theorist Gail Dines laments,

> No anti-porn feminist I know has suggested that there is one image, or even a few, that could lead a nonrapist to rape; the argument, rather, is that taken together, pornographic images create a world that is at best inhospitable to women, and at worst dangerous to their physical and emotional well-being.[62]

To accuse porn of causing violence against women and girls should not be taken in simplistic terms – the claim is rather that some genres of porn shape our sexual desire and expectations in real-life relationships. If a genre of violent pornography is bursting with images of rape, for instance, this in turn feeds a sexual culture where rape in society is at best misunderstood and at worst eroticised.

When it comes to the nature of this harm, philosopher A. W. Eaton argues that the frequent consumption of inegalitarian genres of pornography (those which eroticise unequal gender dynamics) is like smoking.[63] While enjoying just one cigarette won't give you cancer, repeated smoking over a long period of time can certainly increase your chances of getting it. In the same way, repeated exposure to eroticised gender-based violence found in much pornography today can increase the likelihood of consumers committing sexual assault and misunderstanding consent. Studies have shown, for instance, that online pornography today woefully distorts boys' expectations of what girls and women should look like, and what 'good' sex looks like. In 2023, a Children's Commissioner for England report found that exposure to online porn affects young people's beliefs about sexual relationships and body image, but it also found a significant statistical correlation between pornography consumption and sexually violent behaviour. The report claims that these 'sexual scripts' written and disseminated by porn, which instruct what is normal and legitimate in sexual situations, can influence sexual behaviour, predominantly towards women and girls.[64]

Crucially, because this pornography shows inegalitarian sex as *sexy* – as being desirable and worthy of desire – it thus deforms our emotional capacities and resulting tastes: 'if representations can educate our emotions, then they can also *un*educate them', worries Eaton.[65] And as we'll see more in the next chapter, immoral art does this too. Pervasive arousing images, scenes, or actions – whether in pornography or art – can affect not just what we think sex looks like, but what it *should* look like.

The question, then, of whether art causes depravity, is more complex than we might have thought. Much art doesn't directly cause us to do bad things, but it can affect our desires and thoughts and entrench prejudices. These, in turn, can add to a toxic background of misinformation and defective aesthetic tastes, which pervade our culture and social imagination like carbon monoxide.

Fire-starters

While some art slowly moulds our mindsets and feeds wider societal myths, there are other artworks which explicitly *call* for criminality: in Eminem's terms, this art, in a metaphorical sense, *does* load your gun, and perhaps even cocks it too. Incitement – where a person intentionally urges or seeks to persuade another to commit a criminal offence – can plausibly be effected through art, especially hate propaganda in the form of novels and films.

Propaganda can span from 'factual' material like newspapers and online forums to artistic forms like film and music. While it is debatable whether artistic propaganda should be classed as direct or indirect incitement,[66] its messaging is often unambiguous and clearly instructs violence and even genocide.

It was Hitler's unwavering belief in the power of art that propelled him to establish his Ministry of Propaganda, installing Joseph Goebbels as its chief. Two feature films in 1940 were made under Goebbels's eye as part of the Nazi Party's branding. Fritz Hippler's *Der ewige Jude* (The Eternal Jew) is a pseudo-documentary showing Jews in their true 'uncivilised' natural state, and it ends with Hitler's Reichstag speech predicting the annihilation of the Jewish race. Veit Harlan's *Jud Süß* (Süss, the Jew) is a drama set in the eighteenth century which ends with the Jewish villain being hanged and Jews being driven from Stuttgard. 'The film's close made it clear that the example should be followed by later generations,' writes propaganda theorist Randall L. Bytwerk.

The films actively encouraged antisemitic violence and hatred in their wider bid to justify the Holocaust. They had startling effects on huge audiences. After seeing *Jud Süß*, some cinema-goers were reportedly so unnerved that they 'emerged from Berlin theatres screaming curses at the Jews: "Drive the Jews from the Kurfürstendamm! Kick the last Jews out of Germany!"'[67]

Perhaps the most inhumane art made during this propaganda storm was antisemitic children's books. Even more brash than the press at the time, to the point that they even looked crude to some Nazis, children's books published by Julius Streicher's Stürmer Publishing House explicitly called for Jewish extermination. For instance, Ernst Hiemer's *Der Pudelmopsdackelpinscher* (1940) compares Jews to poisonous snakes, bedbugs, tapeworms, and bacteria to be eliminated. One chapter ends with what can only be described as incitement to genocide: 'Tapeworms and the Jew are parasites of the worst kind. If we want to free ourselves of them, if we want to be healthy and strong again, there is only one cure: their extermination (*Ausrottung*).'[68]

The fact that these books were designed as children's bedtime stories is difficult to stomach. Streicher, who was also the founder of *Der Stürmer* – the notorious antisemitic newspaper – was the first member of the Nazi regime to be convicted of inciting genocide at the Nuremberg Trials. He was sentenced to death by hanging.[69]

When accusing an artwork of incitement rather than merely having terrible effects, it's important to look to the artist. We'll delve more into this later in the book, but the artist's character is integral to understanding their creations, and in this case, establishing the *mens rea* requirement of incitement: did they knowingly do it?

Take William Luther Pierce. An American neo-Nazi and ex-university professor who became disillusioned with the government during the Civil Rights Movement, Pierce founded the white supremacist organisation National Alliance. His infamous novel *The Turner Diaries* (1978) tells the story of a violent revolution and race war set in a future America, culminating in the mass extermination of people of colour and Jews.

Denounced as 'the bible of the extremist right' by the FBI, the novel has been credited with inspiring numerous hate crimes and acts of terrorism, including the Oklahoma City

Bombing in 1995, which killed 168 people including 19 children,[70] and the London Nail Bombings in 1999, which killed three people and an unborn baby.[71] The novel has become essential reading for far-right groups, and events and names in the book have been spread across online right-wing media.[72]

While Pierce has denied that his book was instructing specific terrorist attacks like the Oklahoma City Bombing, his wider intention is clear: 'I'd like to see North America become a white continent . . . Terrorism only makes sense if it can be sustained over a period of time. One day there will be real, organized terrorism done according to plan, aimed at bringing down the government.'[73] Given the author's background and beliefs, it's not a far stretch at all to see his novel as an incitement to racist violence, or at least racial hatred.

———

While there are clearer cases of artistic incitement, we need to be careful when throwing the word 'incitement' around – it has legal ramifications, after all. There are some art forms that are unfairly targeted and smeared by this term. Drill music, for instance, has been swept up in a recent moral panic in the UK. Like much rap over the past forty years, this predominantly black genre, with its Chicago South Side origins, has been accused of explicitly inciting violence – particularly knife attacks – among black youth.

Sonically blending trap and grime, UK drill often describes street violence, gang rivalry, and drug dealing. Blamed by politicians and senior police for causing disorder on the streets, the music has been censored across social media platforms, with YouTube taking down thirty music videos identified by

Scotland Yard. In 2021, a report by conservative think tank Policy Exchange stated that at least 37 per cent of homicide cases in 2018 were 'directly linked to drill music'.[74] The Met have even announced an intention to pursue drill artists in the same way as terror suspects.[75] Drill has also been used as evidence in convictions – prosecutors draw on videos and lyrics to highlight defendants' wayward character.[76]

The problem, though, is that there's no clear evidence for these causal claims made against drill as a genre, let alone claims of explicit incitement.[77] While there are exceptional cases of genuine criminality by those who happen to be drill artists (Al-Arfat Hassan recently admitted possessing chemicals for Islamic State terrorist purposes[78]), to launch an attack on an entire genre is too coarse a reaction. The Policy Exchange report, for instance, was condemned by forty-nine criminologists and sociologists in an open letter for being based on 'shaky evidence' and 'falsehoods and misinterpretations', making it 'politically dangerous'.[79]

The former Commissioner for the Metropolitan Police, Cressida Dick, claimed that drill rappers 'describe stabbings in great detail, joy and excitement . . . They say what they're going to do to each other and specifically what they are going to do to who [*sic*].' But in 2021, a report by a legal charity found that drill was being misunderstood by senior law enforcement, and that its misuse to secure convictions was indicative of systemic racism.[80]

Philosophers have been quick to point out that taking such a literal stance towards song lyrics is not standard interpretation. Johnny Cash's 'Folsom Prison Blues' (1955), for example, describes Cash shooting a man in Reno, but of course listeners rarely take Cash to be confessing to a murder. As philosopher Ethan Nowak notes, we don't normally take songs literally like this, but more as creative and aesthetic expressions. Drill music, though, is heard as straightforward testimony.[81]

This 'street illiteracy', where critics unfamiliar with the music take it at face value as direct instruction for assault and murder, risks oversimplifying and distorting the genre's content. One scholar argues that drill's lyricism should instead be understood as an 'artistic performance that reveal(s) an ambiguous relationship to criminality', and that its censure ignores 'the ambiguity, braggadocio and fact-fiction hybridity' characteristic of the genre.[82]

Such misinterpretation and demonising of drill amounts to what philosophers call an 'epistemic injustice', where a person's status as a knower is wrongly undermined: their perceived capacity to impart and possess knowledge – about the world and even themselves – is impaired due to their subordinate position in society. As philosopher Tareeq Jalloh puts it:

> Drillers sometimes label their work as fictional, but they are not believed. Other drillers say their music is merely reflective of the unjust circumstances they find themselves in, and rapping about murder does not make them murderers, but they are not believed . . . stereotypes about the criminality of black boys and men produce these deflated credibility assignments. The driller is not believed because they are stereotyped by hearers – court officials, police officers and media agents – as violent criminals.[83]

'Music saved my life,' writes London rapper Konan. Growing up amid pervasive violence, Konan turned to rap for solace: 'Hearing their lyrics didn't make me want to go out and hurt people, sell drugs and go back to jail. It made me even more empowered to make my life successful in a positive, legal, creative way.'[84] In its defence, artists and fans have said that drill does not cause violence; it emerges *out* of violence. As *Pitchfork* writer Ciaran Thapar remarks:

> Instead of trying to understand and address the unpleasant root causes of youth violence—such as historical poverty, familial instability, and overstretched state schooling—those in power are content to target the music that rises, like steam from a pressure cooker, out of these conditions.[85]

Law enforcement, therefore, risks putting the cart before the horse, at least in this case. Music brashly denounced as criminal saves some people: it pulls them out of violence, and even poverty. In the case of drill, many of its listeners see it as a brutal eyeopener, not a malicious fire-starter.

———

Fire is the result of a chemical reaction between oxygen and some sort of fuel. When these are brought to ignition by a heat source, they combust. Perhaps art's causal link to depravity should be understood as occupying different aspects of this fire triangle: the art can be the heat, fuel, or oxygen.

In some cases, the artwork acts as a lit match deliberately thrown into fuel like petrol or kindling. This is how we can think of incitement – when the artwork explicitly instructs its consumers to commit violence in an already toxic environment. It intentionally triggers the reaction, causing the fire – a culpable instigator. In other cases, an artwork might merely be an accidental electric spark: it arouses depravity in an already troubled person, pushing them over the edge, even though the artwork was not designed for that purpose.

In other cases, artworks can act as fuel or surrounding oxygen, in addition to factors that are commonly associated with causing wrongdoing: socioeconomics, environment, physiology, psychology, and substance abuse. Immoral videogames, for instance, can form part of the background air or fuel, alongside other social and cultural elements that prop up the harmful myths of oppressive systems. Art is just another reactant that combusts – one among many. In these cases, the lit match comes from elsewhere.

We have confronted the second face of our depraved Hydra – in all its wonder, art can ignite a flame within us, but the fuel and oxygen must be there first. Returning to the young Chaerea in Terence's play, it seems that the painting in the chamber was a chance spark, igniting the already impressionable man.

Classicist Robert Germany wrote:

[It's n]ot that we should imagine Chaerea before he saw the painting as morally spotless . . . The point is rather that for a soul already enfeebled by sin, a well-placed work of art can provide a strong or even irresistible incitement to imitation.[86]

But it's not clear that the painting of Jupiter and Danaë in Pamphila's chamber amounted to *incitement* – explicitly calling or urging those who gazed upon it to commit rape. The painting's role in Terence's play was more insidious. Even if not deliberately instructing its viewer to descend into depravity there and then, it still formed part of a broader backdrop of structurally unjust systems, such as sexism – it fed the fuel that ignited within Chaerea.

Even in cases where artworks and artists do not explicitly urge their viewers to follow diabolical orders, they can still invite us to experience the world, especially other people, in frightening and damaging ways. As we move on to the third guise of depraved art, I want you to take on board this notion of artworks having a hateful force even in cases where viewers are not directly aroused or incited into criminality by them. To do this, we're going to analyse art as a kind of speech – communication that can be morally abhorrent in itself regardless of its direct consequences, and which occurs amid pervasive harmful narratives. This 'hate speech' can be very explicit, but it can also be more subtle – even beautiful – and so all the trickier to unearth and resist. We've seen in this chapter that artworks can fan the malignant embers already sitting within our hearts. In the next, we'll examine one particular way that depraved art places the fuel there to start with.

3 | OPPRESSION

Tiziano Vecellio finished applying the last glaze layer to his *Poesy of Europa* in his Venice studio. It was 1562, and the Old Master was the most sought-after artist in Europe. He had spent at least three years working on this large, luminous oil painting. Finally, it was ready to be shipped off to King Philip II of Spain, who had been waiting excitedly.

The tale shown in *Rape of Europa* (1560–62), as it became known after Titian's death, is part of an ancient Cretan myth. Zeus – king of the gods – disguises himself as a white bull and hides among the Phoenician King of Tyre's herds near a beach. While gathering flowers, the king's daughter Europa sees the bull. Believing him tame, she places flowers around his horns, caresses him and climbs on to his back. Zeus seizes this opportunity, and with Europa upon his back, abducts her and swims across the ocean towards Crete. Once they arrive, Zeus reveals his true identity and impregnates Europa. She eventually gives birth to three sons, who later become rulers of different kingdoms in the Mediterranean.

Influenced by Ovid's interpretation of the myth in his *Metamorphoses* (8 CE), Titian's painting shows the moment that Europa is abducted and carried off into the ocean. Faintly in the distance we can see her family, arms flung up in desperation. In the immediate foreground of the frame, we witness Europa's physical distress and the bull's eerily calm demeanour. Europa is dragged away from the shore, helplessly yet erotically splayed on the bull's back. In one hand she clutches a red scarf, which billows above her head. In her other hand she clings to one of the bull's horns to stop herself falling into the dark blue ocean beneath, which teems with sea monsters. Below, a flushed cherub rides a fish and gazes between the princess's outstretched legs. Europa's obscured face tilts up towards the stormy sky, where two other cherubs with bows and arrows fly ahead. The bull looks directly out of the frame at us, his head still garlanded with her flowers.

————

What is wrong with this beautiful picture? Well, it tells us that sexual violence is alluring and erotic. It tells us that 'No' does not count as genuine refusal; that women, deep down, desire such violation. In other words, this painting says things that fundamentally shape how we view sex, gender, and power. How does it do this?

The work was commissioned by Philip II as one of a series of six erotic 'poesies' (poems in paint), all inspired by the *Metamorphoses*. Philip identified with the god Zeus, and so *Rape of Europa* functioned as a kind of portrait of the king – shown as a virile bull who takes a princess and rapes her.[1] But what matters here is not just what Titian shows us. It's how he shows it. This stunning painting blurs the lines between refusal and consent, fear and pleasure. Europa is depicted simultaneously as a frightened and excited victim, who confusedly enjoys the assault. As A. W. Eaton observes in her renowned paper on the ethics of this painting, Europa's precarious posture suggests that the sex will be non-consensual, and yet there is an erotic charge found in the painting's composition. Europa's erogenous zones are foregrounded, and she is surrounded by sensual textures: her wet white dress clings and folds into her curvaceous form. The sea froths around the bull's strong legs, his tail extends outwards from in-between Europa's pubic area, and his horn is grasped by her hand.[2]

There is a potent power dynamic. Europa is being hauled through the sea by the bull, but he moves calmly. Adorned with flowers, he doesn't look too aggressive. While Europa has no control, the bull moves in a way which is cool-headed and determined. His quiet confidence is accentuated by the fact that he looks out at us, dewy-eyed, whereas Europa's face is obscured and difficult to read.

The bull's harnessing of the viewer's gaze is a 'standard artistic device for psychological identification', writes Eaton, wherein the viewer is called to adopt the perspective or point of view of the character looking out of the piece[3] – in this case, to identify with the bull's lust, which is amplified by the fiery colours in the stormy sky.[4] This, contrasted with the ambiguity of Europa's mental state, 'calls upon viewers to be sexually aroused by Europa's helplessness, fear, and vulnerability; to find her both terrified and sexually excited, willing and resisting, and so on', writes Eaton.[5]

In other words, Zeus is shown in a way that purportedly justifies his act: Europa is abducted against her will, but the bull is portrayed as if he knows what's best for his victim. The disparity between his dominant agency and Europa's eroticised refusal and passivity gives us an insight into the mind of a rapist, conveying depraved messages like 'her lack of consent is thrilling', or 'rape satisfies women's secret desires to be taken and ravished'.[6]

Titian himself outlined his wish for the poesies in a letter to Philip II: that they have erotic appeal for the male viewer. Announcing the shipment of the series' second painting, *Venus and Adonis* (1554), Titian described to the king his goal of presenting the female form from all angles. Titian's friend Ludovico Dolce also confirmed that this second painting in the series was meant to be sexually arousing. In a letter to the Venetian nobleman Alessandro Contarini, he wrote:

> I swear to you, sir, that there is no man . . . so hardened in his being, who does not feel . . . a stirring of the blood in his veins. It [the painting] is a real marvel; that if a marble statue could by the stimuli of its beauty so penetrate to the marrow of a young man, that he stained himself, then, what must she do who is of flesh, who is beauty personified and appears to be breathing?[7]

This eroticism is on full display in *Rape of Europa* too: Titian's naturalistic handling of the 'quivering flesh' and 'gorgeous tone' of its central figure has been enthusiastically praised by art historians.[8]

What does all of this tell us? In essence, that you're looking at a beautiful rape myth; valid consent is irrelevant in sexual conquest. Like the bull, the depravity here is just decorated by flowers.

———

Hidden from public view in the Royal Alcázar palace in Madrid, Philip II's erotic art collection caused quite a stir over several royal generations. The highly conservative Catholic society of Spain disapproved of the king's titillating treasures, but while his grandson King Philip IV introduced laws shutting down brothels, he would still frequently retire to his private rooms and enjoy his inherited nudes. Not everyone in the royal household enjoyed these sensual pieces. Philip IV's wife, Queen Elizabeth, apparently found the collection so disturbing that when she would visit her husband, she would order them to be covered over.[9]

Elizabeth's reaction to such scenes may strike us today as simply prudish. But this would be an unfair judgement. It's plausible that she was distressed by the fact that sexual violence was being glamorised by these paintings. It's also possible that her reaction was indicative of many women's frustration at the double standards and sexism within society and the fine art world, particularly in the early modern period. Back then, women were everywhere and nowhere at the same time. 'Why have there been no great women artists?' art historian Linda Nochlin famously asked in 1971. The lazy and yet damaging answer to this tends to take a syllogistic form: 'If women had the golden nugget of artistic genius, it would reveal itself. But it has never revealed itself. Q.E.D. Women do not have the golden nugget of artistic genius.'[10]

The real answer to the question posed by Nochlin, of course, is a sociological one: there have been fewer 'big name' women artists and scholars throughout history because until the nineteenth century, women across the world were largely not permitted to attend art schools or academies, or to receive formal art training such as life drawing classes. They were refused entry into important social circles and higher education, while at the same time battling the norm that they must remain in the domestic sphere. Denying people access to such resources on the grounds of their gender, class, and race, unsurprisingly closes them off from achieving recognised artistic excellence. And yet, for centuries, women (white women at least) were omnipresent in the world of high art: royal courts, academies, salons, and public galleries were crowded with naked girls on the walls, mostly in passive and victimised positions. Women were the painted, never the painter.

This grievance was epitomised at the London National Gallery a few centuries after Elizabeth refused to gaze on Titian's rape imagery. On 10 March 1914, Canadian suffragette Mary Richardson walked into the gallery hiding a meat cleaver in her coat. She approached Diego Velázquez's *Rokeby Venus* (1647–51), brought out the knife, and slashed the painting several times. A hundred years later, at the Musée d'Orsay in Paris, Luxembourgish artist Deborah de Robertis lay down naked in front of Édouard Manet's *Olympia* (1863). De Robertis mimicked the pose of the naked sex worker who defiantly looks out of the painting; she was then put in a prison cell for nearly two days after being arrested for indecent exposure. Unrepentant, she accused the museum of hypocrisy: 'They like nudity in art, they just don't want it to be moving.'[11] Richardson's and De Robertis's actions form part of a resonant lineage of protest against the treatment of women in Western art, and how it has always gone hand in hand with the exclusion of real women from both art circles and the public sphere more widely.

———

It seems, then, that art can *say* things which shape our reality. A painting or sculpture may appear to be an inanimate object. But terrible depravity can lurk in its pretty oil-soaked canvas or monumental carved stone. Art can be forceful, dangerous speech – it can oppress whole social groups through what it says about them. No matter how beautiful it is, a work of art can be sexist or racist; it can sustain social hierarchies. But how is a mere object able to do this? How does it contribute to structural injustice? And does it matter if the artist made the artwork in good faith?

The Artful Birdcage

It is literally impossible to be a woman . . . You have to be thin, but not too thin . . . You have to be a boss, but you can't be mean. You have to lead, but you can't squash other people's ideas . . . You have to never get old, never be rude, never show off, never be selfish, never fall down, never fail, never show fear, never get out of line. It's too hard! It's too contradictory! . . . And it turns out in fact that not only are you doing everything wrong, but also *everything* is your fault.

The philosopher Marilyn Frye famously characterised oppression as a birdcage, where a group is caged in by a society's multiple barriers.[12] The above quote from Greta Gerwig's film *Barbie* (2023) explicitly characterises one such cage, for women.[13]*

---

* Men under the patriarchy can also be enormously harmed, due to being men – social norms like 'boys don't cry' have led to a mental health crisis, with many men tragically taking their own lives. But it's questionable whether men are *oppressed* as men under this patriarchal system. For some theorists, such harms are not forms of oppression because they do not *constrain*, in a cage-like way, the person's options and pathways in life. They can cause suffering, but they don't cause that person to live in a severely limited way, in this case due to being a man.

depraved

Traditionally, oppression has been understood as a dictator or tyrant's exercise of power and control over a group of people – like the Taliban's recent abhorrent restrictions on women and girls' rights in Afghanistan. Today, oppression is understood more broadly as including the formal or informal unfair governance of a social group, where this domination prevents members of that group from having opportunities and freedoms enjoyed by those in more privileged positions, and where the oppressed are more vulnerable to violence and exploitation.[14]

The oppressor itself may not be a ruler or party with cruel intentions. Oppression can manifest instead as pernicious systems and institutions which constrain the self-development and self-determination of whole groups of people. Many of us face interlocking barriers – educational, financial, physical, health-related – simply because of who we are, which prevent us from living a full, good life. As Frye observed, oppression isn't just one kind of suffering; it is complex and multi-layered – this is why it is so difficult for the bird to escape.[15]*

A combination of social prejudice and institutional power via government, culture, and education creates unjust systems that severely discriminate against some groups while benefitting others; systems such as racism, sexism, ableism, classism, heterosexism, and ageism, to name a few. These systems affect our everyday lives and can sometimes be rather subtle. For instance, a man catcalling a woman or girl in the street might look innocent and even well-meaning to some, but to many (if not most) women, it's yet another way that sexism rears its ugly head. While a catcall is often classed as a compliment, it

---

* Some barriers are also legally binding in some countries. For instance, sixty-two countries still criminalise homosexuality to date, with a few which impose the death penalty, such as Iran and Nigeria.

is, in fact, one of many social practices that put women in what Frye calls a 'double-bind': there is no acceptable way that she can respond. If she reacts positively, she's a whore or desperate. If she reacts negatively, the harasser may respond violently. If she does not respond at all, she's a bitch. Either way you're doomed. Such double-binds are characteristic of oppressive experiences, where a person's options in social life are restricted yet all of them still expose the person to censure or penalty. In my own experience, both ignoring and responding to a catcall has exposed me to verbal and physical violence by men.

How we see each other can strengthen (or break) the bars of our cages. This is where art's poisonous role becomes apparent. Our cultural products prop up systems of oppression and constitute one of the many societal barriers. Depraved art in particular can further entrench double-binds and punitive norms for social groups – even, or especially, masterpieces which have stood the test of time.[16]*

If our art constantly represents historically oppressed groups of people as inferior, and in a way that tries to justify and glamorise this power dynamic, then this hierarchy secures a strong foothold. As with the power of advertising and propaganda, if the same story is sold to us again and again, and is told with authority, many of us start to believe it, or implicitly take it for granted. And when the story or image being sold to us is a depraved one, negative connotations and dangerous mindsets can infiltrate our societal norms and laws in the form of outright prejudice and unconscious bias. Art can be wielded as a weapon to keep inferior groups down.

* Material artefacts beyond art also contribute to oppressive systems, such as racist, sexist, and ableist technology, manufacturing, and urban spaces.

Let's return to Titian's *Rape of Europa*. In isolation, this is just a portrayal of an immoral act, albeit an extraordinary work of art created by one of the most revered artists of all time. But the true depravity in this painting emerges from its position in a wider web of cultural domination and white cis-male supremacy. Taken in tandem with movements in art history and historic systems of oppression, artworks like *Rape of Europa* promote and sustain social inequalities.

Exactly how do they do this? I want to suggest that part of the explanation derives from art's power as *speech* and, in the case of immoral art, in its power as a particular kind of *hate speech*. By deploying discriminating and subordinating messages as part of a wider context of structural injustice, many of the artworks we hold dear are active: they count as significant moves in cultural discourse which shape and distort our social reality.

Artistic Speech

One of the most important artworks of the twentieth century is Picasso's masterpiece *Guernica* (1937). The shades of black and grey in this vast painting explode into chaotic shapes and form contorted, writhing figures: a screaming mother holds her dead child in her hands; a dismembered soldier lies on the ground under an impaled horse; someone burns alive in a building engulfed by flames.

The painting portrays the German and Italian air raid that flattened the ancient town of Guernica in the tenth month of the Spanish Civil War in 1937. In what one contemporary newspaper described as 'a three hours' massacre from the air',[17] a third of Guernica's 5,000 residents were killed or severely wounded, and the town was reduced to burning ruins. Picasso began making sketches five days after the bombardment, and then took just five weeks to complete the piece, which was first exhibited to the public in the entrance hall of the Spanish Republic's pavilion at the 1937 World's Fair in Paris (the art in the pavilion was chosen to demonstrate what the country had been experiencing during the Civil War, with the aim of gaining international support in the fight against fascism).[18]

But Picasso's desolate mural doesn't merely show the devastating outcomes of war. Its power lies in what it does as speech. It boldly *protests* the war, *pleads* against human barbarity, and *challenges* the permissibility of warfare and extreme violence. Its forceful messages have been considered too defiant by some. In 2003 a tapestry reproduction of *Guernica*, which was hanging outside New York's Security Council chamber of the UN headquarters, was reportedly covered up by officials during the US Secretary of State Colin Powell's presentation of the American case for war against Iraq. This cover-up shows the acute power and tragic aura of Picasso's piece as a kind of speech: its vehement anti-war message spoke of too close similarities between current and historical events, comparisons which the Bush administration and UN officials did not want the public to draw.[19]

Art can speak like this, even without words. Over the centuries, we've praised art for its unique ability to convey not just emotion but also profound messages. Pope Gregory the Great in 600 CE held that religious paintings were 'books' for the illiterate:

Pictures are used in churches so that those who are ignorant of letters may at least read by seeing on the walls what they cannot read in books (*codicibus*) . . . What writing (*scriptura*) does for the literate, a picture does for the illiterate looking at it.[20]

Paintings which portrayed stories from the Old and New Testaments not only evoked religious emotion to aid in prayer, but also expressed the central messages of the scriptures to those who were unable to read them.[21]

Throughout history, artists have been commissioned to create art that communicates to audiences in this way. Between 1512 and 1516, Matthias Grünewald painted his striking *Isenheim Altarpiece* – a portrayal of the Crucifixion which originally stood in the Monastery of St Anthony in Alsace – to act as a visual language that would strengthen the monastery's healing programme for people suffering with disease. Through carefully chosen imagery, the painting spoke to the patients who would gaze at it daily and pray for relief. Christ's pain and anguish are given centre stage; he is even represented in the altarpiece's *predella* as an amputee, to reflect the condition of some of the onlookers.[22]

While visual art shouldn't be regarded as an ordinary language (visual artworks do not have a stable syntax or anything like a vocabulary), it still shares important features with verbal expression. One such shared feature is its 'illocutionary force'.[23] The actions carried out by Picasso's *Guernica* – its protesting, pleading, and challenging – are normally achieved with words. When we speak, we don't just make meaningful sounds; we do something. When a nervous father shouts 'Look out, it's slippery!' to his daughter when she walks on to a frozen lake, he *warns* her about the ice. When the officer shouts to her troops 'Open fire!', she *orders* them to shoot.

These are what philosophers call 'speech acts' – which were systematically analysed by Oxford philosopher J. L. Austin in the 1950s. I need here to take a brief detour to explain what these special yet everyday things are. When we say, 'Can you pass the salt?' – which Austin calls a 'locutionary act' – we do something *in* saying this: we request or order – which Austin calls an 'illocutionary act', or 'illocution'. The locution and illocution comprise the overall speech act.[24] Our speech acts have downstream effects: my request for salt will have extra-linguistic consequences, like you passing me the salt and my chips getting tastier. Austin called these 'perlocutionary' effects: what we do *by* saying something.

Illocutions constitute effects themselves in that they instantaneously determine what ought to happen: people gain and lose obligations, entitlements, legal statuses, and rights. If I *order* you to pass me the salt, you acquire an obligation to do so. If you *promise* me that you'll bring more salt next time, you acquire the obligation to do this, and I acquire an entitlement to your doing so. If a celebrant declares a couple as *married*, they are married there and then. If a café sign in Jim Crow-era America declares 'Whites Only' to exclude black customers, black people are thereby *ranked* as inferior to whites. In other words, illocutions shape our social statuses and other facts in the world. The power of our speech is almost magical.

The worldly changes inherent to illocutions vary in their 'direction of fit'. In some cases, illocutions simply aim to reflect (or fit) the state of the world – asserting 'my chips are salty' commits the speaker to this already-existing fact. Other illocutions aim to make the world change to fit the speaker's desires – 'I order you to fetch the salt' is designed to get your subordinate to do something. Some illocutions, however, are even more powerful in that they bring about the state of affairs to which they refer: the correct person uttering 'I pronounce you husband and wife' instantly brings about the fact that the couple is married – sometimes, by declaring something to be the case, it is immediately made to be the case.[25]

Normally our illocutions are verbally expressed, but they needn't be. Think of sending flowers to your friend to apologise after a big row, or silently pointing to the salt with a mouthful of chips to request more, or even throwing tomato soup over Vincent van Gogh's *Sunflowers* to protest the climate emergency. The vehicle we use to express our illocutionary intentions just needs to be sufficiently understood by our audience – and this vehicle needn't be an ordinary linguistic one.

So how does this relate to art? Artworks are usually made by people who have intentions, whether broad or specific, for their work, just as Picasso intended *Guernica* to protest war and fascism. Or an artwork might be commissioned by someone else: public sculpture is often commissioned by a person or group other than the artist, but still with a clear intention – normally, to commemorate and glorify a certain figure.

The way an artist portrays something in their art can roughly correspond to a 'locution' – the vehicle that carries the illocution. Picasso's cubist method represents parts of the world: the screaming woman and impaled horse serve to show us a horrific event. It's quite clear to us that Picasso intended with this painterly vehicle to assert that war is barbaric and make a plea for peace. *Guernica* not only represents the air raid; it deplores and denounces it.

So, we can do things with our words, and with our art.[26] But such actions can be toxic, like we find in hate speech. This is a form of communication which incites, promotes, or constitutes contempt and violence towards others based on factors like their race, ethnicity, gender, sexual orientation, or religion. Hate speech targets these individuals and groups and demeans them, expressing contempt and legitimising discrimination.

It can be conveyed in the form of signage and legislation, racist and homophobic slurs, or sexist and ableist jokes, among many other ways.

Hate speech can be hugely dangerous. It can cause concrete harms by being a form of incitement, where it directly leads to violent crime and psychological damage to victims, and to the perpetrators, too. It is these kinds of harms that we investigated in the last chapter. But hate speech also does harm *in* its very expression: remember, it has an illocutionary aspect which immediately shifts social statuses and changes the normative landscape; in particular, it *subordinates* its target victims and sustains oppression. For example, a legislator during apartheid who says 'blacks are not permitted to vote' subordinates black people as a group. This is not just a sentence. Said in the right context, with the right authority, the speech act ranks black people as inferior, legitimates discrimination, and thereby deprives them of important powers.[27]

Like other speech acts, hateful ones needn't just be verbally expressed. Cross-burning, for instance, has been used by the Ku Klux Klan since the twentieth century to threaten and intimidate black Americans, Jews, and Muslims. While the practice had originally been used in medieval Scotland to declare war, it became associated with the KKK after white supremacist Thomas Dixon Jr's novel *The Clansman* (1905), which romanticised and glorified the KKK. The image was further strengthened by D. W. Griffith's film adaptation of the book, *The Birth of a Nation* (1915).

The action of burning crosses became a sinister visual symbol of racial hatred and is still used today despite being banned in several American states. In December 2020, a Mississippi resident named Axel Cox made a wooden cross, doused it in motor oil, and lit it on fire in his front yard to intimidate his black neighbours. He pleaded guilty to a hate crime and was imprisoned for three years.

As well as its clear intended effects of promoting hate and violence towards marginalised racial groups, cross-burning can also be understood as hate speech on an illocutionary level. It is a visual *command* of 'Get out' – which simultaneously *asserts* that marginalised groups are not welcome and thereby *ranks* them as second-class citizens.[28] These are oppressive speech acts, which license and legitimise racial hatred.

Philosophers such as Rae Langton have also argued that some pornography – both linguistic and image-based – constitutes harm to women because it enacts the illocution of subordination through its eroticisation of unequal power dynamics and sexual violence. This, in turn, hinders women's freedom to do things with their words in real life. The frequency with which much pornography expresses rape myths, for instance, distorts understandings of sexual consent and refusal, as we learned in the previous chapter. If women thereby lose this illocutionary power, they are 'silenced', exacerbating their powerlessness and vulnerability to violence.[29]

Art can be oppressive too in its performance of hateful speech acts. What matters here isn't so much the criminality that might directly follow from consuming depraved art, but more the depravity of the art's speech itself and its immediate transformation of what is *permissible* to think and do to others.[30] It can do this explicitly, through its clear invitation to dehumanise the subject it depicts. But it can also do this implicitly, through what it presupposes about that subject. Let's take these two scenarios in turn.

Beautiful Dehumanisation

Artworks can embody oppressive speech because of how they explicitly represent subordinated groups; in particular, their *objectification* of women and people of colour throughout the centuries. Objectification involves several aspects which in most contexts make it morally repugnant. According to philosopher Martha Nussbaum, these include treating a person as a tool for your purposes; as lacking in autonomy and agency; as interchangeable with other objects; as lacking in boundaries; as something that can be bought or sold; and as something whose feelings and experiences needn't be considered.[31] Rae Langton adds more features: identifying a person simply with their body parts, and treating them exclusively in terms of how they appear, as if they lack the capacity to speak.[32] In the extreme, objectifying someone dehumanises them: a violation of a fundamental moral law, according to Immanuel Kant, which holds that humans must be treated as ends in themselves.

These core aspects of objectification can be represented in art and pitched to audiences as justified ways of treating others: the artworks declare that the world is a certain way, thereby making it so. When this objectification is expressed in an alluring manner, reality instantly transforms: it becomes acceptable and legitimate to see and treat certain people negatively.

One prolific Western genre of art that did this was the nude, in its expression of unequal gender relations where women are passive and men are active; as John Berger put it in *Ways of Seeing* (1972), 'men act and women appear'. The genre is dominated by young white women's bodies, so much so that the term 'the nude' has become synonymous with this body type.

Ranging from ancient art to the Victorian period, a defining feature of this genre was its romanticisation and glamorisation of sexual objectification. A. W. Eaton notes several aesthetic ways this can happen, drawing on the core aspects outlined above. Some paintings use visual metaphors, where women are compared to an object which is to be used or consumed, for instance Man Ray's *Le Violon d'Ingres* (1924) where the woman's back is transformed into a violin. Women's sexual parts are also often foregrounded and isolated in the frame at the expense of showing their full faces, like we see in Gustave Courbet's *L'Origine du monde* (1866) and Titian's *Rape of Europa*.

There is often no narrative reason as to why women are shown naked in these works. A classic example is Manet's *Le Déjeuner sur l'herbe* (1863), which shows two fully dressed men having a picnic with a naked woman. As Eaton writes: 'This only thinly disguises the real point of such pictures which, once again, is to offer a titillating view of an unclothed female body.'[33]

Women in these paintings have passive poses: they are mostly shown frontal and reclining or leaning, but with a small attempt at concealment. For instance, Giorgione's *Sleeping Venus* (*c.* 1510) became a staple treatment of the nude in Venetian painting; Venus's arm lies above her head to show her availability and surrender; her other hand is gently placed over her hairless vulva.

This passivity is also given an air of surveillance: the painted woman is the object of someone else's gaze. The nude figure rarely looks out at the viewer, who can be left to gaze at her without being caught out. Famously coined the 'male gaze' by film theorist Laura Mulvey, the act of viewing indicative to so much of our art is politicised and moralised, with an inherent connection to desire and authority.[34] The imaginative viewing position prescribed by nude paintings is presumed to be male, heterosexual, and white. Women are the passive looked-*at*, while men are the active look*ing* subjects. As philosopher Naomi Scheman writes:

> Vision is the sense best adapted to express this dehumanization: it works at a distance and need not be reciprocal, it provides a great deal of easily categorised information, it enables the perceiver accurately to locate (pin down) the object, and it provides the gaze, a way of making the visual object aware that she is a visual object.[35]

Indeed, despite Kant's defining contributions to moral philosophy, he did write that 'the man develops his own taste while the woman makes herself an object of everybody's taste'.[36] Putting it like this, of course, wrongly suggests that this age-old principle is somehow one of women's making.

Many artworks belonging to the nude genre eroticise sexual violation, like we saw in Titian's *Rape of Europa*, where the gendered violence is presented as beautiful, and even sexy. In fact, rape was such a prevalent subject in the Renaissance that it had its very own tradition, or motif: 'heroic' rape imagery. These popular artworks portrayed a powerful god or hero's rape of a mortal woman but eroticised and sanitised this sexual violence.[37] As in Titian's painting, the victim would often be portrayed as willing or acquiescing to the unwanted sexual advances, like we see in Antonio da Correggio's *Jupiter and Io* (1530), where Io is sensually enveloped by Zeus, who is disguised as a dark cloud. Nicolas Poussin's *Rape of the Sabine Women* (1636) even represents the act of rape as heroic and patriotic. The anguished women try to escape, and yet Poussin 'justifies' the incident by showing in the middle-ground a Sabine woman who turns to the Roman who is forcing her, and they stroll off together. With this, 'Poussin reminds the viewer that . . . the Sabines soon accepted their husbands'; this couple serve to downplay the terror of the event, as art historian Diane Wolfthal observes.[38]

This ubiquitous rape imagery was used in Italian upper-class marital gifts to act as a guide for new brides. It would visualise the supposed 'ideal traits' that were expected of the bride by her new husband, like chastity and submissiveness.[39] This erotic domination was not contained to the frame. Its blurring of seduction and rape bled out into early modern society. Testimony from a rape trial in 1477 in Venice reveals that a Francesco Papaciza had previously pursued an Ursia without success. Papaciza had then said that 'either by love or force I want you to give yourself to me', embracing the rape myth that sex can permissibly be sought with threat and violence; a myth that still permeates our society today.[40]

Not only are women objectified in nude and heroic rape paintings, but men are portrayed in the opposite way: as imbued with agency. This asymmetric treatment of male and female figures in art stretches back to ancient times. In the earlier chapter on obscenity, I deferred to the Sumerians and their liberal attitudes towards sex in art. In doing so, I may have given the impression that ancient Mesopotamia was a utopia abundant in egalitarian love, and free from unjust objectification. But sadly, this was not the case. Notwithstanding the progressive nature of the Sumerian civilisation, they were, after all, still a patriarchy. Despite their celebration of the vulva and women's beauty, their unjust social order shone through their aesthetic culture.

This inequality was mainly expressed by the treatment of women's nudity and men's nudity in the ancient art of the

Near East. Unlike the artistic norms for women, where their nudity had no narrative framing and their erogenous zones were centrally indicated, male nudity would appear in narrative scenes that more plausibly required it, such as swimming or religious ritual.

Crucially, whenever men would appear naked in Mesopotamian art, they would always be *doing* something. Where female nudity was exclusively sexual, the undressed male figure on carvings and terracottas had several meanings. Even when they were shown naked in less conventional situations, like battle, their nudity was used to convey their piety, virility, and 'supernatural heroic masculinity'.[41]* As Zainab Bahrani puts it, Mesopotamian art confirmed:

> [the] binary divide where woman is the sign of gender
> – the sexualised other – while man transcends his sex to
> represent humanity . . . the naturalised order is depicted as
> a heterosexual division in which woman becomes the sign
> or metaphor for sexuality itself, and the (human) subject is
> masculine . . . Woman is equated to passivity and to nature,
> to the body itself, while man is a social active being with
> agency.[42]

The lack of narrative around women's nudity in this ancient art, and the emphasis on their body parts like vulvae and breasts, was one of the earliest forms of visual objectification. Despite the Sumerians' admiration of women's erotic allure,

* Bahrani warns us though about interpreting these distinctions simply through the lens of modern patriarchal cultures in the West, and class also complicated matters: Mesopotamia was a hierarchal society with an elite class, and when *elite* women were depicted, their sexuality and eroticised femininity and allure were not emphasised.

women were still ultimately reduced to sex objects as part of their inferior status in this society.

The ancient Greeks also expressed a sexist dynamic in their art, but with a very different rationale. In contrast to the Near East, the vulva in erotic Greek sculpture was almost entirely absent because the female body was considered polluting and repulsive.[43] Masculinity was the norm in this culture, where women were the deviant gender: when Aristotle wove together 'science' with sexism in his *Generation of Animals*, he stated that women were deformed versions of men.[44]

There was no female nudity in Greek art – even breast-feeding imagery was considered too taboo – until Praxiteles' life-sized *Aphrodite of Knidos* in the fourth century BCE. The statue shows the goddess preparing for her bath. Her left hand reaches for a towel, and her right hand and arm shield her hairless pubic area, leaving her breasts exposed. The viewer is cast as a voyeur, having just caught the naked Aphrodite in a private moment – a forbidden pleasure.

Where in Near East sculptures, women would explicitly point to their sexual body parts to unashamedly express their eroticism, in Greek depictions of the female body, women try to conceal themselves – specifically, cover their breasts with one hand and their pubic area with the other. This trope of modesty extended into the Renaissance and became known as the iconic *Venus pudica* pose (*pudica* being Latin for 'modesty'). The Knidian Aphrodite's nudity is portrayed as self-conscious and almost shameful. As Bahrani states, 'The Greek nude females are the first instance in the history of art where a moral statement appears to be made in association with the undressed female body.'[45]

Specifically, the Knidian Aphrodite's vulva is merely hinted at by smooth thin lines of creased flesh, in stark contrast to ancient Near East figurines and images where labia and pubic hair were represented frontally and with detail. This erasure of the female genitalia and its rudimentary depiction in Greek art has been excused as simply a limitation of technique: '[the female genitalia] do not lend themselves so well to artistic depiction as the male . . . [they are] too featureless a form to be artistically useful', writes archaeologist Catherine Johns.[46]

I think this does a disservice to ancient craftsmen, though – I'm sure sculpting vulvae was not beyond their capabilities. In all likelihood the vulva's erasure was due to ancient Greek society's wider fear of female sexuality: Greek words used to refer to the vulva were indirect and derogatory.[47] This fear would be abated in art by oversimplifying female sexual features, while the voyeuristic stance of the viewer distanced them from the inherent 'danger' of women.

———

Despite these geographical differences, the erotic objectification in all these pieces is still unfairly gendered and racialised; in being a form of hate speech, these representations *target* groups of people and rank them as inferior beings, affecting what is permissible to think about them – and how we act towards them. Since the *Aphrodite of Knidos*, the female nude has far exceeded the male nude in art. There are very few works of art where male figures are shown to be naked in a sexualised and docile manner.* Can you think of many – if any – historical paintings or sculptures of a naked man lounging

* A striking example of this would be Camille Felix Ballanger's *Death of Abel* (1975) where the male figure echoes Alexandre Cabanel's famous *Birth of Venus* (1863).

or sleeping in a lush landscape, basically doing nothing; head cocked back and coyly hiding his penis?

We can see how this pervasive sexualised treatment of women in art further entrenches and exacerbates women's inferior position in society. Isolated cases of objectification in culture needn't be considered more problematic for women than for men, but taken altogether, they form a glaring asymmetry: women are assigned the role of the sexual object, without a choice in the matter. Artistic traditions such as the nude and heroic rape, then, function to build a bar in the cage, in their expression and perpetuation of this gendered objectification. As art historian Lisa Farrington puts it:

> The persistence of male action and female inaction in much of Western art reflects the male artist's belief (and the belief of the patriarchal society of which he is a product) that the social, economic, and political mobility of women should be limited, and certainly should not exceed that of men.[48]

Together with gender oppression, these paintings and sculptures promote racial oppression, mainly in their general omission of people of colour (especially from the early modern period onwards) but also in their treatment of black and brown people as 'other', again through objectification. In most Western art across the centuries, non-white women are represented in a highly problematic way, or not at all.

People of colour were often actively erased.[49]* Much art of the Renaissance whitewashed its central characters, from the

---

* There are sketches and paintings of black people, but from the eighteenth century onwards they largely focus on studies of fieldworkers, servants, and slaves.

mythological Ethiopian princess Andromeda to the Judean Jesus Christ. Despite Andromeda's being black, she was almost exclusively depicted as white in Renaissance art; her dark skin was largely ignored by artists until the second half of the seventeenth century.[50] The dominant images of Christ that have circulated for centuries mostly portray him as light-skinned with blonde or reddish hair and European facial features, despite his Judean heritage. This erasure continues into the modern era. As theorist bell hooks laments of twentieth-century media: 'to stare at the television, or mainstream movies, to engage its images, was to engage its negation of black representation'.[51]

This whitewashing in art reflected a racist beauty ideal which is still prevalent today. While beauty paradigms vary across cultures and times, the white Eurocentric beauty paradigm, with its roots in slavery, has dominated for centuries. The period spanning the sixteenth and nineteenth centuries saw a move towards classical racialism in the Age of Imperialism, where 'other' races and genders were seen as deviations from default white masculinity and thereby declared lesser human beings. As philosopher Paul C. Taylor argues, this phase of racism and imperialist violence had an *aesthetic* dimension: considerations about human beauty were fundamental in creating racial meaning and division, as a person's bodily beauty was considered to indicate their moral and intellectual aptitude.[52] Colonial discourse, which associated blackness with animalism and sexual deviance, and whiteness with humanity and civilisation,[53] was infused with judgements of beauty – a lofty quality reserved only for the powerful and morally superior.

Art was a sure-fire way of validating and legitimising these sinister sentiments. Where people of colour *were* shown, they were normally portrayed as second-class citizens, further entrenching racialised messages about beauty.[54] In Renaissance and early modern nudes, the white female body was mostly presented as the ideal: exalting pale skin over darker skin.

For instance, in Manet's *Olympia*, a naked white sex worker looks out at us as she reclines on a bed.[55]* Beside her, behind the bed, a clothed black servant presents her with flowers. The aesthetic presentation and dynamic between the black servant and the white woman in this painting has been widely interpreted by scholars as an expression of racist views about sexuality and beauty. A poem which appeared in the exhibition catalogue accompanying the painting's first display highlights how Manet apparently used the black woman's body to emphasise the idealised beauty of the white woman:

> Spring enters on the arms of the mild black messenger / She
> is the slave who, like the amorous night / Comes to adorn
> with flowers the day beautiful to behold.[56]

Olympia famously caused an uproar when it was first shown at the Paris Salon in 1865 because of the defiant gaze of the depicted white woman, modelled by Victorine Meurent – she's a mortal unclothed woman, not a lounging classical goddess; she is naked rather than nude. Instead of being presented in the familiar passive position, she harnesses the viewer's gaze, expressing her agency. Scandalously, she owns her sexuality, and her body is only available for a price.

---

* Various parts of the painting suggest that the figure is a sex worker: the orchid in her hair is a symbol of female sexuality, her jewellery implies a wealth typical of high-class courtesans and the name 'Olympia' was associated with prostitutes in nineteenth-century France.

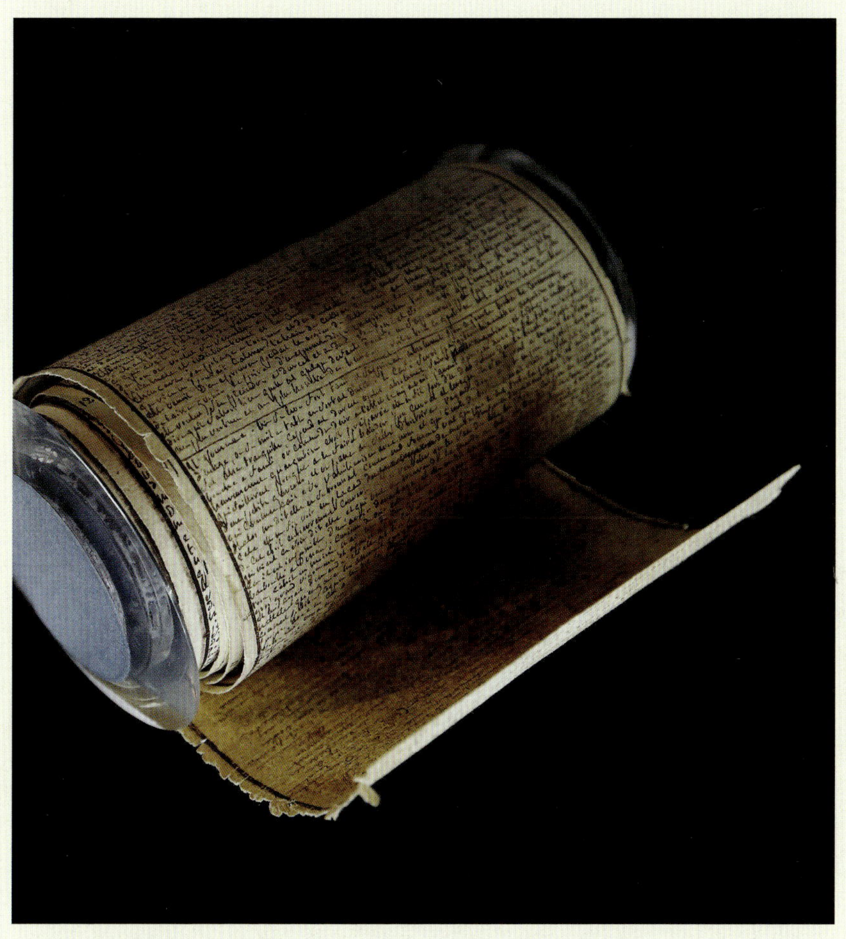

A secret, painstaking creation of utter depravity: the Marquis de Sade's
novel about a savage orgy – *The 120 Days of Sodom* – was saved after
the storming of the Bastille prison in 1789. This 40-foot-long script and
Sade's other literary works went on to inspire avant-garde artists but
also real-life serial killers.

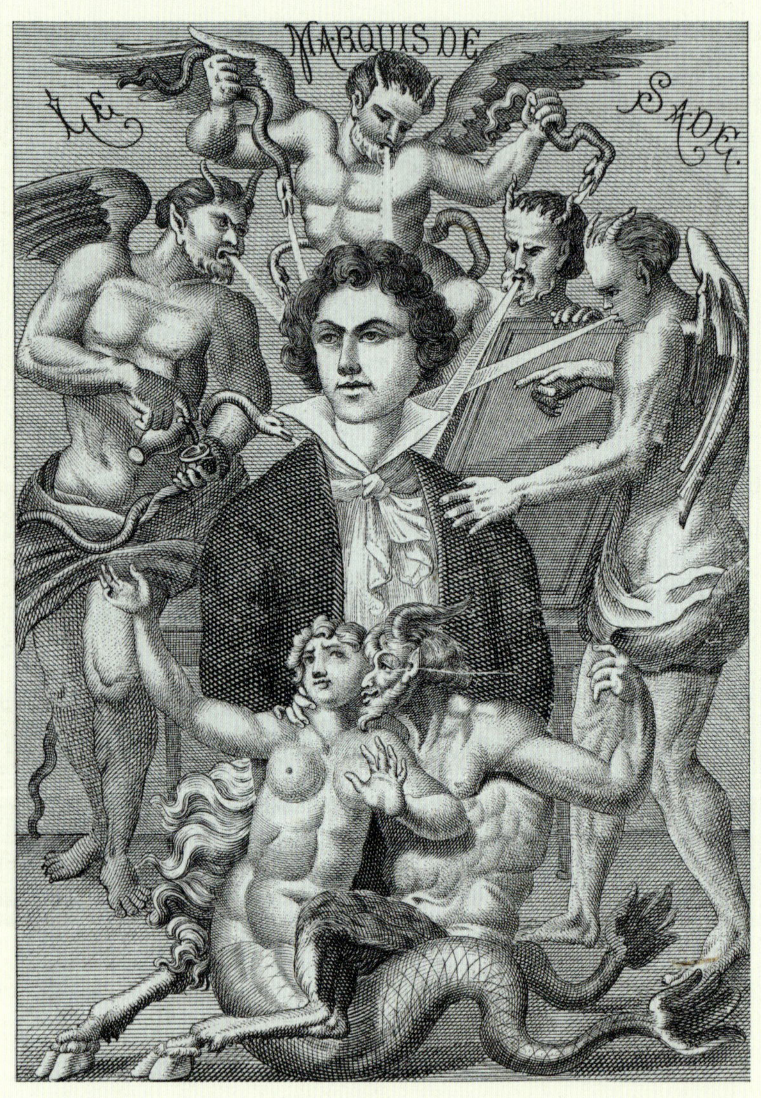

The Marquis de Sade was a nobleman with a mind so sordid that he gave his name to the pleasure derived from the pain of non-consenting others: sadism. He is shown in this nineteenth-century French engraving as a young man surrounded by horned and winged demons. Their mouths emit strange jets over his body, while a satyr in the foreground entwines himself with an unwilling mermaid.

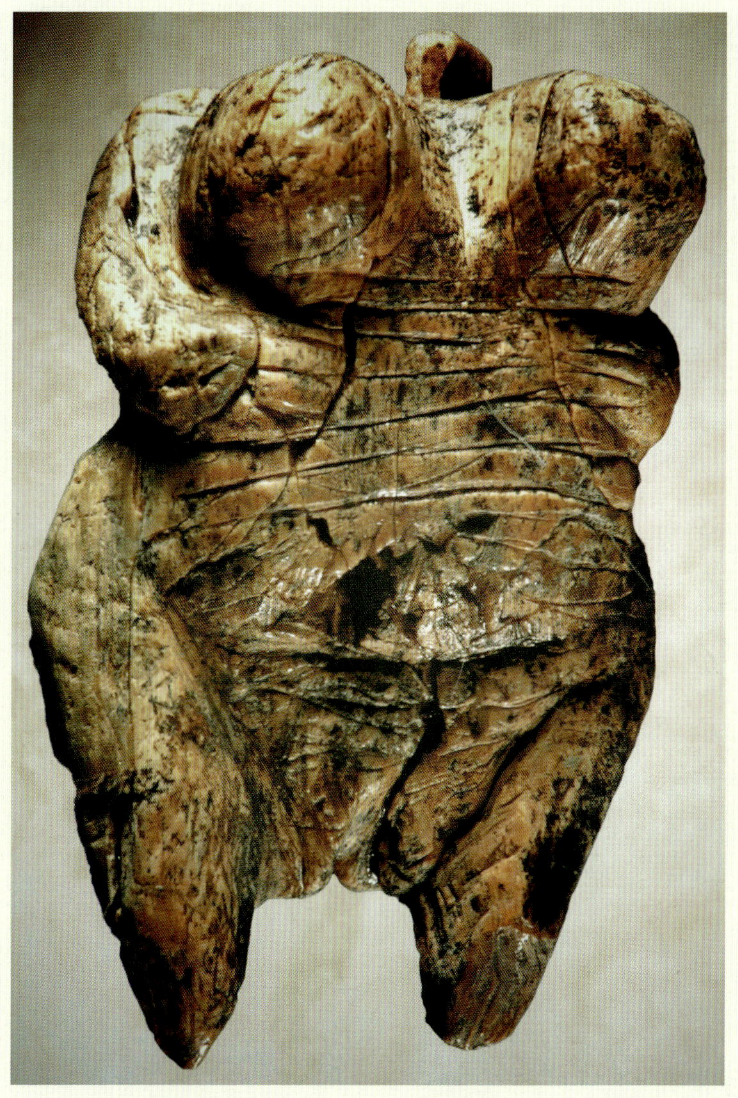

Prehistoric pin-up or poignant self-portrait? You could hold this small amulet carved from a mammoth tusk in the palm of your hand. It is still debated why this 35,000-year-old artwork was made and what it means. Whatever the answers, this masterpiece connects us with our distant ancestors – despite our differences, the desire to create art is what binds us together.

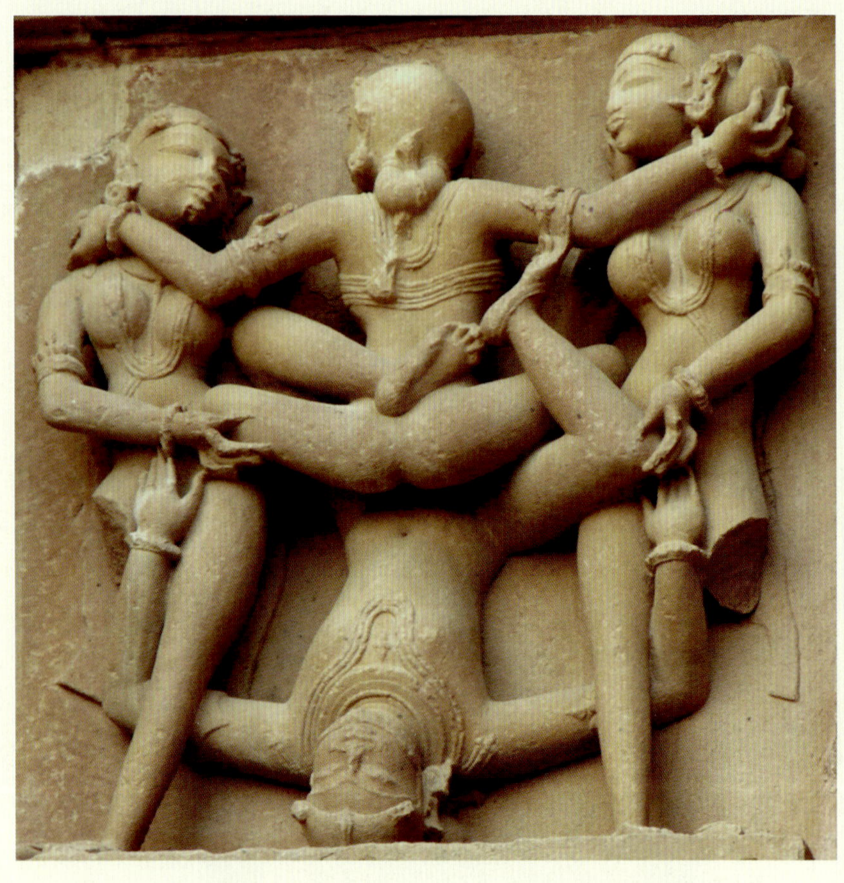

One of the raunchier carvings of the Khajuraho monuments in Madhya Pradesh, India. Mostly built between 885 and 1000 CE, this group of Hindu and Jain temples celebrate joint deities and tenth-century everyday life – many of the sculptures show farming, dancing and animals. While the few sexually explicit carvings are largely taken to express spirituality and love, the British engineer Captain T. S. Burt described the works as 'disgraceful' when he re-discovered them in 1838.

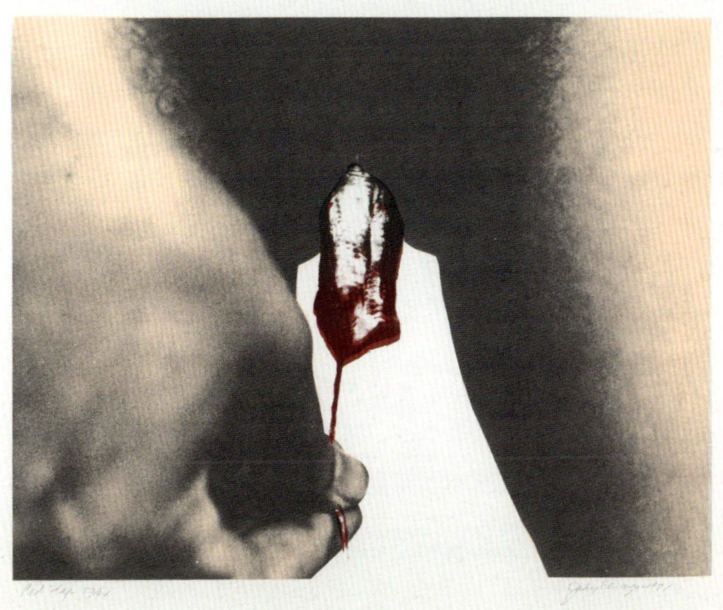

Repulsive or mundane? While the blood of dominant bodies, such as those of white men, has been associated with strength and honour, the bodily fluids of marginalised peoples have been rejected as dirty and obscene. Judy Chicago's groundbreaking *Red Flag* (1971), which shows a bloodied tampon being removed, exposes this double standard and forces the viewer to examine the perception of the female body as abject, and even find beauty within its stark corporeality.

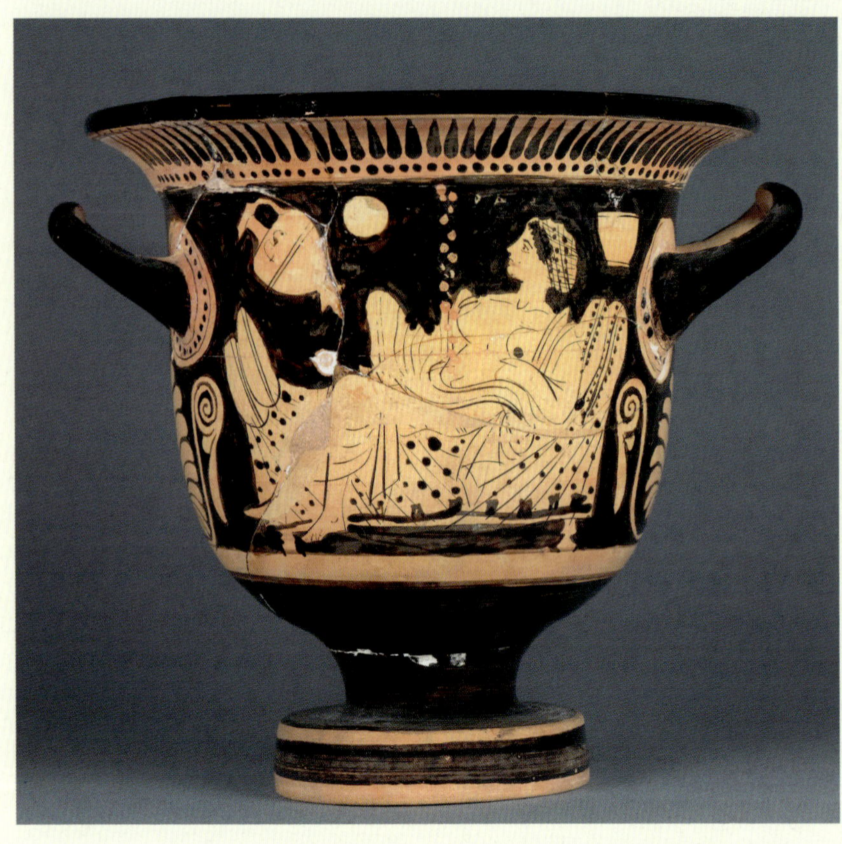

This ancient Boeotian bell krater from *c.* 430 BCE shows the moment that
the mythical princess Danaë is impregnated by Zeus from above . . .
by a golden shower, no less. A painting of this event also features in the
Roman comedy play *Eunuchus*, written by Terence in the second
century BCE. So erotic that it may as well have been physically throbbing,
the painting sends the protagonist mad with lust and he rapes a young girl.
Surely we can't blame the artwork for his wrongdoing – or can we?

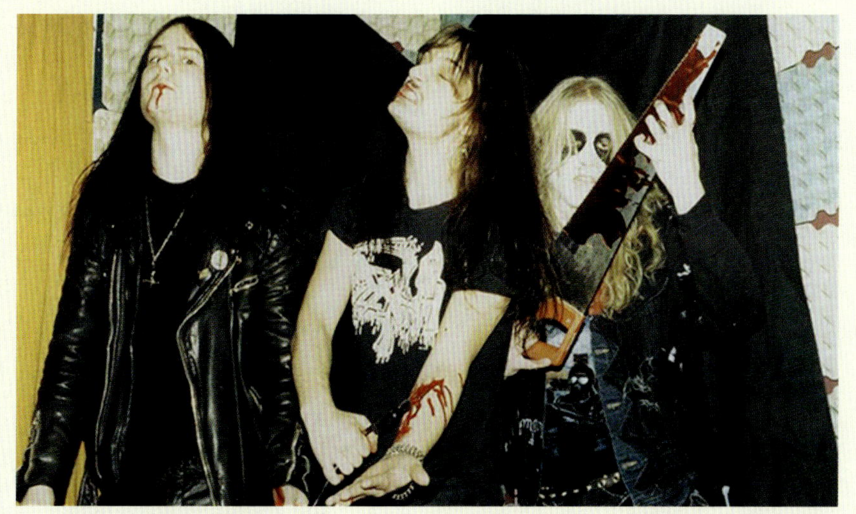

Euronymous, Necrobutcher, Dead: members of the Norwegian black metal band Mayhem in 1987. Their extreme strain of heavy metal, which has Satanism as its official religion, explores themes such as freedom, the wildness of nature, and deep misanthropy. Mayhem also screeched about loving to lick bloodied 'cunts' crawling with maggots. This sonically innovative music was perhaps too provocative: several of its creators and listeners were moved to burn down churches, commit suicide and even kill each other.

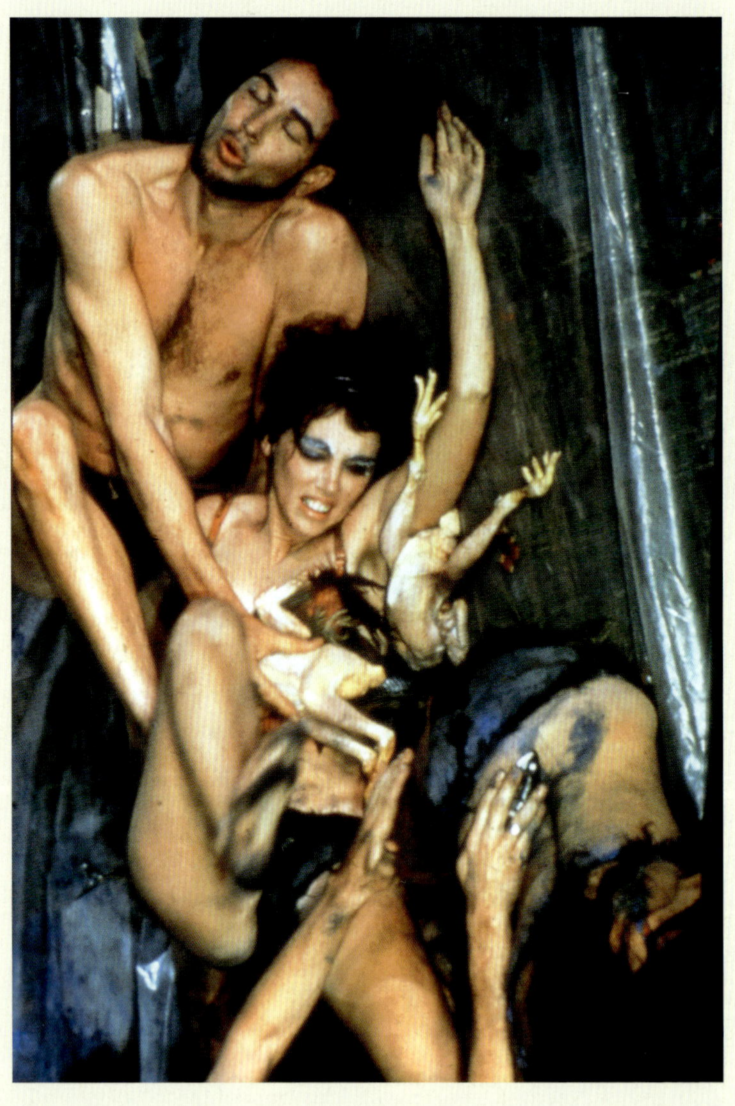

Jubilant and repellent. Carolee Schneemann demolished the stubborn boundaries and assumptions of the Western artworld by rejecting historic aesthetic restrictions on the female body. However, in her *Meat Joy* (1964), she used dead animals as part of the performance. Is this wrong? Or does an artwork dependent on real-life exploitation or cruelty make it all the more trenchant?

This was hugely controversial and progressive at a time where the most respected art was 'academic' in its nostalgic return to classicism and antiquity. Yet, the white sex worker's confrontational gaze is contraposed by the black servant's lowered gaze towards her mistress. As well as not being presented as an ideal of beauty, the black maid – widely known to have been modelled by a woman named Laure – does not look out at the viewer at all: she is passive. bell hooks observed that 'There is power in looking'; slaves in the US were denied the right to look at their enslavers, and were punished for looking directly at them.[57] While hooks identifies sites of resistance to this domination – black people can preserve their agency by critically looking back – Manet's *Olympia* does not afford the black maid this freedom to confront her spectators on the same level as her employer, Victorine: Laure looks at her mistress, but she is not permitted to look at *us*. So, *Olympia* may have challenged the oppression of women, and the wider role of art in society, but it did not go far enough: only white women were afforded this power in the painted world, and only white erotic desire was catered to.[58] *

The black servant in *Olympia* can be interpreted as an example of wider racist perceptions and ideas that have dominated the Western social imagination over the last three centuries. These central ideas of anti-blackness constitute what sociologist Patricia Hill Collins calls 'controlling images'. These core stereotypes 'are designed to make racism, sexism, poverty, and other forms of social injustice appear to be natural, normal, and inevitable parts of everyday life'.[59] Racist stereotypes, which fully emerged during the transatlantic slave trade and early modern

* Some studies of this painting do argue though that Manet took care to show that Laure was not enslaved.

European colonisation, were created to support the dominant group's interest in maintaining black and brown subordination.

Some racial stereotypes which were particularly prevalent in nineteenth- and twentieth-century America will be familiar. The 'Mammy' figure, a racial caricature of African American women, is an obedient and nurturing domestic servant. She is large with pitch-black skin and white teeth and wears a calico dress and head scarf. She lives to serve her master and mistress – her white family are her world. The character was posited as 'proof' that black people – in this case, black women – were contented as slaves.[60]

While nineteenth-century France did not have a direct equivalent of the American Mammy figure in its social imaginary, its society held many anti-black tropes (such as savagery, unintelligence, hypersexuality) due in part to its colonisation of the Caribbean and its eventual loss of Saint-Domingue (now Haiti) in 1804 after enslaved Africans staged an insurrection against French colonial rule.[61] The maid in *Olympia*, while not strictly speaking enslaved at this post-abolition time, is still interpreted as the subjugated caregiver, invoking the spectres of slavery and the Mammy figure.[62] Conceptual artist Lorraine O'Grady asserted: 'Forget "tonal contrast". We know what she is meant for: she is Jezebel *and* Mammy, prostitute and female eunuch, the two-in-one.'[63]

Juxtaposing the Mammy was the 'Jezebel' figure or 'Hottentot Venus'. This was the portrayal of black women as naturally hypersexual, an enduring stereotype used to justify sexual violence in slavery that was exemplified most notoriously by the appalling objectification of Sarah Baartman in England and France in the nineteenth century, as we will see later.[64] Historically, white women were portrayed as models of self-respect, modesty, and purity, but black women were often portrayed as innately promiscuous to sanitise and deny the possibility of their rape.[65]

Another pervasive anti-black image in the US was the caricature of a black man lying in a field, eating watermelon and avoiding labour. The image was used to characterise black men as innately idle, dim-witted, and inarticulate, and while not contented with their enslavement, too lazy to challenge it. According to the Jim Crow Museum of Racist Memorabilia in Michigan, this stereotype of the 'c**n' – the racist slur which is an abbreviation of 'raccoon' – served to dehumanise black men and legitimate their enslavement.

Depraved imagery stemming from these anti-black stereotypes was everywhere across the US and Europe throughout the nineteenth and twentieth centuries, from cinema to kitsch household objects. Anti-black caricatures would appear as characters in Warner Brothers children's cartoons and Hollywood films and novels, but also on greeting cards, postcards, toys, and kitchenware, and in advertising products for breakfast foods. The Jezebel figure would appear on metal nutcrackers and swizzle sticks for stirring drinks, and even fishing lures.

Possibly the most enduring cultural expression of these stereotypes is the performance of blackface. Originating in nineteenth-century US minstrel performances (though some scholars note its origins in medieval Europe),[66] white performers would insultingly mimic black people by making up their faces with burned cork, and wide red or white lips. Their performances would light-heartedly present a derogatory conception of blackness, drawing on the familiar ideas of laziness, ignorance, sexual promiscuity, happy-go-luckiness, and contentment with oppression.[67]

This demeaning practice became widespread family entertainment, performed by household names like Judy Garland, Fred Astaire, and Shirley Temple. It is still mishandled in more recent times: the former Prime Minister of Canada Justin Trudeau on several occasions donned blackface and brownface at parties during his youth, and YouTube celebrity Jenna Marbles quit the platform in 2020 after tearfully acknowledging her 'shameful' impersonation of Trinidadian rapper Nicki Minaj.[68]

Dehumanising images like these can be so poisonous that today their mere display is socially and sometimes legally prohibited. The 'Censored 11' Warner Bros cartoons were taken out of circulation in 1968 due to their extremely offensive use of ethnic stereotypes. And recently, a police raid on a pub in Essex, England, resulted in the removal of several golliwog dolls from a bar display after a complaint.

The golliwog figure, which began life in the nineteenth century as a doll-like character created by American British author Florence Kate Upton and was later popularised by Enid Blyton's children's books, became a striking anti-black image with its minstrel attire and grotesque appearance. Influenced by the blackface tradition, it appeared as a children's toy, and on wallets, sweet wrappers, perfume bottles, and jewellery across the US, the UK, and Australia.[69] While owning and displaying golliwog figures is still legal in the UK unless they directly incite racial hatred and violence (which is difficult to prove), children's books containing the image have been withdrawn from public libraries, and many shops have stopped selling the figurines and dolls.

In addition to the objectification we saw above in the imagery of the nude and heroic rape traditions, dehumanisation in racist depictions like the golliwog also functions by caricaturing and exaggerating stereotypical features of the oppressed social group. For instance, antisemitic pictures that were used during the Middle Ages and then in Nazi propaganda served to demonise Jewish people by portraying them as ugly and frightening villains. Caricatures originating as far back as the thirteenth century show Jews with large hooked noses and horns, and as having a miserly and greedy demeanour while attempting to gain global control. More recent antisemitic imagery portrays Jewish people as 'other' by using tropes like zoomorphism, where Jewish people are depicted as animals like octopuses and snakes, and literal demonisation, identifying Jews as bloodsucking vampires.[70]

People with disabilities have been misrepresented in the story of art as well: their conspicuous absence from artworks, particularly before the twentieth century, falsely suggests they did not play any role in society. Where they *are* shown in art – whether in paintings and novels or films and TV shows – these portrayals are often highly objectionable. For hundreds of years, stereotypical representations of disabled people depicted them as inherently pathetic or even as wicked and evil.* Christian paintings – notably those of the sixteenth and seventeenth centuries, such as Hieronymus Bosch's *The Garden of Earthly Delights* (1490–1510) – would show ugliness, physical anomalies, and disfigurements as expressions of human sin.[71] More generally, the 'bad guys' in stories ranging from *Treasure Island* to the James Bond novels and films tend to have difficulties with their mobility or have other visible impairments,

---

* There are of course exceptions to this: visual art in the Enlightenment period exhibited a kinder portrayal of disabled people, such as Francisco Goya's painting *The Madhouse* (1812–19) and the Chinese portraitist Lam Qua's detailed depictions of patients with tumours in the nineteenth century, which have been heralded as both medically accurate and humane.

while people with dwarfism have been used to create unsettling atmospheres in many horror films.[72]

These artworks again serve to marginalise those who don't have 'typical' bodies or neurodevelopment by showing them to be somehow *other* – as figures of ridicule, pity, or fear. While the intentions of some of the artists behind these works have been subject to debate, it is widely agreed that artistic representations have contributed to the oppression of disabled people throughout history. As noted in a report by the British Council of Organisations of Disabled People, such art and media 'dilutes the humanity of disabled people by reducing them to objects of curiosity', thereby hindering others' compassion towards them, undermining their opportunities in society, and sapping their self-esteem.[73] In my terms, these artworks have *subordinated* these diverse groups of people over the centuries, further cementing their historical status as second-class citizens.

Dehumanising images are today rife in online spaces, too, with a proliferation of Islamophobic memes objectifying Muslim people. In 2018, a UK Conservative councillor posted a meme on Facebook which visually compared a woman and child wearing burqas to garbage bags. He was suspended by the party as a result, but then later reinstated.[74] The sole aim of such images is to inspire hate and/or fear of the oppressed – to *see* them as sub-human, as the enemy, and to thereby justify their poor treatment. This use of visual metaphor is a simple yet powerful aesthetic device that achieves this 'seeing-as': Jews are represented as animals, Muslims as garbage bags.

The effects of these images throughout modern history have been devastating, and it is their peculiarly aesthetic expression of poisonous stereotypes which makes them so toxic.[75]

This has led to what philosopher and activist W. E. B. Du Bois called a 'double consciousness': 'this sense of always looking at oneself through the eyes of others, of measuring one's soul by the tape of a world that looks on in amused contempt and pity'.[76] Those who are oppressed simply wish to be seen as human, but instead are plagued by the dominant group's negative impression of them. As British Nigerian historian David Olusoga has said about blackface performances in film and TV:

> The people who invented racism – the slave owners and the racial scientists – they could write their books but no one really read their books. *This* is how you transmit to millions and millions of people ideas about who people are, what they are like. This is how you generate stereotypes. This is how you convince people that others are not like them. It's art, and art is not a cherry on the cake of life, art really is life, and this is racism literally made into an art form.[77]

Expressing such views through art and entertainment, inviting us to see these sentiments as natural and appealing, makes them much more insidious and powerful as a form of social domination. When it comes to oppressive speech, a picture is worth a thousand words.

Trojan Horses

Up high against the sky, a bronze angel with large open wings supports a dying Confederate soldier in her right arm. Her left arm is defiantly outstretched, holding a laurel wreath. This monument in downtown Salisbury, North Carolina – called *Fame* or *Gloria Victis* – is a familiar symbol which was placed at the centre of a busy traffic intersection in 1909, expressing sombre commemoration of the 2,500 Confederate soldiers from the state's Rowan County who fell during the American Civil War. The angel figure in the sculpture is the Greek goddess Pheme (or Roman Fama). The daughter of Elpis (Hope) in Greek and Roman mythology, Pheme would bring people favourable world renown or wrathful scandalous rumour. Both the Greek *pheme* and Latin *fama* are related to the infinitive 'to speak'. And speak this sculpture does, like a toxic foghorn.

In 2018, the monument was covered in white paint, apparently as a response to the distribution of Ku Klux Klan flyers in nearby black neighbourhoods. A couple of years later, shots were fired near the statue during the 2020 Black Lives Matter protests following the murder of George Floyd, allegedly by a white nationalist. Around this time, an online petition claimed that the statue supports 'white supremacy and memorializes a treasonous government whose founding principle was the perpetuation and expansion of slavery'.[78]

On the other hand, the Fame Preservation Group – a local historical society – argued that the statue is part of Salisbury's identity, and simply represents those who fought against an invading federal military force; for them, its removal was tantamount to an erasure of North Carolina's political history.[79] In a CNN news item, one member of the group insisted that the statue was 'just an inanimate object'.[80] Despite the preservation group's efforts, in 2021 the monument was relocated to the town's Old Lutheran Cemetery, where since 1996, 176 Confederate soldiers have had tombstones.

The preservation group's suggestion that the sculpture was anodyne and inanimate was misguided. Like much

Confederate art, *Fame* does not merely represent the Confederacy and its values – it *does* something. It glorifies and venerates the Confederacy. But in revering a war fought in support of slavery, the statue implicitly ranks black people as inferior citizens; monuments such as these do not depict subordination, they literally subordinate. How should we make sense of a bronze sculpture having such depraved force?

In this chapter, I've been suggesting that the arts are one of the many buttresses of oppressive systems; their seductive portrayals function as 'illocutions' which determine how we can legitimately think about and act towards marginalised groups of people. We've seen how visual artworks can perpetuate sexist and racist norms in how they represent women, people of colour, Muslims, and Jews. But the depravity of much hate speech lurks in the shadows. Degrading and offensive representations of target groups are not always explicitly presented or stated; sometimes, they are implicitly presupposed.

For instance, consider a bigoted coach who shouts at a male football player 'even a *girl* could make that shot!' after the player misses a goal. In saying this, he implies that girls and women are bad at sport, even though he doesn't explicitly state it. This familiar sexist trope is smuggled into the situation, functioning as what Rae Langton calls a 'backdoor speech act'.[81] If nobody challenges the coach, his illocution is accepted into the situation's background of assumptions. It becomes accepted in that moment that women are weak, which in turn affects what is permissible to think and infer about women generally. These pernicious backdoor speech acts subordinate target groups and legitimise further discrimination.

Cultural artefacts like paintings and public sculpture can sneak oppressive speech acts in through the backdoor too – an

artwork might act as a Trojan horse for deplorable messages.*
In 1778, Spiridione Roma's painting *The East Offering its Riches
to Britannia* was installed in the East India Company's London
headquarters on the ceiling of the revenue committee room. It
shows Britannia as a pale-skinned, regal young woman with a
mighty lion at her feet, signifying the white European feminine
archetype in a position of authority over Asia. India is represented by the dark-skinned bare-breasted woman kneeling at
Britannia's feet, offering her a crown of rubies and pearls.

The painting was commissioned as propaganda: it expresses the myth that the Company's relationship with India was
'consensual and benevolent' and 'without coercion or violence',
according to art historian Alice Procter. It is a visual argument
that India was the 'jewel in the crown' of the British Empire,
and that Britain's exploitation and pillage of India was justified.
As well as being an outright lie, this aesthetic agenda employed
by the Company also presupposes that such domination was
'generous, necessary, even inevitable'.[82] To justify colonial control of a nation and its people, this group must be assumed to be
naturally inferior to the settlers. While the painting explicitly
shows India as subordinate to Britain, it also smuggles in shady
speech acts of subordination: that this is the way things naturally are and ought to be. Remarkably, this piece now hangs in the
Foreign, Commonwealth & Development Office in Whitehall,
London: a controversial adornment for a department dedicated
to contemporary international diplomacy.

Let's return to the Confederate monument *Fame*. The tall
statue is cast in bronze and, before it was relocated, it dominated a traffic intersection with its imposing scale. As a visual

* I'd like to thank Sean – one of my Cardiff University undergraduate
students – for this great description of the backdoor speech-act concept.

locution it uses familiar aesthetic conventions to announce its message: the angel lifts the dying Confederate soldier as if to Heaven, and in its other hand brandishes a laurel wreath, which is an ancient Greek symbol of triumph. This statue clearly honours the fallen Confederacy and what it stood for.

But as I've argued, this commemoration only scratches the surface. By honouring and celebrating an unrecognised republic which supported racial division and human enslavement, this statue's speech act presupposes that such slavery is justified or even admirable. This depraved message lurks within the bronze sculpture as a 'backdoor' act of subordination. For if it is permissible to enslave a racial or ethnic group, this is supposedly because that group is in all ways lesser than the oppressor.

So often, hatred in art is present in its low-profile speech; through explicitly testifying or asserting that a commemorated event or ideal is laudable, it implicitly declares that a socially marginalised group is subordinate. These artistic speech acts are common: many of our galleries and public spaces are dominated by paintings and monuments that tout oppressive social norms like racial hierarchies. We can't say that artworks are 'inanimate' and innocuous because they don't literally point a gun. Depravity bubbles beneath their surfaces and is all too often overlooked or dismissed. Just because an artwork is beautiful doesn't mean it's harmless. And just because it's in a visual medium doesn't mean it's silent.

Intimacy

In September 2014, the sound of drumming, whistles, and horns filled the air outside London's Barbican Centre. Protesters held placards stating: 'EXHIBIT B, THE MOST RACIST

SHOW ON EARTH . . . #BOYCOTTBARBICAN' and 'AN EXHIBITION OF WHITE PRIVILEGE'. The crowd had gathered to object to Brett Bailey's *Exhibit B* (2013), an installation which had already toured other European capitals and had been met with similar controversy. The exhibition at the Barbican was shut down before it even opened to the public, after the protests were deemed a security concern.

Based on historical examples of human zoos and nineteenth-century ethnographic displays, *Exhibit B* was composed of thirteen *tableaux vivants*. Each one involved black actors representing a period in the brutal history of European relations with Africa since the seventeenth century. The artist said of an earlier version, *Exhibit A*: 'What I'm looking at in this work is how Europeans have represented the African body and how those distortions have led to a particular sequence of actions and have legitimized some of the most terrible atrocities.'[83]

One tableau in *Exhibit B* represented a naked Sarah Baartman enclosed in a glass cabinet and rotating on a plinth. Known by the pejorative name 'Hottentot Venus', Baartman was a young Khoikhoi woman who was brought to London from South Africa in 1810 by a British doctor to take part in public shows and perform domestic duties, although it's unclear whether she was coerced or went willingly.[84] She was exhibited as entertainment for white viewers at 'freak shows' in Paris and London and marketed as 'the missing link between man and beast';[85] her curvaceous form was showcased to peddle pseudo-scientific racialised theories and contribute, as we have seen, to the controlling image of black women's hypersexuality. Even in death, Baartman was appallingly objectified: her body was dissected by French naturalist Georges Cuvier, and her genitalia became an obsession in France.[86] Her body was put on display in Paris until 1976, and only finally laid to rest in her homeland in 2002.

Another tableau in *Exhibit B* showed an enslaved man in an iron mask, surrounded by a still life of fruit. The scene evoked Dutch *vanitas* paintings, drawing the viewer's attention to the jarring distinction between opulent Dutch Golden Age culture and the brutality of the transatlantic slave trade which provided the Netherlands with its riches.[87]

Brett Bailey is a white South African man whose art explores the history of colonial and post-colonial Africa; his *Exhibit B* was intended to expose imperialist violence. But many viewers were disturbed by the piece and objected that it was racist despite Bailey's stated aims. After the moral outcry when his show reached London, Bailey responded in the *Guardian*:

> The intention of Exhibit B was never hatred, fear, or prejudice. It is about love, respect, and outrage. Those who have caused Exhibit B to be shut down brand the work as racist. They have challenged my right, as a white South African, to speak about racism the way I do. They accuse me of exploiting my performers. They insist that my critique of human zoos and the objectifying, dehumanizing colonial/racist gaze is nothing more than a recreation of those spectacles of humiliation and control.[88]

Many viewers and those involved in creating the piece were on Bailey's side. They argued that while the work was triggering and difficult to swallow, it nonetheless formed a necessary eyeopener to Britain's racist history. The Scottish newspaper *The Herald*, for instance, praised the piece as a 'beautifully arranged and produced show' and as 'compulsory viewing'.[89]

But others insisted that the work's literal use of chained-up and caged black people, and the fact that the artist was a white man, meant that the artwork re-enacted the very racial power relations it was attempting to critique.

When an artwork is interpreted as toxic, does it matter if the artist had different intentions for it, like Bailey did with *Exhibit B*? And does the artist's identity matter when considering this question?

———

Sometimes, the artist's intention carries more weight when it comes to how their art is interpreted. Recall Andres Serrano's *Piss Christ*, which we visited in an earlier chapter. The photograph of a plastic crucifix immersed in the artist's urine was taken by many to be outrageously blasphemous. But Serrano himself is Catholic and has been, in his own words, a 'follower of Christ' his whole life. He insisted that *Piss Christ* was not blasphemous at all but rather serious Christian art, representing the gruesome reality of the crucifixion. Much like Grünewald's *Isenheim Altarpiece*, *Piss Christ* aims to reveal Christ's true agony and suffering. Serrano told the *Guardian*:

> What it symbolises is the way Christ died: the blood came out of him but so did the piss and the shit. Maybe if Piss Christ upsets you, it's because it gives some sense of what the crucifixion actually was like.[90]

Piss Christ is still shocking, but the fact that Serrano is a Christian suggests a plausible alternative interpretation of his work, and that the moral outrage it caused was misplaced. The same goes for Chris Ofili's *Holy Virgin Mary*, the painting of a black Virgin Mary partially made from elephant dung. While this work (among others at the 'Sensation' exhibition in New York) was called 'sick stuff' in 1999 by the then Mayor of New York City, Rudolph W. Giuliani, Ofili complained that the uproar against it was misguided. Like Serrano, Ofili grew up Catholic, and continues to practise the faith as an adult. As for his chosen material, he used elephant dung in much of his art around the time he painted *Holy Virgin Mary*, largely in reference to a formative visit he made to Zimbabwe in the early 1990s. With this context in mind, the Catholic League for Religious and Civil Rights' denouncement of the work as an attack on religion seems to be a misunderstanding.[91]

So why should we listen to Serrano and Ofili more than we do to Brett Bailey? Perhaps the reason we defer to the artists' authority in these cases is that they belong to the very group they are making art about. Both Serrano and Ofili are Catholic, and so we might think this gives them a privileged position from which to speak artistically about Catholicism and related theological themes.

Bailey, on the other hand, stands in a problematic racial dialogue with his own work. While the black actors willingly consented to their role in *Exhibit B*, the fact that the artist and orchestrator of the event was a white South African man meant placing a white man in a position of authority. This, combined with the work's (assumed) largely white audience, arguably undermined Bailey's artistic goals. Of course, white people should engage with the history of racism and imperial violence, but doing this by composing scenes that 'simply imitate the history and leave Black performers silent seems unproductive at best', as Alice Procter puts it.[92]

Even if we defended Bailey and insisted that his work's re-enactment of racial violence makes his art *more* effective as social commentary, I think the more pressing harm here is to do with a breach of intimacy (a term we will come back to) and a lack of first-hand emotional knowledge. As Bailey is white, he was not in the appropriate position to make art about black pain. How can a white man truly understand the anguish of racial subjugation without having experienced it? Du Bois famously observed this point in his autobiography *Darkwater: Voices from Within the Veil* (1920). In an essay on democratic theory, he argues that extending the right of democratic participation to women and black people was vital on epistemic grounds. He wrote:

> only the sufferer knows his suffering and . . . no state can be strong which excludes from its expressed wisdom the knowledge possessed by mothers, wives, and daughters . . . The same arguments apply to other excluded groups.[93]

When it comes to democratic decision-making, Du Bois argued that the best policies will be derived from the collective knowledge of all, rather than the social elite. To truly understand social injustice, and how to remedy it, we must listen to the members of those disadvantaged groups, for this is where the pertinent wisdom lies. Only the sufferer knows his suffering.

This has come to be known as 'standpoint theory', a term coined by feminist philosopher Sandra Harding in 1986. Originating with the Marxian idea that to truly understand the class system we must listen to the experiences of the proletariat (as the bourgeoisie cannot simply imagine what it's like to be in their position), standpoint theory holds that those who are oppressed have vital and unique insights about the world. In the same way, artists who do not belong to the marginalised group they make art about are at an epistemic, and indeed emotional, disadvantage, and may risk being insensitive to their subject.

One famous case of a white artist making art about black pain is Dana Schutz's *Open Casket* (2016), which was shown at the Whitney Biennial in New York. The painting portrays the mutilated face of Emmett Till, the fourteen-year-old African American boy who was horrifically lynched in 1955 in Mississippi after being falsely accused of flirting with a white woman. Schutz's painting is based on a photograph from Till's funeral, which shows his body laid out in an open coffin at the request of his mother, Mamie Till, who wanted everyone to witness the consequences of the appalling racist murder: 'Let the world see what I have seen,' she told the funeral director.

Schutz was accused of cultural appropriation in her use of black pain as material for her painting. Artist and writer Hannah Black wrote in an open letter to the Whitney Biennial's curators that 'the painting must go':

Although Schutz's intention may be to present white shame, this shame is not correctly represented as a painting of a dead Black boy by a white artist — those non-Black artists who sincerely wish to highlight the shameful nature of white violence should first of all stop treating Black pain as raw material. The subject matter is not Schutz's; white free speech and white creative freedom have been founded on the constraint of others, and are not natural rights. [If] Black people are telling her that the painting has caused unnecessary hurt, she and you must accept the truth of this.[94]

As Black points out, the subject matter here was not Schutz's to experiment with. While Schutz intended to present white remorse, having a white artist paint a black boy's mutilated face in such confronting detail was perhaps not the best way to do it. Schutz's artistic speech turned toxic due to the circumstances of this artwork's creation; not being black, she was not in the right position to have standpoint knowledge of racial violence. She may have had empathy in her *attempt* to put herself in Mamie Till's and the wider black community's shoes, but there's only so far this empathy can go.

In 2012 the Afro-Swedish artist Makode Linde displayed an extremely controversial work of art at the Modern Museum in Stockholm. In celebration of World Art Day, his *Painful Cake* was shown at a reception attended by the Swedish Culture minister. The work comprised the artist, who is a black man, wearing golliwog makeup and forming the head of a caricatured black woman – the rest of whose body was made of cake – referencing the infamous image of the 'Hottentot Venus'. The piece was part of the artist's wider project called 'Afromantics', which transposes blackface imagery on to Western icons such as Beethoven, Betty Boop, and the twelve disciples. When viewers cut into the cake, the artist let out piercing screams, referencing the ongoing abhorrent practice of Female Genital Mutilation.

Strangely, the Swedish Culture minister smiled and laughed as she cut into what's now known as the 'Hottentot Venus Cake', while onlookers awkwardly grinned and filmed the spectacle on their phones. At one point, the minister fed a slice of cake – which had just been cut in a clitoridectomy gesture – to the artist himself, in a bizarre representation of cannibalism.

An uproar in Sweden and the international media followed, and the event was reported to the Parliamentary Ombudsman, with the National Association of Afro-Swedes demanding the minister's resignation. The international debate was again divided between those who admitted that the artwork was distressing but insisted that it exposed contemporary racism and so was not racist itself, and others who deplored the work for being racist and degrading to women despite the artist's goal for the piece. The minister defended the artist:

> I am the first to agree that Makode Linde's piece is highly provocative since it deliberately reflects a racist stereotype. But the actual intent of the piece – and Makode Linde's artistry – is to challenge the traditional image of racism, abuse and oppression through provocation. While the symbolism in the piece is despicable, it is unfortunate and highly regrettable that the presentation has been interpreted as an expression of racism by some. The artistic intent was the exact opposite.[95]

Despite Linde's explicitly anti-racist aims, something again went wrong with this work; a depravity that outstrips the horror he was aiming to evoke.

Even though *Painful Cake* was created to make an anti-racist point *and* was made by a black man, it could be argued that the only kind of artist who should ideally create and display such an upsetting piece is a black woman. The 'Open Letter from African women to the Minister of Culture' posted on the Afro-Nordic blog *MsAfropolitan*, for instance, argued that the artwork became an appalling spectacle of misogynoir.

> As representatives of African women on the ground, we have the experiential privilege to convey to the Swedish

Embassy's Ministry of Culture the fury that we have seen, particularly from African women who are dismayed at the fact that this project which was supposed to bring awareness of the very painful and complex issue of genital cutting has ironically, had the complete opposite effect. The fact that the artist is black does not in any way diminish the gravity of this racially demeaning project . . . the racial overtones of this project re-inscribe the exploitation and dehumanisation of black African women, which clearly cannot be denied . . . No one, including the artist seems to have consulted Black African women at the forefront of the movement to end the practice of female genital cutting . . .[96]*

The main problem the signatories of this letter touch upon appears to be the grotesque and insensitive nature of the artwork's execution – the golliwog and Hottentot images were indeed a shocking combination. But the artist's gender is also a factor: it reinscribed the violence his work was trying to denounce.

Given that oppression operates in interlocking ways across multiple systems like gender, race, and class, the knowledge and experience of oppression that black men have in a white supremacist patriarchy, for example, will be different to that had by black women. As Patricia Hill Collins puts it in her seminal book *Black Feminist Thought*:

[Because] Black women have access to the experiences that accrue to being both Black and female, an alternative epistemology used to rearticulate a Black women's standpoint

---

* The term 'misogynoir' was coined by the writer Moya Bailey in 2010 to capture the misogyny directed towards black transgender and cisgender women, particularly in American visual and popular culture.

should reflect the convergence of both sets of experiences. Race and gender may be analytically distinct, but in Black women's everyday lives, they work together.[97]

Having a black man speak on behalf of black women in the form of art, at least in this extreme case, can be considered a breach of intimacy – Linde overstepped the line.

This is one way we can understand the harm of cultural appropriation – the representation of cultural practices or experiences by cultural 'outsiders'. Philosophers C. Thi Nguyen and Matthew Strohl observe that intimacy can be generated between people, and these intimacies can be wrongly breached. Like reading your friend's diary without their permission, a breach of intimacy is a violation: in this case, of someone's right to privacy. In the same way, social groups can have forms of intimacy which can be breached by non-members: 'what makes a practice intimate is that it functions to embody or promote a sense of common identity and group connection among participants in the practice, and thereby renders it meaningful and valuable to these participants'.[98]

In the case of cultural appropriation, if members of an oppressed group set a boundary and request or imply that non-group members refrain from adopting or using a cultural product that has importance for that group's identity, this prerogative should be respected. A white person donning a Native American headdress at a music festival, for instance, is widely considered unacceptable because the adornment is a sacred custom, which is meaningful to the practices that unite the indigenous peoples of the Great Plains and Canadian Prairies. Failing to respect this boundary constitutes a breach of intimacy.

Something similar can happen when artists make art which

represents the experiences of oppressed groups to which they do not belong. Despite Makode Linde being black, his not being a black woman meant that many saw *Painful Cake* as a violation of an implicit boundary. As with Schutz's *Open Casket*, the agony of FGM and the despicable objectification of the female black body was perhaps not Linde's story to tell, especially in such a brutal manner that made use of now-prohibited imagery like that of the 'Jezebel' or 'Hottentot Venus'.

So, artistic speech can become depraved even when it is expressed in good faith.[*] It matters *who* brings the art to the world. Now, this is not to say that artists and authors should never tell stories from a perspective different from their own. But when doing so, they must be extremely careful with their execution of the work. They must listen to those they represent. Otherwise, they risk doing more harm than good.

———

When Titian created *Rape of Europa* and his other beautiful nudes, he would not have been fully aware of the dangers he was contributing to. At the end of the day, he was hired to do a job, and he did it spectacularly well. But regardless of an artist's intentions and awareness around their art, it can still scream – or whisper – depraved messages.

* The role of the artist's intentions in determining artwork meaning has been debated by philosophers for decades. I personally adhere to the alleged anecdotal view held by conceptual artist and philosopher Adrian Piper, who observes of her own work: 'My work is an act of communication, and it's important to me the way what I assert lands, and where it lands within someone who sees it. On the other hand, I also recognize fully and live by the principle that once the work leaves my studio, I cannot control the effects it has.'

Isolating each painting, each sculpture, each carving, each figurine, each performance, might make them look innocent. But taken together, these artworks that have been produced over thousands of years have slowly, insidiously reinforced the bars of our birdcages. When oppression is propped up by alluring beauty, by frightening dehumanisation, by engaging entertainment, and through civic speech, it creates toxins that spill out into society, and are difficult to eradicate.

At the heart of artistic speech is the magical ingredient of illocution. Whether or not they directly cause criminality, depraved artworks can oppress social groups because of how they shape social reality: this art affects what is *permissible* – what it is *legitimate* to think about and do to the oppressed. In response, we should adopt what bell hooks calls the 'oppositional gaze' – we must defiantly and critically look back at Titian's bull, and acknowledge it for what it is.

Treating immoral art as a peculiar kind of hate speech – a type that can even be sexy and beautiful – prompts the question: *who* is the speaker? An artist's creation often grows to be bigger than them, but it is still gifted to us with their hands. And while artists like Bailey and Titian meant no harm, many artists do. So now we must face perhaps the most important head of our depraved Hydra: the problem of the immoral artist.

4 | MALEVOLENCE

The child waited on the bed. The sun had set, and a twilight darkness slowly enveloped her. The sounds of cicadas filled the room, and she breathed in the sweet scent of the *tiaré* blossom growing outside the wooden hut. He was late. As she stared at the door through the dim light, she felt a tightening in her chest. She clutched her white dress; her breath stopped.

The door finally opened – he had returned: the painter.

———

A wide head at the level of the cheekbones. Like that of a cat. Generally the skin is green, in some way related to that of the snake . . . Lives almost as do animals . . . Like she-cats, she bites when in heat and claws as if coition were painful. She asks to be raped. She is totally indifferent to any consideration you might have for her.

Giving her a good beating every week [makes her] obey a little. She thinks very poorly of the lover who does not beat her.[1]

depraved

These descriptions of Tahitian girls and women are reportedly the words of the renowned nineteenth-century post-impressionist Paul Gauguin. The French painter first travelled to Tahiti in 1891 to escape what he saw as degenerate European culture – and his wife and children – and immerse himself in what he considered to be Eden; to enrich his art, and his soul.[2] During his return to France after that initial stint on the island, Gauguin explained to a journalist why he'd fled there:

> I was captivated by that virgin land and its primitive and simple race; I went back there, and I'm going to go there again. In order to produce something new, you have to return to the original source, to the childhood of mankind.[3]

But what met Gauguin was disappointing for the disillusioned artist. French colonial rule had fundamentally changed island life over the preceding decades. Christianity had been widely assimilated, and local traditions and beliefs had been banned. Yet Gauguin wished to keep alive the myth of the untouched paradise. Much of his art from this Polynesian period tried to advertise – or yearned for – a false image of Tahiti as a utopian oasis free from the claws of European custom and culture.

Not long after his first arrival in Tahiti at the age of forty-three, Gauguin met a local girl named Teha'amana, also known as Tehura. She was thirteen years old, and she soon became Gauguin's 'native' wife, or *vahine* (the role of these girls for French colonists at the time was to provide them with sex and food). Their marriage lasted two years, and Teha'amana bore his child. On Gauguin's return to Tahiti in 1895, she refused him. He then lived out the rest of his life in French Polynesia, and never saw Europe again.

It is still debated exactly how Gauguin contributed to the European imagination and mystification of Polynesia. He has been praised as pioneering the 'primitivist' aesthetic style – a use of flattened perspectives, vivid colours, and indigenous symbolism – which defined nineteenth- and twentieth-century Western art movements inspired by non-Western cultures. Some defend this aesthetic approach as a sincere attempt to authentically explore worlds newly discovered by European imperial powers, whereas others worry that this approach has perpetuated an exoticised othering of those who differ from Eurocentric norms.[4] Gauguin's views of Tahiti have been described as 'orientalist' in part because of his ignorance of names for cultural and religious products, and the names of the various islands' inhabitants. But some argue that his was a genuine engagement with the islands and its people, knowing them better than most professional anthropologists at the time.[5]

Regardless of the complexity of Gauguin's 'primitivist gaze' – in his genuine longing to become part of these 'exotic' communities but also in his exploitation of them – it is certain that he was a sexual predator. When he created some of his best-known paintings in the South Pacific, he used his colonial privilege to sexually abuse girls as young as thirteen, possibly infecting them with syphilis. Another of his wives after Teha'amana – fourteen-year-old Vaeoho, also known as Mary Rose – was allegedly bought by Gauguin from the girl's father in the Marquesas Islands 'for six yards of cotton cloth . . . three dozen ribbons, a dozen pieces of lace, four reels of thread, and a sewing-machine'.[6]

Gauguin's paintings of these girls came to represent his vision of them as pure, divine femininity. As theorist Jane Duran writes, 'their youth alone gave them precisely the innocence for which Gauguin was looking, an innocence that he came to regard as characteristic of the culture as a whole'.[7]

We might think that Gauguin's abuse of these girls was by the by; a series of unfortunate events that had nothing to do with his brilliance as an artist. But this would be wrong. His sexualised attitude towards his child brides is smack bang in the middle of much of his art, like his *Manaò tupapaú* (*Spirit of the Dead Watching*, 1892). This oil painting shows Teha'amana, who, according to the artist, was lying in fear one night when he arrived home. In the painting she awkwardly lies naked on her stomach on a plush bed, and ambiguously looks sideways out at the viewer. Behind her is the ghost of an old woman, and shades of purple and luminous light dance on the wall. In Gauguin's travelogue *Noa Noa* from 1893/4, we get insights into his motivations in making this painting:

> Tehura's dread was contagious: it seemed to me that a phosphorescent light poured from her staring eyes. I had never seen her so lovely; above all I had never seen her beauty so moving. And in the half-shadow, which no doubt seethed with dangerous apparitions and ambiguous shapes, I feared to make the slightest move in case the child should be terrified out of her mind. Did I know what she thought I was, in that instant? Perhaps she took me, with my anguished face, for one of those legendary demons or specters, the Tupapaüs that filled the sleepless nights of her people.[8]

Despite the many merits of this painting, you are nonetheless looking at the depiction of a dark-skinned girl in an abusive relationship with an older white man. As art historian Nancy Mowll Mathews, among others, has speculated, the submissive fear in Teha'amana's eyes is likely not a reaction to a spirit in the room, but to Gauguin's known aggression and ownership of her.[9]

In the last months of his life, Gauguin lived in a bamboo hut in Atuona on Hiva Oa. He had decorated his door with sculptured panels of sequoia wood, which portrayed naked women, flowers, and animals, with an inscription reading: 'Maison du Jouir' – the House of Sensual Delight (or, depending on your translation, the House of Orgasm, House of Come, or House of Love). It was there that in 1903, racked with pain from possibly syphilis-induced sores, the artist died of a heart attack at the age of fifty-four.

It is difficult to like Gauguin as a person. The man emerges from his own writings and others' testimonials (not to mention his own art) as a pretentious and arrogant bully. In 1893 fellow painter Camille Pissarro lamented that Gauguin 'is always poaching on someone's ground; now he is pillaging the savages of Oceania'.[10] He is also often blamed for pushing the vulnerable Vincent van Gogh over the edge during their stormy friendship.

But the reality behind Gauguin's alluring and colourful creations is sometimes ignored, the focus instead placed on the paintings themselves and their innovative style and legacy in modern art. Shouldn't we pay more attention to the artist behind the beauty?

Origin Stories

The problem of immoral artists is as old as art itself. Great art has for centuries been made by people who behaved badly. Caravaggio killed a man in a brawl, supposedly over a woman or a tennis match (it's not clear), Virginia Woolf expressed anti-semitic views, Eric Gill sexually abused his own teenage daughters, Miles Davis battered his wives, and J. K. Rowling has been denounced by many as transphobic.[11] But these artists have created masterpieces which stand the test of time, whether through mesmerising use of the chiaroscuro technique, pioneering modern narrative devices, or paving the way for new movements in jazz or hugely influential children's literature.

Although it may not seem like it sometimes, these accomplishments are still the products of flesh-and-blood people. Flawed people. And we often forget this when we put great artists on a pedestal up and away from the morally bound Earth of us mortals – we tend to give artists a moral pass. But artists are mortal. Gifted, yes, but also ordinary in many respects. They eat, they sleep, they shit, and they make mistakes.

Some artists are extraordinary not just in their creative wisdom but in their misdeeds. Many have taken advantage of their power and authority, ruining lives through sexual violence, abuse, emotional manipulation, and even participation in genocide. So where does this leave their art?

The question of whether we can separate the art from the artist has never been more relevant. In 2019, Michael Jackson's songs were banned by several radio stations across the world. The bans occurred following the release of *Leaving Neverland*, a documentary which follows Wade Robson and James Safechuck and their allegations of child sexual abuse by the late singer. Many artists have been similarly censored or cancelled for their misdeeds in recent years. Movements such as #MeToo have forced misconduct into the spotlight and implored us to no longer sanitise or excuse unacceptable behaviour. This leaves consumers of art in a tricky position.

Do we do something wrong if we enjoy and dance to Michael Jackson's music? Should we refrain from watching films directed by Roman Polanski, who was charged with drugging and raping a thirteen-year-old girl?[12]

When we discover that our favourite artist has supposedly done something bad, we feel conflicted about how to react. I've written some of this book while listening to Michael Jackson's music. One of my favourites – 'Beat It' (1982) – fills me with nostalgic joy, transporting me back to my 90s childhood where I practised moonwalking with an old friend in her living room, young and carefree. The art we love defines the way we navigate the world – it holds precious memories and encapsulates our hopes and dreams.

Have I been wrong to continue enjoying Jackson's music? To fully answer that question, we first need to understand how an artist's character infects or enhances their creations. A later chapter will grapple with the ethics of consuming and censoring immoral art and artists, but before we do this, we need to get a handle on how an artist's own depravity is even relevant to their art in the first place.

———

'You have an interesting face. I would like to do a portrait of you. I am Picasso.' Marie-Thérèse Walter met Pablo Picasso when she was seventeen, he forty-five, outside an upmarket department store in Paris in 1927. After his flirtatious interaction with Marie-Thérèse, Picasso painted her in his studio nearby, and they began an extra-marital affair unbeknownst to his first wife Olga Khokhlova. This liaison with Marie-Thérèse lasted about eight years. The pair had a daughter, but Marie-Thérèse was soon cast aside by Picasso, who had moved on to his next mistress – the surrealist artist Dora Maar.

Having secret love affairs and deceiving your partner(s) is a very bad thing to do. But it is less Picasso's tumultuous love life and more his problematic attitude towards women in general that has caused outrage, pushing the artist's remarkable life and art on to the stage of public scrutiny. The main accusation put to Picasso in recent years is that he was a misogynist. This much shouldn't be surprising, given that many people, including some women, are misogynists. But Picasso's beliefs about women were particularly damning. He once told one of his partners – the abstract painter Françoise Gilot – that 'women are machines for suffering' and that 'for me there are only two kinds of women: goddesses and doormats'. When Gilot left Picasso after ten years, he demanded that art dealers boycott her work in a bid to destroy her reputation as an artist – she said 'no' to the cultural giant and it led to her 'civil death'.[13]

Women for Picasso were a means to an end; muses and objects of god-like adoration, there to serve his sexual and creative appetite. Picasso's granddaughter Marina writes in her memoir that her grandfather submitted women 'to his animal sexuality, tamed them, bewitched them, ingested them, and crushed them onto his canvas. After he had spent many nights extracting their essence, he would dispose of them, bled dry.'[14]

Picasso's misogyny isn't just found in his unsettling sexist beliefs, but in his actions too. He was physically and emotionally abusive, kidnapping one woman, Irène Lagut, out of possessive jealousy, and frequently locking up his first serious partner Fernande Olivier in his apartment. He demonstrated a familiar pattern of domestic abuse and then abandonment of his lovers once they became ill or lost their youthful vitality. Several of the women in his life did not escape unscathed: two were dismissed as mad, and two committed suicide.

When we learn facts like these about our favourite artists, it is hard to ignore them. An artist's life is often interwoven with the art they produce for the world. Picasso said his paintings were like the pages of his diary, and we can plainly see his moral convictions expressed as painterly entries.

Tate Modern's *Picasso 1932 – Love, Fame, Tragedy*, for instance, presented a single intense year of the artist's life. The exhibition included beautiful portraits of soft and curvaceous forms representing his secret lover Marie-Thérèse. *Nude Woman in a Red Armchair* (1932) shows Marie-Thérèse's lilac flesh twirl and wind into the enveloping chair in which she sits. In direct contrast, there were jagged, rigid, and violent depictions of his then wife Olga. *Woman with Dagger* (1931) shows a serrated and contorted grey female form, supposedly portraying Olga, attacking a rival below – supposedly Marie-Thérèse.

Knowing Picasso's biography and moral character affects how we interpret and value his art, particularly his portraits of his lovers. Knowing how he treated women can taint our aesthetic experience of these revolutionary works. We feel torn between recognising the greatness of his creations and the chauvinist reality lurking behind them.

There is a popular belief today that we shouldn't react like this. To do so is irrational because it doesn't track anything robust or real in the art. Rather, we should interpret an artwork based on its internal aesthetic merits alone and not bring anything outside the painting to bear on how we witness it. The art and the artist are, and should be, entirely separate.

This sentiment emerged in the latter half of the nineteenth

century, when art criticism and theory – influenced by Immanuel Kant's writings about beauty a century earlier – focused on an artwork's internal features. The appropriate stance towards art was simply examining what it looked or sounded like, rather than its relation to supposedly irrelevant things like morality or the artist's character. The ethical realm was not to touch the aesthetic realm, for subsuming art under the shackles of morality ignores the true essence of art, which is that it affords a special kind of experience where we become immersed in an artwork in a 'disinterested' way – we behold it for its own sake.

Reinforced by the literary practice of twentieth-century New Criticism, theorists such as Clive Bell and Roger Fry released works of art from their artists' intentions and creative contexts. For these thinkers, we should sever the text of a novel and the painterly or sculptural forms from their maker. Under this formalist approach, we should judge Picasso's paintings for their aesthetic appearance alone and their place within the frontiers of artistic experimentation. How Picasso acted towards his subjects, or his beliefs about women, have no bearing on the significance of his creations. So, feeling that inner tension over a painting made by an artist who abused women is inappropriate – it doesn't trace any moral attitude within the work itself.

In a 2009 *New York Times* article discussing Roman Polanski's trial, the poet and novelist Jay Parini adopted this formalist stance. Using Picasso as an example, Parini argued that an artist's moral character has no bearing on their products. The depraved or saintly enlightenment of an artist is 'another subject' altogether: 'Nobody looks at a Picasso painting in a museum and says, "I should not take this work seriously because Picasso cheated on his many wives and was abusive to his son."'[15]

I'm going to show you that this gets the nature of art totally wrong. Artworks are more than just their surfaces, or what immediately meets the eye. They do not drop out of the sky; they are created by a person with an identity and background, at a certain time and place. Out of historical situations, they are *born*.[16] There is more to a painting than the way its colours and shapes are put together on a canvas or panel. There is more to a poem or novel than its text.

Why should we think that this view of art is true? Well, to show why, we need to conduct a thought experiment. I want you to imagine British Pop artist Allen Jones's infamous group of three sculptures *Hatstand*, *Table*, and *Chair* (1969). This provocative artwork consists of three fibreglass white women dressed in fetish clothing, positioned as pieces of furniture. *Hatstand* stands erect with her arms upturned as hooks. *Table* is on her hands and knees with a pane of glass across her back. *Chair* is on her back with her legs up in the air, a seat cushion on her thighs. When this installation was exhibited in 1970, there was a major backlash. Feminist protesters attacked the work – *Chair* was damaged with paint-stripper – for being outrageously sexist and objectifying.

Now imagine that in another world, much like our own, those very same sculptural forms are composed and arranged in an identical way, but this time they are created by a woman in the wake of the #MeToo movement in 2018. It seems right to say that we would have a very different artwork here, in this alternate world. One that does not itself objectify women but that instead protests sexism and exposes how women are treated in society as sex objects.

So, we can imagine that the same constructed sculptural forms – the same type of composition – would manifest in two different artworks. We ascribe different meanings to them, even though they look exactly the same. We'd likely value them differently too – maybe we'd prefer the latter piece, as it contains a deeper political message. What this hypothetical scenario shows us is that it matters who makes the art. Its origin and creative context are integral to how we understand it.

This sentiment is reflected in another thought experiment. Philosopher and art critic Arthur Danto asks us to imagine walking into a museum and seeing a row of identical red square canvases. The first one is a historical painting called *Israelites crossing the Red Sea*. A second one is called *Red Square*, a minimalist work. Another is also called *Red Square* but is a punning Communist tribute painted in the manner of Kazimir Malevich. Another is called *Kierkegaard's Mood*, and another *Red Tablecloth*, painted by a sour disciple of Henri Matisse. The last is a primed canvas by the Renaissance painter Giorgione, left unfinished.

All these red objects look the same, but they have very different artistic properties.[17]* The first canvas represents something clear: the sea. The second canvas belongs to the minimalist movement and is simply a red square. The third is a political symbol. The fourth has metaphorical, emotional content – what does it mean for a person's mood to be red? The fifth mockingly references another artist's style. The last isn't art at all.

* Danto arrived at this realisation when confronted with the brilliance of Andy Warhol's *Brillo Boxes* in the 1960s. Warhol's action of piling up copies of commercial packaging in Manhattan's Stable Gallery in 1964 posed the question: What is art? The work made 'a revolutionary and ludicrous demand, not to overturn the society of artworks so much as to be enfranchised in it, claiming equality of place with sublime objects.' It challenged how we should understand and value a thing as art (Danto 1981, p. 208).

Many of the significant qualities in these artworks are not found in their expanse of red pigment alone. External features must enter our aesthetic experience to fully understand and value them. Reducing Picasso's *Nude Woman in a Red Armchair* or *Woman with Dagger* to their genre-defining visual forms obscures how these are even works of art at all. Merely engaging with a work's surface may mean we can glean all sorts of fascinating things from it, but if we don't engage with the work's history, we're not treating it as a work of art but as something else entirely. You cannot separate the art from the artist because the artist is a necessary part of the art. The balmy curvaceousness of *Nude Woman in a Red Armchair* is only the beginning.

The formalist approach to the problem of immoral artists, namely, that there *is* no problem, is completely on the wrong track. Artworks are partly constituted by historical and moral facts outside of the literal object before you; the artist's moral character is among them. As philosopher W. E. B. Du Bois observed in his 'Criteria of Negro Art' – written in 1926 to argue for the responsibility of black artists to create anti-racist art during the Harlem Renaissance – artists create art that reflects their whole self.[18] This includes their social roots – where they came from, and where they are going.

The Devil Is in the Detail

So, the artist's morality is relevant to their art. But where do we draw the line? How exactly does the artist's immorality taint the fruits of their labour? The content of Picasso's paintings isn't determined *only* by Picasso happening to have sexist beliefs. Rather, much like the language we use must be suitable to communicate our beliefs about things, for the artist's moral character to somehow affect their artwork, the work in question must support or bear 'evidence' of this character. Can we *see* or *read* or *hear* the morality itself in the art? As the philosopher Berys Gaut puts it, painters can be brutal or caring towards their subjects through their artistic medium: 'It is the *way* that a work conveys its ethical or other insights that makes them of aesthetic relevance.'[19] Artistic choices such as prose style, metaphor, lighting, poses, brushstrokes, and composition can convey significant attitudes towards the portrayed subject.

Of course, people can express an attitude in one setting and a different one in another. Picasso may have mistreated the women in his life, but still hypothetically have been able to capture authentic love in his art. The same artist can be compassionate towards his subject but nasty towards her outside of the art. However, 'the test must be whether, in the light of one's knowledge of the artist's attitudes outside his work, one can detect in the work traces of these attitudes', argues Gaut.[20] By inspecting an artist's work, we might *see* or *hear* moral perspectives. And many of Picasso's paintings of his partners are clearly bound up with complex attitudes towards women.

The Dream (1932) is one of Picasso's many portraits of Marie-Thérèse. The painting shows the artist's lover sleeping in an armchair. Her head lolls to rest on her shoulder, her hands clasped in the shape of a vulva. Her face looks calm, although Picasso has transformed half of it into the form of a phallus. This dozing woman simply cannot get sex off her mind.

And in *Nude Woman in a Red Armchair*, Marie-Thérèse's body is entwined with the furniture, blending into it seamlessly; the chair caresses her as she becomes almost inanimate. While it may be alluring, this compositional technique recalls Man Ray's *Le Violon d'Ingres* (1924), where a woman's body becomes a musical instrument. Bearing in mind the historic oppression of women and the artistic genre of the nude which sustains this sexual inequality, these works are not immune from the cultural pattern of reducing a woman's body to a thing, a thing without agency or subjectivity.

This immoral sentiment towards women – this objectification – is expressed by Picasso through his painterly style and the formal treatment of his sitters. As Gaut notes of Picasso, 'Someone who was previously ignorant of the biographical facts could come, after learning them, to see attitudes in the paintings with greater focus and clarity than she previously had done.'[21]

We can call this approach to the relationship between immoral artists and their art an 'empiricist' answer to the problem – the idea being that we need to see evidence of the artist's immorality in the work itself for there to be a meaningful connection. We can trace the artist's moral attitude towards their subject matter in the way they have given it to us: in the chosen colours, composition, form, and symbols.

This approach to the problem of immoral artists can be used to illuminate several such cases, like films and songs by artists whose misdeeds are similar to that which is shown in the art itself. Woody Allen's child sexual abuse allegations,[22] for instance, bear upon our ethical and artistic appreciation of *Manhattan* (1979), where Allen plays a character with similar proclivities in a manner that expresses indifference to the acceptability of this kind of relationship. And think how R. Kelly's child sex offences relate quite plainly to his own music in lyrics like those of 'Age Ain't Nothing but a Number', a song written for his child bride Aaliyah's album in 1994.

In the same way, we can *see* the connection between Gauguin the man and his portraits of his child brides. We know that while Gauguin was creating these pieces, he described the Polynesian women and girls he met as 'animal-like' and deep-down desiring rape and violence; he frequently painted his 'Frightened Eves', as Nancy Mowll Mathews puts it. Interpreting his work in this wider context reveals how Gauguin's immoral attitude is relevant in a direct, clear way to his portraits of his victims. The fact that he used his patriarchal and colonial privilege to abuse these very girls cannot be robustly detached from the exoticised portraits of them.

The tension we feel towards artists like Picasso and Gauguin is not merely appropriate; it should be demanded. To fully understand their art, we must consider the context in which it was made. Next time you see one of their portraits of their partners, remind yourself that you are looking at the expressions of men who used and abused women and girls. In the art these lovers are reduced to object-like forms – a chair, a penis – or their fear is eroticised.

Now this is not to say that Picasso did not love his partners, in some way, or that Gauguin saw his Tahitian girls as *merely* exotic objects. And this is not to say that these paintings are not great artistic achievements. But we have a social and moral responsibility to scrutinise them. For, among other things, they represent humans with complex emotions and subjectivity as decorative objects – or they are just simply portrayals of sexual violence. And who do we benefit by dismissing these ominous realities?

More Than Meets the Eye

We're not out of the woods yet. Problems arise when an artist's misdeeds or immoral character don't clearly show up in their art. With Picasso and Gauguin, their art portrays the women or girls they abused. But what about art made by a troubled mind that doesn't immediately indicate such literal evidence of any depravity?

Let's think about the following case. Graham Ovenden was a British artist best known for his nude/semi-nude photographic and painted portraits of pre-pubescent girls. He was also a convicted child sex offender. Consider one of his headshots – *Head of a Girl, Michelle* (n.d.) – and let's assume that this painting did not involve using (or abusing) a real model, and that it doesn't sexualise the portrayed child in any obvious way. Because there's no visual indication of a sexualised attitude towards the girl, the empiricist would have to say that Ovenden's misdeeds in his life have no relevance to this particular artwork.

But suppose, as is likely, that Ovenden's motivation for the painting was to derive sexual pleasure from it – even though there's no visual indication of eroticisation. Wouldn't this make a difference? Philosopher Ted Nannicelli writes – and I agree – that it does:

> it seems entirely plausible that the painting is morally flawed as a result of the morally reprehensible motivation from which it was likely created — that is, the sexual gratification Ovenden anticipated taking (and likely did take) by painting [it].[23]

We can see this subtle connection between the immoral artist and their art by conducting a similar thought experiment to the one we did earlier with Allen Jones's women-furniture. Imagine two perceptually indistinguishable headshot paintings of a child, who is portrayed in a non-sexualised and neutral pose. Let's assume that the first was made by an artist with no paedophilic proclivities when representing the girl – perhaps a loving older sister. But imagine that the second was made by Ovenden, whose motivation was to gain sexual gratification. It seems right to say here that the former artwork would be innocuous, but the latter would not be innocuous at all; the artist will have 'created something morally defective – an instance of child pornography', as Nannicelli puts it.[24]

Being aware of the circumstances surrounding a work's creation affects the nature of the work. In this case, it determines whether or not the work is pornographic – a property generated by something outside of the work itself: the artist's motivation to make something for his own sexual arousal. Intention can determine a work's category or genre, such as its being poetry or satire. And in Ovenden's case, because of his (assumed) intention in making the piece, we can judge that the portrait is pornographic and not simply the innocent portrayal of a girl's face.

So, this different approach – let's call it the 'motivation approach' – to the problem of immoral artists moves away from what we can straightforwardly see or hear in the work: it invokes an ethics of production centred upon an artist's motivation in making the work in question. But what about artworks made by a depraved person which were not created with such a specific immoral motivation? To answer this, we must turn to quite possibly the most immoral artist of all time.

A Wolf in Sheep's Clothing

Munich, 1919. Likely still feeling the effects of a mustard gas attack from when he was in the Ypres trenches, Adolf Hitler is an unemployed artist struggling to make ends meet.

Angry and disillusioned with the dire state of Germany after losing the First World War, he leaves his cold studio to attend a meeting of the German Workers' Party – the right-wing organisation that preceded the Nazi Party.

The rest is history, as they say. But let's return to Hitler's studio – what do you see? There are watercolour paintings and sketches of pretty Germanic landscapes, with soaring mountains and small chalets nestled in woodland. There are colourful still lifes of alpine flowers and detailed drawings of city scenes and architecture. On first impressions, Hitler's work just looks like generic postcard art. Nothing jumps out in these paintings that indicates depravity.

Hitler's art has never been popular: critics and theorists have dismissed it as mediocre and amateur. But many of us see these paintings as tarnished by who made them. In 2019, the Nuremberg auction of five landscape paintings attributed to Hitler failed to attract buyers, and the sale was attacked as being in bad taste. And yet, compared to easier cases like Gauguin's and Picasso's portraits of the very women or girls they treated badly, it's less clear that Hitler's atrocities are at all relevant to his art.

There's nothing here for our empiricist to grab on to: even though the artworks were made by Hitler, there is no obvious antisemitic or Nazi standpoint noticeable in these paintings; no antisemitic caricatures or Nazi symbols like swastikas which would be a clear trace of Hitler's immorality (in fact, it's precisely because there are no such symbols that it's legal for these paintings to be sold in Germany today). Rather, many people dismiss them as 'innocuous' or 'unobtrusive',[25] and, well, just no good.

There isn't anything significant for our motivationist to grab on to either. It's unlikely that Hitler intended his artworks to promote Nazi and antisemitic ideals or function as Aryan propaganda each and every time he sat down to create them. Unlike Ovenden's de facto aim for his child portrait to be sexually titillating, Hitler's early paintings were the exercises of a young artist who was trying to put food on the table; someone who desperately wanted to get into art school, and famously failed.

Both schools of thought we've considered, in their different ways, would concede that while these works were created by one of the most barbaric people in history, there's no robust link between his savagery and his art. Beyond the mere fact that he created these paintings, we needn't engage with their meaning or aesthetic value any differently to how we might with a pretty Sunday painting made by a good, ordinary person. It seems the malevolence of the creator here leaves the art untouched.

This is wrong, though. Both approaches we've looked at so far are insufficient for trickier cases like Hitler's art. We can still assume that Hitler did not have conscious antisemitic motivations when painting each of his works. But I want to suggest a more subtle connection between the malicious mind and its art: depravity can lurk in the artist's *style*. To understand this connection, we need to look more closely at Hitler's whole creative practice, including the art that he himself loved.

Hitler mainly painted small, realistic, detailed pieces in watercolour and oils, of cityscapes, scenic German and Austrian landscapes, delicate flowers, and women. Many of his works were made in Vienna a few years before the First World War, and he began selling some in 1909. It was around this time that Hitler was becoming political, while also becoming disillusioned with the contemporary artworld, particularly modernist art. He says in his *Mein Kampf* (1925) that it was while he was in Vienna that he started to develop his antisemitic inclinations.

As well as his growing hatred of Jews, Hitler's bittersweet nostalgia for a 'traditional' pastoral Germanic nationalism was reflected in his passion for certain genres of art. He adored German and Italian Renaissance art, Graeco-Roman Classicism, and Neoclassicism – an eighteenth-century art movement based on the ideals of art from Rome and ancient Greece, characterised by straight lines, precision, definition, and realistic palettes. His artistic influences and preferences were not arbitrary: around this time, the art of antiquity was being hijacked to ground the emerging Aryan myth that the ancient Greeks and Romans were originally Nordic – that it was Germanic peoples who in fact gave birth to civilisation.[26] *

The art historian Frederic Spotts describes Hitler's painterly style throughout his life as a 'literal Naturalism . . . rooted in the naturalistic German tradition – concrete and identifiable subjects, clean lines and attention to detail'.[27] His whole oeuvre was inspired by a belief in the so-called 'Germanic spirit' – a mystical, rural, and ancient nobility facing a decaying future after the Age of Enlightenment and the Industrial Revolution. This romantic concept existed before the formalisation of the Nazi Party and was expressed in writings by the traditionalist German architect and painter Paul Schultze-Naumburg. It formed the basis of Hitler's belief that 'Aryan art', with its stylistic sources in classical Greece and the European Middle Ages, was the epitome of beauty.

This Aryan style infamously reached its peak when Hitler came to power later in his life, where he gave his own artistic preferences the authority of law. The Great German

---

* In *Mein Kampf*, Hitler wrote that there was a 'racial unity' linking Greeks, Romans, and Germans, where he saw the former two as originating from the Nordic race.

Exhibition, which was held in Munich eight times between 1937 to 1944, showed pre-approved paintings of Germanic and Austrian landscapes, soldiers, and blonde nudes, all of which conformed to Hitler's aesthetic taste and expressed his conviction that Greek and Roman figures embodied the racial ideal. The exhibition was designed to purge his empire of 'degenerate' non-representational, abstract modern art, which was seen by the Nazis as a form of Jewish aesthetic violence.[28] In contrast, the Great German works expressed National Socialist values of 'blood and soil', of racial purity and obedience, and Heimat themes (love of the homeland) showing *volk* at work in the fields. As Klaus Fischer writes:

> In looking at Nazi architecture, art, or painting one quickly gains the feeling that the faces, shapes, and colors all serve a propagandistic purpose; they are all the same stylized statements of Nazi virtues—power, strength, solidity, Nordic beauty.[29]

Hitler's early paintings, then, are examples of what I'll call 'proto-Nazi' art, where his taste – his aesthetic ideology with its background of German romanticism and pre-First World War nationalism – blossomed. His nostalgic style, influences, and go-to subject matter sat firmly within this emerging Aryan art tradition.

With this in mind, we can see that Hitler's depravity is deeply connected to his art. In the Graham Ovenden case we examined earlier, the artist's motivation to make pornography was conscious and directed towards his painting. But do these motivations need to be conscious and directed in this way every time for a work to be imbued with the artist's moral character? I don't think so. Even if Hitler did not specifically intend each of his paintings to have a proto-Nazi meaning, his early works as a whole still stem from connected Aryan styles and fascist mythology, and were made by a man who substantially contributed to (and indeed wrote) this mythology.

The (im)moral motivation in question needn't be a specific one directed at an individual work; it needn't have been conscious when that painting was made. Rather, we can look to the holistic motivations that form part of the artist's wider practice. So long as this practice is connected in some way to the artist's misdeeds, the depravity is baked into the art itself. When we look at Hitler's art, we see the world through his eyes.

We can run another philosophical thought experiment to test out this idea. One of Hitler's watercolours from 1914 is of Neuschwanstein Castle, a nineteenth-century palace in the foothills of the Alps in southern Bavaria. The painting is precise and realistic, with a gentle naturalistic palette. But imagine that the very same painting in another world is made instead by a politically neutral Bavarian farmer who simply wants to capture his surroundings with his new set of watercolours.

Our understanding of these two works would be very different depending on who made them, even though they'd look exactly the same. Knowing that Hitler is the origin of the actual piece reframes our understanding of it – this fact reveals its proto-Nazi style to us, as an instance of a developing romantic Aryan aesthetic (the depicted castle itself is a classic example of the Romanticist interpretation of medieval architecture). The farmer's painting, on the other hand, wouldn't belong to that 'style' in this deeper way, even though it is, on the surface, identical.

Many people criticise Hitler's paintings simply for their crudeness – countless articles have been written about how he gets important rules like perspective all wrong, rendering crucial angles wonky and stilted, which leave his paintings 'spatially dead'.[30] But should we really care? Hitler's technical ability should be the least of our worries. His diabolical character lurks in the art movement and style in which he practised. Such a sinister style can even be rather charming – on first glance, Hitler's seemingly unthreatening paintings wouldn't look out of place at a summer village fête art stall.

A journalist in the *Guardian* wrote of Hitler's paintings that because they're in fact quite 'sweet', doubt should be cast on whether aesthetics and morality should ever interact, and confirms 'that there has never been any relation between form and content . . . if Hitler can do loveliness, then it has nothing to teach us. Beauty is simply beauty.'[31] But this journalist has reached a mistaken conclusion here. As I've argued, there is a monster prowling within Hitler's pastoral scenes – a monster which so many have missed. And such ugliness can look, on first glance, rather sweet indeed.

––––––––

The various ways that an artist's immoral character can 'show up' in their art are abundantly evident in the music genre of black metal, which we encountered in the earlier chapter on causation and criminality. As we saw there, some black metal is created by immoral artists. Sometimes this moral fact is clearly present in the music itself, simply because it is bombastically expressed in the songs. Take, for instance, 1389, an openly National Socialist Black Metal (NSBM) project from Bosnia and Herzegovina by Vožd Jovan Pogani. Many of his lyrics are anti-semitic and explicitly celebrate white supremacism in their

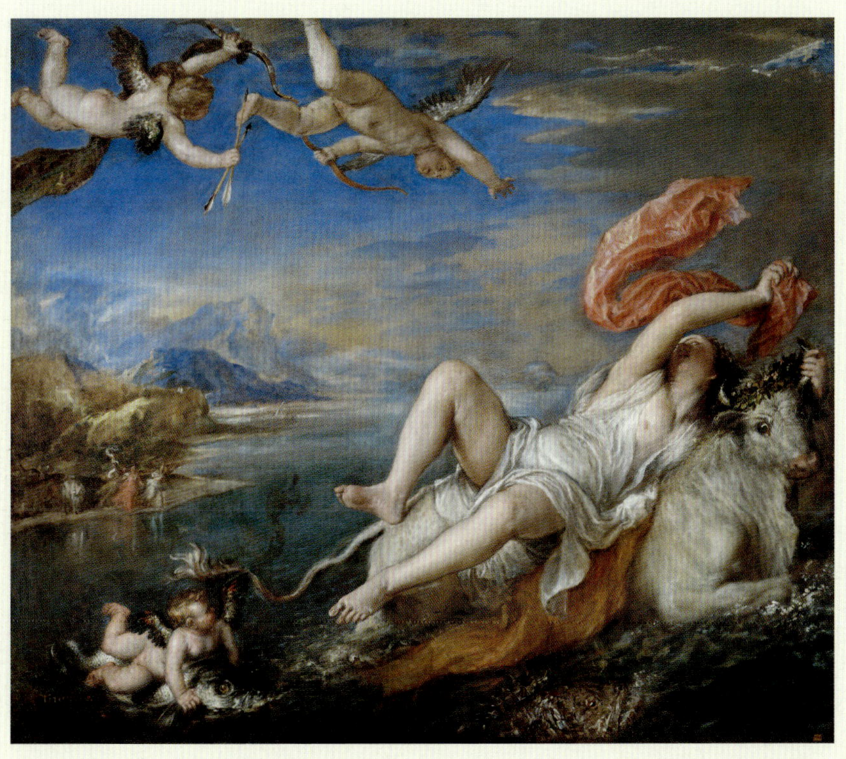

Does 'no' really mean *yes*? Eroticisation of sexual violence was pervasive in Renaissance art, particularly the tradition of 'heroic rape imagery', where a god would sexually assault a mortal woman. In Titian's *Rape of Europa* (1560–2) here, we can see the princess Europa being abducted by Zeus, disguised as a bull. As beautiful as the painting is, and despite our love of Titian, this work is an instance of hate speech in its legitimisation of a rape myth.

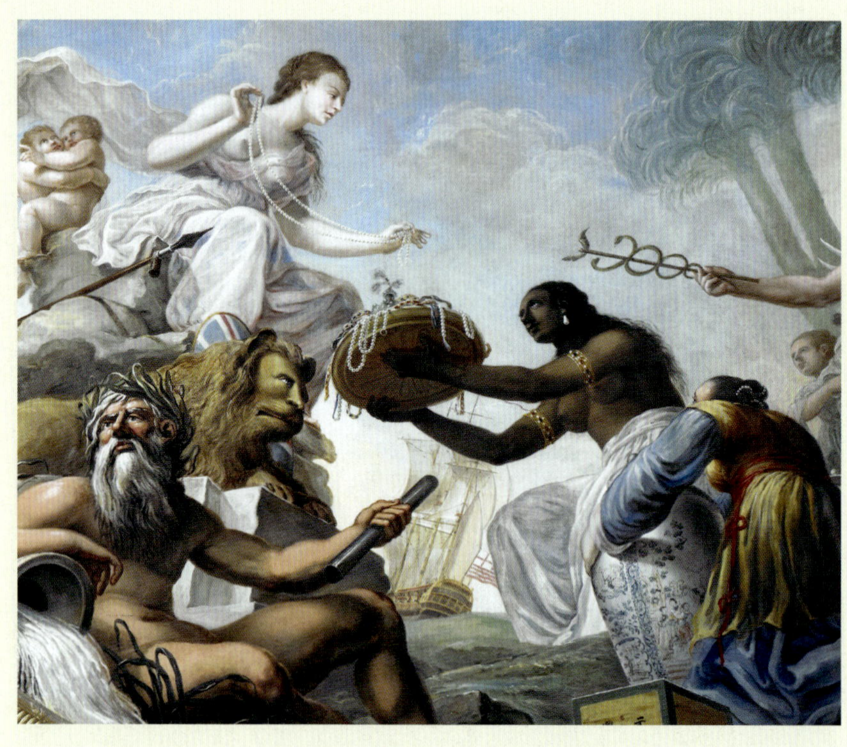

Pretty propaganda. Spiridione Roma's *The East Offering its Riches to Britannia* was installed in the East India Company's London headquarters on the ceiling of the revenue committee room in 1778. A pale Britannia sits high and regal while a dark-skinned woman representing India kneels at her feet, peacefully offering Indian goods and labour to the British Empire. The painting, as well as vastly misrepresenting the historical reality, sneaks in acts of subordination and implies this power dynamic is the way things naturally are and ought to be.

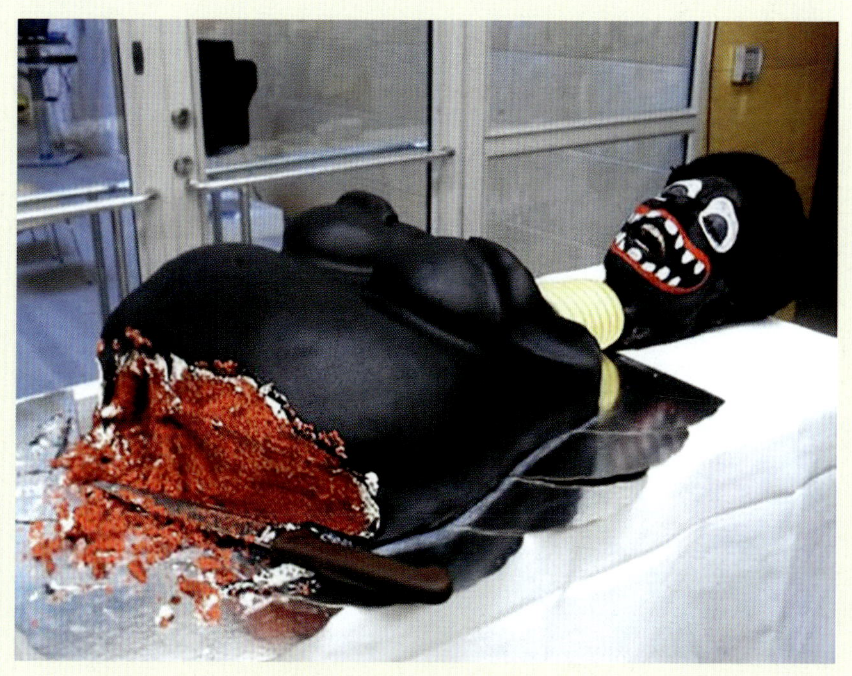

Powerful and disturbing, or offensive and harmful? Makode Linde's *Painful Cake* was a hugely controversial performance at Stockholm's Modern Museum in 2012. The artist's head – adorned in golliwog makeup – screamed as 'his' caricatured black female body made of cake was cut into by white audience members. Linde had good intentions for the work: he designed it as a general form of post-colonial critique, and specifically a commentary on female genital mutilation. And yet, some criticised the work for *re-inscribing* the dehumanisation of black African women, in part because of the artist's gender.

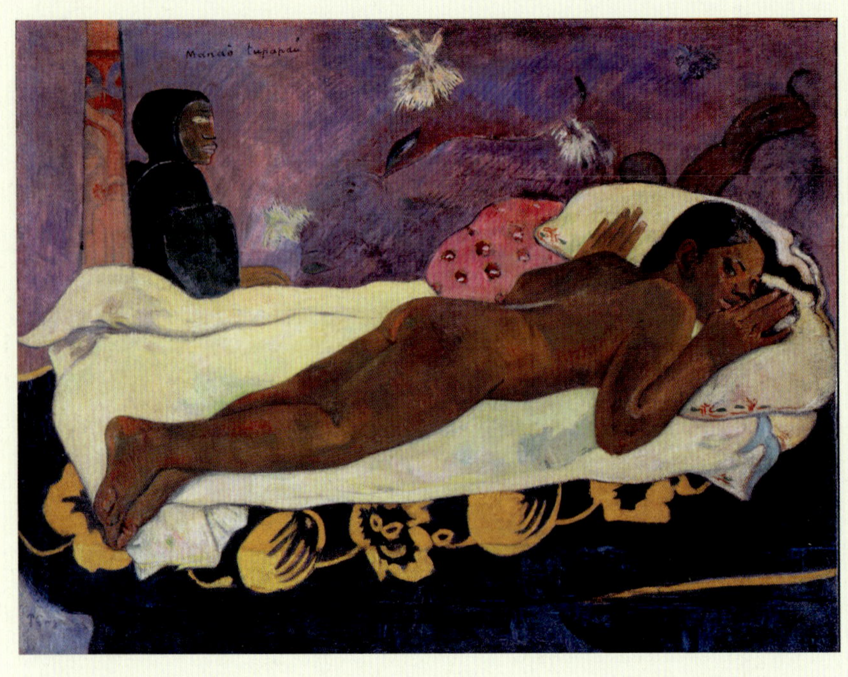

Can you separate the art from the artist? Fourteen-year-old Teha'amana
often waited fearfully in the dark for the forty-four-year-old painter
Paul Gauguin to return home. His painting *Manaò tupapaú* (*Spirit of the
Dead Watching*, 1892) shows this very moment. He may have loved his
child bride, but their relationship was one of abusive colonial exploitation.
Is this painting a window into his reality, or hers?

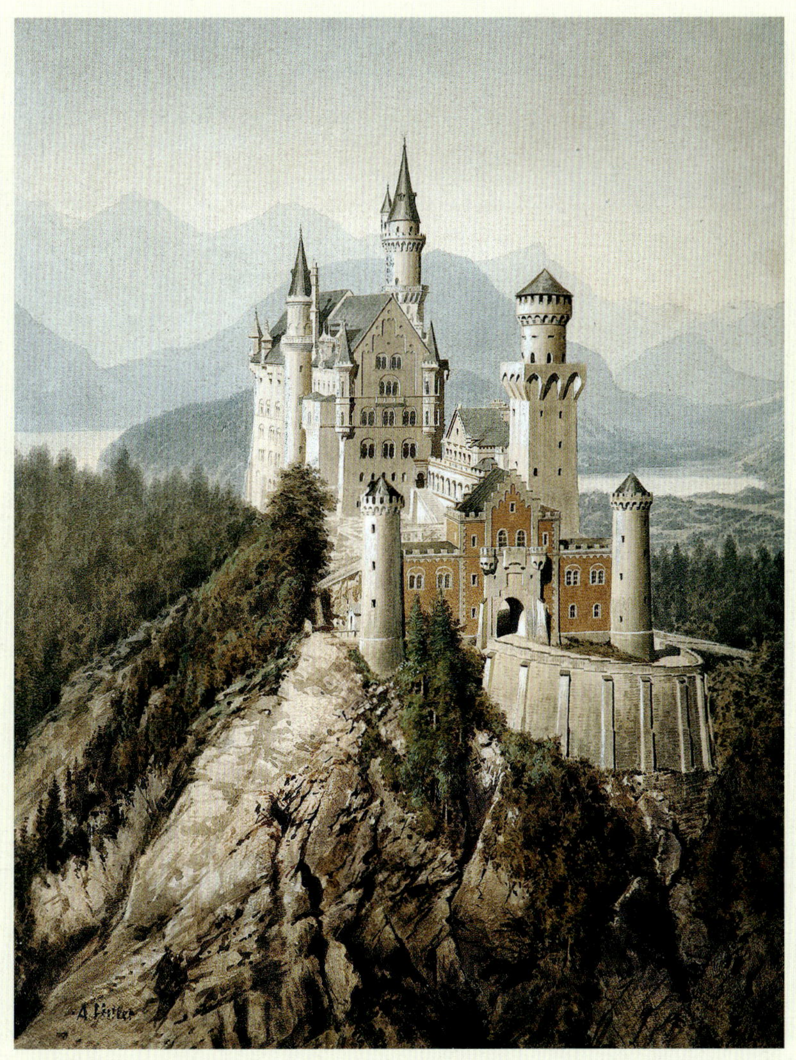

Adolf Hitler's paintings look innocent on the surface: here we can see his watercolour of Neuschwanstein Castle from 1914. But, armed with his paintbrush, Hitler was in fact expressing his depraved vision of a desired return to the pastoral 'homeland' – a romantic world populated with the so-called Aryan race, traditional architecture and nostalgic 'pure' art. His artworks may have looked pretty (or rather dull) but this actually makes them all the more insidious.

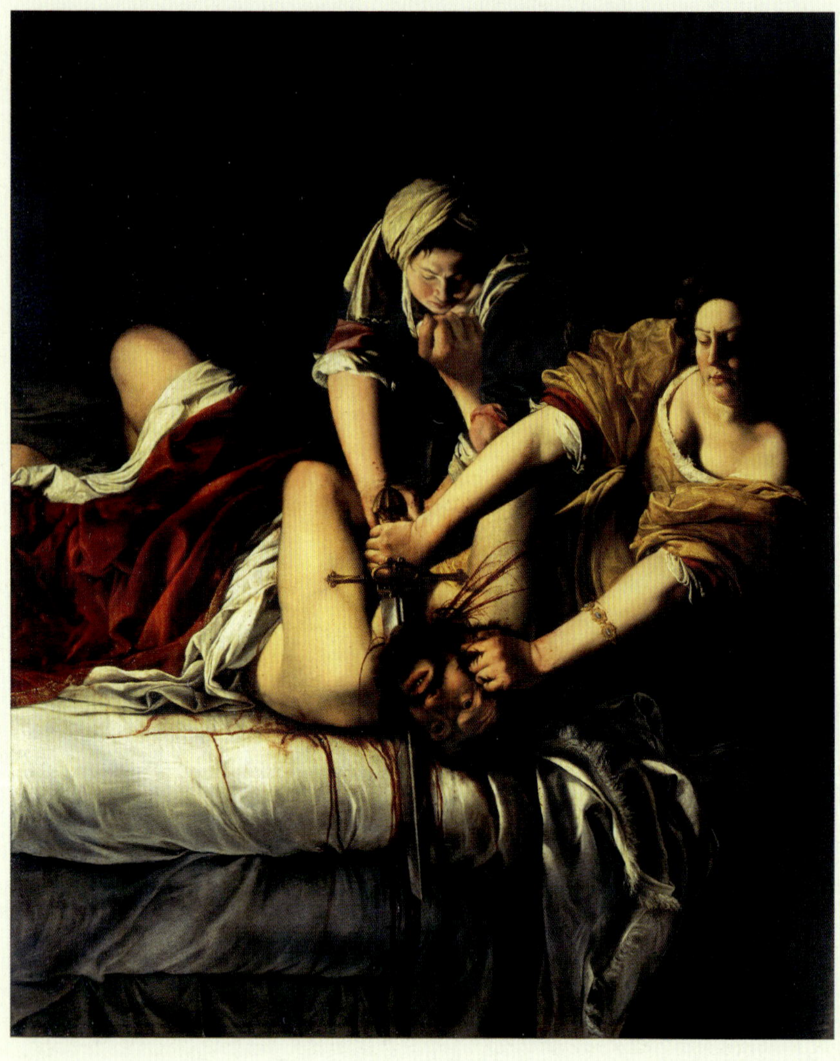

This is her revenge. Artemisia Gentileschi's *Judith Beheading Holofernes* (*c.* 1620) shows the Old Testament story of the Jewish widow Judith decapitating the invading Assyrian general. The work has been interpreted as a self-portrait, with Artemisia as Judith, and her rapist as Holofernes. As a form of counterspeech, this work addresses the violence endured by women at the hands of men for thousands of years, both on and beyond the canvas.

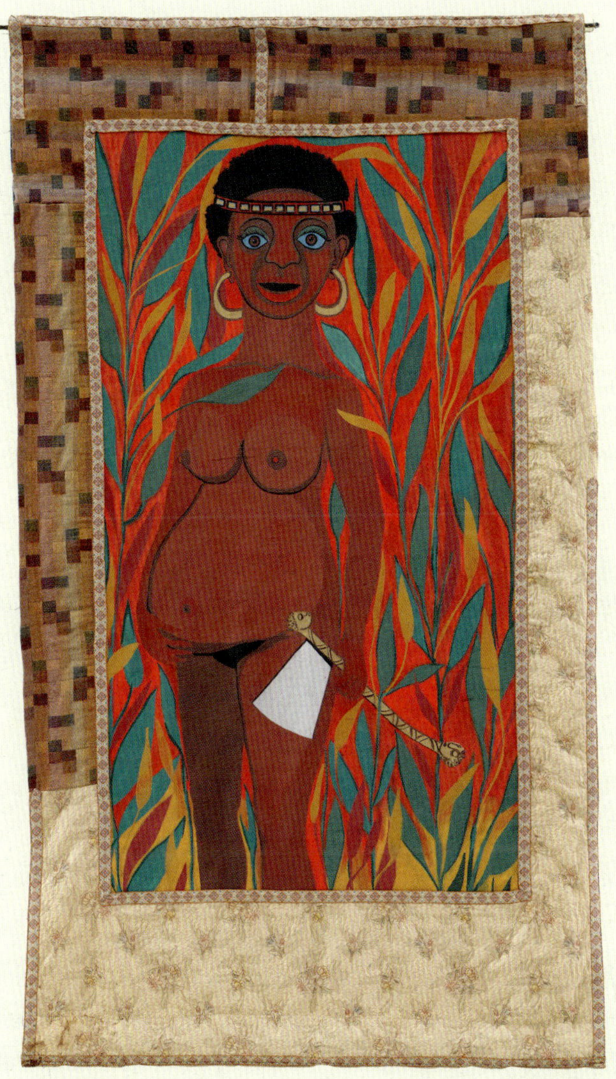

Faith Ringgold is a time traveller. In her *Slave Rape* (1972) thangka series, she goes to the fields of the transatlantic slave trade and arms black slaves with weaponry to fight off their enslavers. In *#3 Fight to Save Your Life*, Ringgold places an axe in the hand of a pregnant enslaved woman. This kind of art forms a compelling resistance to depravity, putting us in contact with past atrocities but in doing so reimagining what liberation could look like.

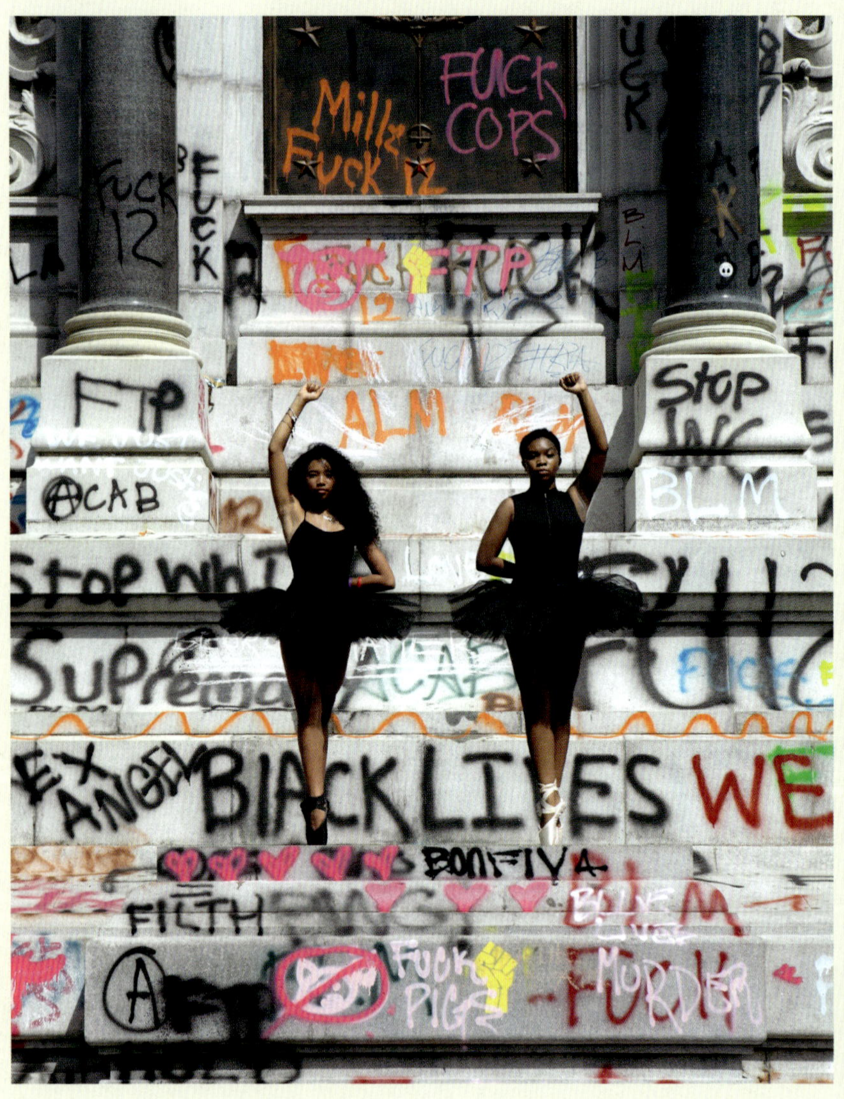

This is metaphysical iconoclasm. Ballerinas Ava Holloway and Kennedy George posed on pointe in front of a monument to the Confederate general Robert E. Lee in Richmond, Virginia during the height of the 2020 Black Lives Matter protests. Ava and Kennedy's intervention transformed the depraved monument into something beautiful.

worship of Hitler. Likewise the bluntly titled album *Fuck You All, We Are NSBM!!!* (2012) by 1389 and Tank Genocide.

But sometimes the musician's moral character is not so obviously relevant to the meaning and aesthetic properties of their music. Consider Burzum, one of the original bands from the early Norwegian black metal scene. This one-man band is the product of the openly neo-Nazi and homophobic Varg Vikernes, who we saw was also the murderer of Mayhem's original lead vocalist, Euronymous. Despite the shocking personal (and criminal) record of its creator, Burzum's thematic imagery and lyrics about Norse mythology are not considered to be explicitly political. So, some fans of Burzum report being able to separate the art from the artist in this case – as if Burzum's musical works are not tainted by the views of its white supremacist creator.

But even if we grant that Burzum's literal content is not explicitly white supremacist, it's plausible (and likely) that Varg Vikernes had broader immoral motivations and made morally relevant stylistic choices when creating his music. The clue to this is found in his preoccupation with the natural world, fantasy, and pagan mythologies – he screeches an awful lot about forests, fiery skies, cold winds, and lakes. Vikernes said in a 2010 interview that 'Burzum is not a political or religious band, or even an anti-religious band'.[32] However, his love of the natural world is conceivably linked to his broader fascist philosophical outlook. Just as Hitler did, Vikernes has harnessed elements of the eighteenth- and nineteenth-century Romantic movement – namely, a nostalgia for the wild natural world – and infused it with racist sentiment.

Scholars have traced the use of the forest in particular as a metaphor by the Nazis to express their 'blood and soil' ideology: their goal for the 'racially pure' to settle in their so-called homeland.[33] As Johannes Zechner writes: 'Inherent in this forest ideology . . . was a strong racist component: the capability to care for nature was exclusively attributed to Aryan racial ancestry.'[34] Indeed, some majorly sketchy and explicitly National Socialist Black Metal bands put the forest at the heart of their aesthetic identity, the Ukrainian NSBM band Hate Forest being a case in point.[*]

This racist hijacking of the Romantic ecological aesthetic is, I think, a plausible interpretation of Burzum's musical project. Its lyrical, artistic, and sonic themes evoke the ancient spirits of nature and the self's relation to Nordic wildness. I don't think it's a huge leap to say that Vikernes's music therefore has a neo-Nazi ecological aesthetic, even if this isn't explicitly expressed. So, even in tricky cases like this, we can still find depravity – it just lurks among the trees.

Harder Cases

My parents used to own two signed limited-edition prints of Rolf Harris's paintings: a landscape called *Blue Hills*, and a portrait of two old men sat on a wall called *Lifelong Friends*. Both were artist's proofs; Harris will have confirmed the quality and accuracy of these copies of his originals. My parents always enjoyed looking at these pieces, and they paid a lot of money for them.

But after learning the shocking news in 2014 about Harris's conviction for child sex offences and possession of child pornography, my parents felt uncomfortable about having these

---

[*] I imagine they in fact love the forest.

paintings on display in their home. Eventually, they decided to cover them over with eighteenth-century prints of the city of Bath, to at least save the frames.

I think that my parents' reaction was appropriate, and I imagine it resonates with you as well. But the problem here is that Harris's immorality was not present at all in these works. In fact, Harris wrote explicitly about *Blue Hills* that he painted it purely from imagination and with leftover paint from another session. There was nothing whatsoever to do with paedophilia in the paintings: no straightforward visual evidence and no suspicious aesthetic ideology lurking in his style (what would a paedophilic painterly style even look like?).

Cases like this abound. Many songs, films, and paintings have been made by depraved people, but the works of art themselves bear no trace of the artists' misdeeds. So how do we deal with cases like this? Do such works transcend their creator's depravity?

Not quite. I'd suggest that the artist's immorality affects how we engage with the work as an *object*, but unlike the previous cases we've considered, the artworks themselves are not tainted by this immorality. What do I mean by this? People make things. Artworks, tables, pots, sweaters, curtains, cars, computers, footballs, and so on, are created by people (sometimes with the help of machines). We can call these things, loosely speaking, 'artefacts'. Some of these artefacts are art. Some are not art. But all artworks are artefacts – things created by people – special kinds of things, yes, but still things.

Sometimes, an artwork has been made by a problematic person. Perhaps it was born at the hands of a paedophile, an evil dictator, or an abuser. And while the artwork's meaning or artistic features themselves may not be marked by the artist's depravity, the artefact which *carries* that artwork – the canvas, the panel, the clay, the bronze, the set of chosen words or musical notes – *is* tainted.

The very fact that we value original works of art over their copies is precisely because the artist touched or conceptualised that original object. A few years ago, I was in the Museum of Modern Art in New York. I remember turning a corner and what I saw took my breath away. It was Vincent van Gogh's *The Starry Night* (1889), right there in front of me. I felt I could finally be close to the man himself. I could see the way he'd dipped and dragged his paintbrush through his buttery oils; I could see his dazzling expression of emotion.

In the same way, if you were to hold a Hitler watercolour in your hands, you'd be handling the very marks of this abominable man's creativity. A direct trace of his existence on canvas or paper is right there in the flesh. You'd feel the same if you were holding anything at all that Hitler made, or perhaps if you sat in a chair he owned or touched the fabric of his uniforms.

We care about where objects or artefacts come from. Even if they weren't originals, the fact that my parents' prints were still images created by Harris and had been given the seal of approval by the man himself was enough of a reason to hide them from view. They were, indirectly, the products of Harris's hand.

My experience of looking at Harris's *Lifelong Friends* and *Blue Hills* in my family home before they were covered over was clouded by knowledge of his child sex offences. I could no longer fully appreciate them knowing who had produced them. In the same way, you may feel some disgust when trying to listen to a Michael Jackson song. These reactions may not address any content in the artwork itself, but they do track the fact that the artwork as a thing – an artefact – came from a troubling place.

‘Yes, Picasso was a misogynist. So what?’ According to *Telegraph* columnist Michael Deacon, acknowledging the problematic behaviour of great artists proves that ‘the woke Left . . . haven’t got a clue about art’.[35]

I’m afraid it’s Michael who hasn’t got a clue about art. I hope I’ve convinced you that it’s actually these dismissive approaches to the problem of immoral artists that betray their own ignorance. To truly understand art, we must look to the creator. We must acknowledge their character in our interpretations – doing so will reveal endless riches. We can never fully separate the art from the artist: to do so is a conceptual mistake and does a disservice to the very nature of art itself, not to mention its victims. Michael needs to listen to art historians, and – if he can stand them – philosophers.

We’ve seen that the act of creating is unavoidably an ethical endeavour. And now we reach our final face of depravity: where the way an artwork is *made* is itself an abomination.

5 | CRUELTY

A waitress dishes out the raw remains of chickens and fish at a playful orgy. The pop songs 'My Boy Lollipop' and 'Baby Love' soundtrack writhing human forms that embrace each other and the carcasses. The legs of headless chickens flop into orifices and dead mackerel flap at prancing feet – one finds itself lodged firmly between a woman's thighs. Wet paint is smeared over the floor and clings to the cavorting bodies. Human and animal limbs entwine in a glistening spectacle, emitting a sickly sweet aroma.

Carolee Schneemann's *Meat Joy* caused such a stir when it was first performed in Paris in 1964 that a man in the audience leapt from his seat, dragged Schneemann to the side, and began to strangle her. At a second performance in London, Schneemann and her performers were chased off the stage by police. This work of 'kinetic theatre' was, for Schneemann, 'an erotic rite – excessive, indulgent, a celebration of flesh as material'.[1] It captures perfectly how Schneemann's practice defied patriarchal norms, representing womanhood as monstrous yet beautiful flesh imbued with agency. As well as challenging the traditional objectifying imagery of the nude and the marginalisation of women in the artworld, Schneemann pushed the nature of painting to its extreme. In a jubilant yet repellent collapsing of the boundary between subject and object, the artist's body as performer became part of the art itself.

One of the ground-breaking elements of this early feminist artwork was its use of dead animals, which opened up possibilities for new forms of expressive media. Despite *Meat Joy*'s merits – particularly its visceral messages about sexual liberation and its overturning of traditional aesthetics – some have been troubled by its use of animals as material. While the sight of dead chickens and fish is familiar in the supermarket or on our dinner plates, to see these animals used in the spectacle of art is more disturbing.

Many works of art have been made in problematic ways like this. Some tread the line between moral impermissibility and artistic excellence, while others are simply barbaric. From the problematic use of ivory in medieval sculpture across the world to twentieth-century conceptual art that involves setting live animals on fire or taking advantage of vulnerable people, artists have often relied on exploitative practices or physical violence for their creative acts.

If a work of art has its origins in such cruelty, does that make it inherently worse? In some cases, could it even make an artwork *better*? Are unethical means of production more acceptable when used in the name of art? The way an artwork is made often influences its meaning and merit, and we feel that a balance must be struck between the value of the artwork and the cruelty involved in its creation. And yet, many of us are happy to eat meat, so why draw the line at killing an animal for art?

Sympathy for Rats

Düsseldorf, 1965. Conceptual artist Joseph Beuys sits in the middle of a locked gallery, caressing a dead hare. Beuys's face glistens in honey and gold leaf, as for three hours he quietly talks to the animal about the pictures on the wall, while viewers watch and listen to his murmuring through the gallery's windows.

How to Explain Pictures to a Dead Hare is indicative of Beuys's radical and varied approach to artmaking, which combined pedagogy, performance, and sculpture in a form of socio-political commentary. The dead hare for Beuys was a multi-faceted symbol encompassing women, birth, and the physical world; the honey, a symbol of thought. By whispering to the corpse Beuys challenged the limits of language and conceptualisation, going beyond the rational in an attempt to communicate with the dead, and with nature.[2]

It's not clear where the hare came from. But given how other artists have sourced animals for their art, it is possible that this hare was killed specifically for Beuys's artistic action. What is so unnerving about Beuys's piece, though, is how gentle and tender he was with the dead hare, which he cradled like a baby. Beuys later said in an interview while advocating for animal rights, 'Yes, I speak for the hares that cannot speak for themselves.'[3]

Already resisting a simple explanation due to its rich symbolism and strange composition, Beuys's performance becomes even more impenetrable when we factor in the ethics of its creation: even if the hare wasn't killed purely for Beuys's piece, some might object to its body being used as a prop. On one hand, knowing that a sentient being was killed – or at least that its death was being exploited – for the performance might have made some viewers so uncomfortable that they were unable to engage with the work on its own terms. The dead animal could act as a barrier to aesthetic enjoyment and the contemplation that Beuys called for. On the other hand, it may have been precisely this discomfort that drew viewers in – a morbid fascination that enhanced rather than ruined the aesthetic experience.

In some cases, artists seem to revel in the mere appearance of animal cruelty, even when it's not clear that any actually occurred. Take Alejandro Jodorowsky's Mexican acid Western film, *El Topo* (1970). The cult classic features several disturbing scenes including one showing hundreds of slaughtered rabbits in the desert. The bloodied creatures really were dead. But were they killed for the film? It's not clear. Jodorowsky has given contradictory statements over the years. In a 1972 book recounting the film's making, he claimed that he'd killed the three hundred rabbits with his bare hands. But then in a 2008 interview, he said the animals had already died from a myxomatosis outbreak and had just been bought for the film. And in 2014, he spoke of his regret at asking his son to kill the rabbits. We'll never know what happened to those poor creatures, but the director defended the use of their carcasses regardless, arguing that 'we should give everything to art'.[4]

Perhaps the best-known case of killing in the name of art is Damien Hirst's *The Physical Impossibility of Death in the Mind of Someone Living* (1991). The work comprises a preserved tiger shark, which was caught off the coast of Queensland, Australia, and suspended in formaldehyde in a glass vitrine. Due to improper care, the original piece deteriorated, and the decaying shark had to be replaced by another that was caught off the same coast a few years later. To this day, it's not clear how many sharks have been killed for Hirst's whole oeuvre, but it may be as many as seventeen.[5] Hirst's very own fishmonger, the shark hunter Vic Hislop, reportedly kept a few sharks on ice should any more replacements be required – including a great white shark,[6] which is a species at high risk of extinction.

My first in-person encounter with *The Physical Impossibility* was in New York in 2009. As a long-time lover of sharks, I was ready to hate it. But what met my sceptical eye was startling. The piece was bold and frightening, but it was also desperately sad – an apex predator of the ocean and supreme balancer of its ecosystem had become a helpless object; inert, frozen in time. I could see its jaws slightly agape, and its dead eyes staring past me into nothingness. It was unnerving to observe this magnificent creature suspended like this, and difficult to comprehend that it wasn't alive.

I hated the work because of its cruelty, but I still thought it was remarkable. Its spectacle approximated what philosophers call the Sublime – a powerful sight eliciting both awe and horror – presenting the inconceivability of death at just safe enough a distance, through a glass barrier. Isn't that one of the things that art should aim to do? Simply placing a formidable fish in the church-like space of an art gallery confronts us with the unfathomable; the vast ocean is brought to the concrete metropolis, death itself is brought to the living.

This disorientating experience felt wrong, but through this wrongness I was forced to contemplate humans' irreversible violence towards the ocean, and the nature of fear and mortality. And I experienced these thoughts in a different way from when I watched programmes like David Attenborough's *Blue Planet* series: these documentaries might make us feel upset and angry at humanity's destruction of the natural world, but with Hirst's shark, the horror was more immediate, more unsettling – it cut deeper.

As with some of the likely reactions to Beuys's hare performance, the gruesome sight of Hirst's shark is what draws people in; its macabre presence is precisely what gives the work its aesthetic value. And yet it's undoubtable that Hirst's shark installation is morally flawed. As Ted Nannicelli notes, an artwork can be ethically tarnished because its production involves killing or exploiting an innocent animal, but the display of an animal's remains can also be read as a callous act of disrespect. The moral vices that arise from such exploitation must not be overlooked. Animals are sentient: they feel pain, and so have interests that should be respected, as famously argued by philosopher Peter Singer. Hirst's shark corpse is literally objectified – transformed into an artwork to be gawped at and bought and sold. As we saw in an earlier chapter, objectification is, most of the time, morally repugnant – the shark was stripped of its dignity in a show of disregard for its sentience.

It's important to recognise that artworks which exploit live and dead animals *are* morally flawed in this way. But these artworks can still have social, political, and emotional value, and many critics would argue that this value outweighs the cruelty involved in their production. One question, though, is whether the moral flaws could and should be avoided or minimised. Could the work's message have been expressed in a different way, without using animals as a means to an end?

With Hirst's shark, it's not clear at all that a replica would have achieved the same effect. What makes the work so entrancing is that it's a real, dead shark – the point is that we're supposed to stare actual death in the face. The same can be said for Schneemann's *Meat Joy* and Jodorowsky's *El Topo*: knowing that the dead animals were real was key to the art-works' aesthetic absurdity and shock factor. Bodily reality is what produced these difficult pleasures. Schneemann's sub-version of the smooth, tamed beauty of the nude genre which defines the Western history of art is so effective because she brings the body to life – 'a lived body that gets dirty, is prey to illness and injury, and that ages, dies, and rots', says philosopher Carolyn Korsmeyer.[7]

The moral disgust surrounding the use of animals in art can be precisely the thing that makes such works aesthetically successful. But even if we grant this, some artists clearly go too far, to the point that no experience conveyed by the art could justify the suffering endured to get there. Whereas Beuys once formed a political party in which most of the members were animals,[8] other artists have expressed utter derision or indifference towards their artistic kills. Damien Hirst has described cows as 'walking food' and 'death objects', which he uses aplenty in his installations.[9] In total, it's estimated that he has used 1 million animals and insects during his career – he famously quipped that 'it's amazing what you can do with an E in A-Level art, a twisted imagination, and a chainsaw'.[10]

In Hirst's case, it's the sheer magnitude of animals killed for his art and his apparent disregard for their lives that forms a glaring ethical flaw in his whole practice. Surely an aesthetic experience, no matter how valuable, isn't worth such sustained cruelty?

Our intuitions about the permissibility of animal abuse in art will be further tested when the animal is killed right in front of us. In 1976 at California State University campus in Los

Angeles, Kim Jones – performing as his persona 'Mudman'– stripped, covered himself in mud, and placed pantyhose over his head and a wooden lattice on his back. He then brought out three live rats, doused them with lighter fluid and set them on fire. The rats screamed. He screamed. The rats died a gradual, agonising death. Jones – sorry, Mudman – then covered their scorched remains with soil and stones, slowly got dressed, and walked away.

The piece was, unsurprisingly, hugely controversial. The university's gallery director was fired, and Jones was taken to court and convicted of animal cruelty, incurring a small fine. In a 2005 interview Jones reflected on these reactions: 'I knew they would be upset. When I did it people just went nuts.'[11]

What was the point of this barbarity? According to Jones, it was an artistic repetition of an act common among US soldiers in the Vietnam War – the artist had been a US marine and had served a tour there from 1967 to 1968. Rats would plague the soldiers, crawling over them while they slept and stealing their food. The soldiers would sometimes burn the rats to death out of frustration and to relieve boredom.

Jones wanted to bring this grim aspect of war to the art space, to force his audience to face the reality of torture, and to test whether they'd feel sympathy for the rats or attempt to prevent the killings. They felt sympathy for sure, but they did not intervene. Their status as mere spectators mirrored the position of witnesses to war – when we watch war crimes and immense brutality on our TV screens, so many of us become overwhelmed and feel powerless to stop it.

The message of this piece is admittedly an important one. The rats became a symbol of the animal – human and non-human – and a metaphor for both the soldiers and Vietnamese civilians facing the terror of war, with the audience as passive witnesses to the suffering. The work also illuminated our willed ignorance and hypocrisy when it comes to animal cruelty: '*Rat Piece* made the pain of rats – usually killed out of sight – visible, even shareable, in a rare way,' writes scholar Martin Harries.[12] As Peter Singer notes, 'Few people feel sympathy for rats.'[13] Perhaps a few more felt it after Jones's performance.

In a similar vein to *Rat Piece*, the Chilean Danish artist Marco Evaristti placed live goldfish in ten blenders in his performance *Helena & El Pescador* (2000) at the Trapholt Art Museum in Kolding, Denmark. The audience were permitted to press the blender buttons to obliterate the fish. One person did, killing two. After complaints from the campaign group Friends of Animals, the director of the museum, Peter Meyer, was fined for cruelty to animals. His fine was later cancelled however after a court in Denmark ruled that the exhibit was not an instance of animal cruelty, because the fish were killed instantly and would not have felt any pain. Surreally, an expert witness from the maker of the blenders – Moulinex – testified that the fish will have indeed perished within a single second, in a bizarre promotion of the product's quality.

Helena & El Pescador aimed to test people's moral sense of right and wrong and to force them to 'battle with their conscience', according to the artist. Overall, the piece was a 'protest against what is going on in the world, against this cynicism, this brutality that impregnates the world in which we live'.[14] Again, we might think that this is a true and important message, made all the more powerful when expressed in such an upsetting way. But does the work's lesson really justify its cruelty?

Peter Meyer went on to defend Evaristti's work in the name of free speech: 'An artist has the right to create works which defy our concept of what is right and what is wrong,' he told the court.[15] Yes, artists – as people – ought to have freedom of expression under the Universal Declaration of Human Rights. But the problem reduces to one of conflicting rights. If you think that animals have any rights, and these are being violated by the rights of artists' creativity, then maybe the former should take priority: a basic right to life is superior to a right to create art.[16] Some scholars, therefore, hold that artists have a moral imperative *not* to create art that violates the rights of animals.[17] Artists might be somewhat special, but they shouldn't get a moral pass.

Even if the drama of some animal art would be lost if it didn't have such an unethical provenance, there are other ways to express similar messages about ecological violence and speciesism – the discrimination against non-human species – that avoid committing harm. Contemporary artists Julia deVille and Angela Singer (no relation to the philosopher), for instance, weave together aesthetics and activism in their ethical taxidermy pieces to challenge our beliefs about animal rights and the meat industry. The animals are 'ethically sourced': they have died of natural causes or are at least not killed specifically for the art, perishing as roadkill, as stillborns, or of old age.

DeVille's neo-Victorian memento mori pieces comprise jewel-studded lambs, rats, calves, deer, dogs, cats, mice and birds, often served on large silver trays, in ice-cream scoops, or in bowls. While still using dead animals, deVille like Beuys expresses a tenderness towards them – their placement in glinting household objects and adornment with precious gems is delicate and gentle. She celebrates these animals' lives while disrupting our gaze over them:

My work is not about turning people vegan or vegetarian, I am simply trying to *decondition* people, so they see the reality of the way they consume animals, in a manner that leads them to make more informed decisions, decisions they are morally aligned with.[18]

Angela Singer's works are more confrontational and just as morally forceful. Her manipulated 'botched' taxidermy pieces expose the aggression humans inflict on animals in trophy hunting, by viscerally presenting the animal's wounds using glass beads and wax. These pieces range from decapitated bodies and severed heads to rabbits and lambs shown frontally with their bubbling bloody insides pouring out in the form of red beads. *Sore* (2003), for instance, comprises a trophy stag's head soaked in blood with its antlers sawn off. The work demands that we scrutinise our desire for supremacy over non-human animals.

The potency of Singer's art is achieved through its 'abject' aesthetics: unsettling experiences that provoke disgust and repulsion and which force us to consider our relationship to ourselves and others in the world.[19] While the concept of the abject was originally tied to the maternal human body in feminist theory, as we saw in Chapter One, Singer's art brings the abject to the non-human animal. Her pieces are unexpected and jarring – collapsing the boundary between human and animal, between us and them. Beuys hints at similar themes when he explained his *Hare* performance:

I have understood that the hare and with it all of nature are organs of human beings without which the human being cannot live . . . he needs nature and also the animals just like

> he needs his heart, his liver and lungs, so therefore one can
> see the hare as an external organ of the human being.[20]

The animal we stare back at is an intimate part of us. We are not in nature, we are nature.

Singer's depiction of injury with red wax and beads rather than through the actual suffering of an animal is hugely affecting. When asked about what she thinks of Hirst's exploitation of animals, she replied that Hirst doesn't seem interested in the responsibilities and ethical issues raised by taking lives for art: 'He summed up his position with his statement that the "idea is more important than the actual piece."' Here, though, Singer and deVille show that we can have the 'idea' and its aesthetic punch without the unethical origin. And such art can still constitute persuasive political activism. As Singer urges: 'discussion alone isn't enough. We live in an era when so many animals are endangered; we all need an urgent wake-up to do what we can to stop the oppression, exploitation, domination and torture of animals.'[21] But regardless of how animal art is made, it's not entirely clear that its immorality is any worse than our daily domination over animals outside of the art gallery. Of those who might be alarmed and offended by Jones's rat fire or Hirst's preserved shark, many will eat meat, dairy, and fish. While some people need meat and dairy for health reasons (the vegan diet does not suit everyone), many of us indulge in being carnivores when we don't need to. The steak tastes too good.

Why is art that kills or harms animals any different? Eating part of an animal because you fancied roast beef on a Sunday doesn't seem *that* morally different from going to see Hirst's slaughtered cows in an art gallery for contemplation. Enjoying fish and chips on a Friday evening doesn't appear morally different from watching Evaristti's live fish perish in blenders. In fact, most commercially caught fish – wild and farmed – which become our delicious fish suppers have slowly suffocated to death or been gutted while still conscious. That's a fate worse than immediate death via efficient art-blender. And this is not even to mention the pervasive exploitation of animals in entertainment domains like circuses, marine parks, and zoos, where animals are held captive and forced to perform for our amusement.

Animal art is perhaps more susceptible to our moral condemnation because it's just weird – sharks in glass boxes and chickens in an orgy dance are, to put it mildly, unusual phenomena. But are these performances, films, sculptures, and installations really, deep down, any less absurd than TV broadcasts advertising edible animal parts, complete with seductive music, saliva-inducing imagery, and discount slogans? In art's defence, it implores us to openly reflect rather than blindly consume.

Animal art might be morally unpalatable, but so is our unthinking treatment of animals on a daily basis. At least the art is challenging us to do something about it. As Jones said of his *Rat Piece* audience: 'They could have stopped me.'

Against Nature

In the notably mild December of 2018, twenty-four blocks of glacial ice from the Arctic waters of Greenland – some the size of trucks and weighing up to 6 tons – were arranged in a circle in front of the Tate Modern in London. Each chunk of ice was unique in its glistening beauty. Some were opaque, some transparent, some craggy, some globular. But they were all melting.

This temporary installation was part of Danish Icelandic artist Olafur Eliasson's project *Ice Watch*, which had earlier iterations in Copenhagen and Paris. In collaboration with geologist Minik Rosing, Eliasson had the ice fished out of Greenland's Nuup Kangerlua fjord. The blocks had detached from the ice sheet and were composed of compressed snow. This meant that each block held tiny bubbles of ancient air, stored up to 100,000 years ago, which contained less than half as much CO_2 as we have in our air today. Rosing and Eliasson encouraged viewers to interact with the ice – by putting your ear against it, you'd have been able to hear pure, unpolluted air popping and fizzing. Eliasson said: 'The ice is amazingly beautiful – you can smell it, you can kiss it, and essentially put your hands on it and touch Greenland . . . and witness the ecological changes our world is undergoing.'[22] By connecting people to the deep, distant past of the planet – visually, tactilely, olfactorily, sonically – this artwork on the Thames was designed to jolt us into tackling the climate emergency. Global warming is increasing the number of these floating chunks of ice, which contribute to rising sea levels. By transforming the ice into art, Eliasson wanted to make the climate emergency intimate and emotional:

> I've been studying behavioural psychology, and looking into the consequences of experience . . . It turns out that data alone only promotes a small degree of change. So in order to create the massive behavioural change needed [to tackle climate change] we have to emotionalise that data, make it physically tangible.[23]

While many of us care about our planet and the very real effects of the climate crisis, it can still feel distant to those of us whose homes and livelihoods are not at immediate risk. Even images of climate destruction can further increase our numbness or hopelessness. But art like *Ice Watch* can bring the emergency home – making it big, cold, and solid. Eliasson and Rosing wanted *Ice Watch* to be about hope: while they cited the alarming statistic that 10,000 blocks of ice just like the ones on display are falling from the ice sheet every second, they didn't think inducing fear was the right way forward. Rather, inviting viewers to peacefully engage with the ice blocks and contemplate their beauty offered a vital space to create a positive narrative – one that might give rise to solutions. Art must step in to play this role when our politicians and corporate giants fail to act.

However, some have pointed out a glaring moral error with *Ice Watch*, despite the good intentions behind it. How much carbon energy was expended in *making* it? Combined with its other iteration nearby in the City, the artwork's total carbon footprint for its London stint was reportedly 30 tons. This is a significant amount, and the artwork's timing made the irony all the more potent: it arrived in London to coincide with the Intergovernmental Panel on Climate Change's warning that we had just twelve years to mitigate the worst effects of the climate crisis.

The clock was ticking, and *Ice Watch* may have undermined the very point it was trying to make. Some, therefore, have accused *Ice Watch* of being ethically compromised, saying that this moral hypocrisy hinders its artistic value. At the very least, if its creation directly undermines the main point it was designed to make, that seems like a pretty big artistic flaw.[24]

This criticism may be too hasty, however. While *Ice Watch* had a carbon footprint, the estimated energy cost for bringing a single ice block to London was equal to one person taking a return flight from London to Greenland. If you've ever had any disposable income, you've probably had a holiday abroad or two, or maybe you've flown somewhere for work. Or think of all the celebrities and influencers you've seen post on social media about their third holiday this year. Yes, ideally *Ice Watch* wouldn't have had any carbon footprint at all insofar as its moral value was concerned. But insofar as its artistic message is successful, perhaps the fact that it *does* have a carbon footprint equivalent to a person's plane ticket actually reinforces its environmental message. Given the work's effects on thousands of viewers, it's surely far better to bring the real ice sheet to the banks of the Thames at the cost of thirty trips, rather than at the cost of thousands of trips to witness the dying ice sheet in situ.

You might think, though, that for an artwork to be truly morally good, and therefore fully effective as political activism, it ought to not harm or exploit the planet at all. *Herald/Harbinger* (2017) by artists Ben Rubin and Jer Thorp, for instance, is a permanent public installation in Calgary, Canada, capturing the astonishing soundscape of the melting Bow Glacier 136 miles away – the source of 60 per cent of the city's drinking water. The artists set up a solar-powered seismic observatory near the glacier, which monitors the shifts and cracks in the moving ice.[25] With just a five-minute delay, the whooshing and gurgling of the glacier is amplified outside an office building in a city plaza, accompanied by visuals on LED panels that respond to the sound waves. The artwork brings the city into conversation with nature, where the two soundscapes co-exist and tumble over each another in a beautiful polyphony. Eventually, though, as the glacier recedes over the next century, its signal will fade, leaving the artwork deathly silent.

This 'living wake' for the dying Bow Glacier draws our attention to the climate crisis, while not itself producing a carbon footprint.[26] It has what philosopher Emily Brady calls 'aesthetic regard' for nature, in its delicate union of humanity and the natural world, where the artists show respect towards nature while using it as their material.[27] Some art goes even further by actively restoring and caring for nature. Patricia Johanson's *Endangered Garden* (1997) is a publicly accessible linear park containing sculptures that support the flourishing of local flora and fauna. As well as increasing the aesthetic enjoyment of Candlestick Cove in San Francisco, where it replaced a sewage pumping station, this ecological artwork-cum-garden regenerates the habitat of native endangered species. In this way, the artwork's artistic value is enhanced: it has what ancient philosophers called 'functional beauty' in that it is well designed for a morally good aim – its beauty derives from its virtuous purpose.[28]

Earth and Land art like *Ice Watch* and *Endangered Garden* can be an effective form of environmental activism as well as providing us with unique aesthetic experiences. Such artworks range from small sculptures complementing the wilderness to monumental gestures and marks on the land itself. The use of the natural world as material offers a way for artists to bring us closer to our beloved planet.

But it can also be an excuse to wreak havoc. Take for instance the land art of Christo and Jeanne-Claude. For their 1983 piece *Surrounded Islands*, they surrounded eleven islands in Miami's Biscayne Bay with bright pink polypropylene fabric, transforming the archipelago into a series of pink lily pads. The work took three years and a lot of money to complete. It also encountered a federal lawsuit from a wildlife paramedic and angry opposition from wildlife groups and environmentalists, due to the harm the 6.5 million square feet of plastic sun-blocking material could do to the marine ecosystem.[29]

depraved

In the end, the two-week installation reportedly did not cause any harm: ecological testing and consultations suggested that the artwork did not pose a threat to local seagrasses, ospreys, or manatees (apparently the manatees even *enjoyed* the fabric, possibly to the point of lust).[30] Christo and Jeanne-Claude countered the environmental objections by restoring the islands to their original state after the project, and cleaning 40 tons of existing waste from each island during the process. Moreover, the artwork rejuvenated the cultural profile of Miami with a legacy that still lasts today.[31]

Even with the knowledge that no physical harm was done by *Surrounded Islands*, some critics still see Christo's and Jeanne-Claude's art as an 'aesthetic affront' to nature. Rather than constituting a symbiosis of art and nature like Johanson's *Endangered Garden*, Christo and Jeanne-Claude's works 'forcibly assert their artifactuality over against [*sic*] nature, by their size, their engineering complexity and their synthetic components', according to philosopher Donald Crawford.[32] That is to say, in its aesthetic destruction of the natural setting, this kind of land art has committed a separate harm.

But some works of land art are more violent towards nature, in that they harm the local ecosystem as well as leaving an ugly scar. Take for instance Michael Heizer's earthwork *Double Negative* (1969–70), where the artist made a large incision 50 feet deep and 1,500 feet long into Nevada's Mormon Mesa. At the time, no environmental impact statement was required for the art piece, but many now worry that it has weakened the mesa, causing further erosion.[33] Construction of the work involved dynamite and removing 244,000 tons of earth and rock, which will have killed vegetation and disrupted habitats – particularly that of the endangered desert tortoise.

Rather than working in harmony with the mesa or raising ecological and geological awareness, *Double Negative* is an experiment that seeks to finish what the nineteenth-century impressionists started when they took art outdoors, away from the confines of the gallery and the studio: to make art of the outdoors itself. While the piece is an important endeavour from the perspective of art history, it has been accused of being egotistical; it embodies an unbalanced power relationship where the artist uses the land as their medium without respect or aesthetic regard for it.[34] Art historian Suzaan Boettger describes Heizer's works as not having any connection to the 'idea of nature or of the earth as a source of living being itself'. For land artists like Heizer, the earth is just another canvas: 'a flat, hard surface on which to boldly make one's mark'.[35] Some art historians have even described Heizer's art as a 'masculine gesture',[36] an act of 'macho aggression', and a 'raw assertion of male authority over Mother Earth'.[37]

While we might cringe at this gendering of the destruction, the message of these critics is clear: some land art is depraved in its objectification of nature, just another manifestation of human supremacy over the biosphere. *Double Negative* forms a vast monument to anthropocentrism, the belief that humankind is somehow exceptional and superior to all other nature.

Artistic creation is a unique and defining feature of humanity, but surely this power must be wielded for good. If artists are going to use the earth itself to express their artistic visions, they should ideally ensure they do not harm it in the process by using it purely for art's sake. Even better, they should have aesthetic regard for it: respecting and protecting the biosphere while sculpting and moulding it.

All Too Human

Four women enter the El Gallo Arte Contemporáneo in Salamanca, Spain, and straddle black chairs. Naked from the waist up and with their backs turned, they allow themselves to be tattooed with a single horizontal black line which passes continuously over each of their backs. They smoke cigarettes, chat, and laugh while the female tattooist inks them for life.

The women are sex workers and heroin addicts. They have consented to this tattoo in exchange for money: about 12,000 pesetas (approx. £46), the price of a heroin shot. Normally charging 2,000–3,000 pesetas for fellatio, for this half hour of a different kind of labour these women can sustain their addiction.[38]

This was an artistic action, or 'happening', by Santiago Sierra: *160 cm Line Tattooed on 4 People* (2000), which was recorded as a single-channel black-and-white video. During the filmed event two men can be seen passing through the video frame, taking photographs of the women and measuring their bared backs.

The women did consent to this performance – something that non-human animals cannot do. But many still find the way in which the artwork was created unethical. It makes a spectacle of human exploitation and enables heroin addicts to have more of the drug. Things are further complicated by the subsequent purchase of the piece as an art product: Sierra himself benefits financially, while the participants in the work remain marginalised and disadvantaged after their one-off wage.

This, however, was Sierra's point. His broad body of work exposes the exploitation of human labour in the global capitalist economy, stressing the division between the global north and global south. He hires people to perform pointless tasks that are sometimes degrading and painful: to clean people's shoes, sit in a cardboard box, hold heavy weights, lie in the trunk of a car. The people he employs are often the invisible and subjugated in society: the poor, the homeless, sex workers, asylum seekers, and illegal immigrants.*

160 cm Line's unethical production, including the artist's ethically dubious relationship with the 'performers', constitutes the artwork itself. Its moral flaw is not just incidental but forms its very identity. The work confronts ideas of freedom and choice: was the consent of those sex workers valid? Their economic and medical situation casts doubt on the freedom of their choice to participate in a conceptual artwork made for worldwide consumption. This singular event therefore serves as a microcosm of structural injustice in the world at large.

Many critics celebrate Sierra's art precisely for this immorality – for the unfiltered window it gives on to the global market economy; for its 'ethnographic realism'.[39] But others are not so charitable. By transforming this ethical dilemma into an aesthetic spectacle – and indeed, a commercial product – Sierra has been accused of replicating and capitalising on the very relations he aims to critique. Just as we saw with Brett Bailey's *Exhibit B* in an earlier chapter, it is vital to get the artist's role in this kind of immoral art right.

Yes, the sex workers consented to this artwork – but consent comes in different strengths. As we've noted, while these women were not physically coerced or forced into having their backs tattooed, they agreed to it because they lacked wealth and were imprisoned by a drug habit. In this way, their consent

---

* More recently, a planned work by Santiago Sierra – *Union Flag* (2021) – was to involve soaking a Union Jack flag in the real blood of First Nation peoples. But it was cancelled amid strong denouncement by Aboriginal communities. Presumably the participants were going to consent to the drawing of their blood, but other members of the targeted group rejected this.

was *morally defective*: valid nonetheless, but faulty in that it arose out of non-ideal conditions like poverty and addiction.* Their consent was not affirmative: they did not participate in this artwork for the joy of getting a tattoo, or as a full exercise of their creative agency – they did it because they needed another fix.

We might think that, regardless of the value of the messages put forward by this art – its value as political speech – we should focus instead on the simple fact that it further erodes the dignity of its participants, a moral wrong not redeemed by the artwork's supposedly laudable content.[40] By prioritising the didactic element of such works, we risk dismissing their ethical corruption in violating the dignity of others and taking advantage of their vulnerability.

The problem of the artist's moral responsibility over how their art is made is further complicated when the work itself spirals out of the artist's control. Marina Abramović's infamous *Rhythm 0* (1974) consisted of her issuing the following instructions to an audience in a gallery in Naples:

> There are 72 objects on the table that one can use on me as desired. Performance. I am the object . . .
>
> During this period I take full responsibility.
> Duration: 6 hours (8 pm – 2 am).[41]

* For more on the concept of defective consent, see Victor Tadros, 'Consent to Sex in an Unjust World', *Ethics*, 131/2 (2021), pp. 293–318. Tadros explores this concept in relation to sex, and how unjust sexual ideology often renders women's consent to sex *defective*, even if still valid. This preserves 'proper respect for the exercise of agency, even where it is the result of injustice' (p. 308).

Included on the table was a rose, perfume, bread, grapes, and wine, but also scissors, nails, pins, and a pistol with a bullet. Abramović remained passive throughout the piece. At the start, the audience were gentle – they gave her the rose to hold and kissed her cheeks. But things soon turned malicious. One person cut Abramović's neck and sucked her blood. There were sexual assaults on her body. Her clothes were cut away with knives. When one person loaded the pistol and put it to Abramović's head and placed her own finger on the trigger, a fight broke out. Once the performance ended and Abramović ceased being a 'puppet', the audience ran away, unable to confront what they'd just done. Abramović was traumatised and noticed that her hair had suddenly greyed afterwards.[42]

Rhythm 0 exposed the savagery that lurks in the corners of some people's psyches. Perversity simmered in the hearts of those audience members who went too far. Why did they make the decision to violate Abramović rather than respect her when they had an entirely free, uncoerced choice in that moment? The work clearly involved immorality, in what was done to the artist. But was the artwork itself morally flawed because of this? Abramović was the artist behind this piece, so was she ultimately responsible for the viciousness that unfolded? Did she create the unethical work?

She certainly did not create the actions that ended up constituting the artwork. She was, by design, powerless: the audience knew this, and to suggest that she was responsible for what others did to her would be absurd. This contrasts with her *Rhythm 10* (1973), performed a year earlier in Edinburgh, where she played the Russian game of jabbing knives between her splayed fingers. The bodily harm inflicted there was by Abramović – she cut herself twenty times.

Abramović is still loosely speaking the author of the *Rhythm 0* work, but we might decide that 'the work' here is merely the concept shaped by Abramović's open-ended instructions, and not the particular iteration of the work that occurred in its one-off 1974 performance. If the artwork was performed again, there's every chance it would involve entirely different actions and therefore possess better moral properties. In a happier possible world, the piece would end up being empowering rather than objectifying, with a respectful audience. The work in its open-endedness is morally neutral: Abramović did create *Rhythm 0*, but it's not an unethical work in its essence.

Another way to think of it, however, is that the work itself *was* that singular, sinister, one-off happening, but that Abramović was just one of its many creators. The audience members in that Naples gallery became artmakers too, dragging the work down into a debased realm.

———

While the message of an artwork might be laudable, it's vital to acknowledge that the work can still be flawed insofar as its creation involved unethical acts – even when this immorality might actually make it *better art*.

Even so, we need to be careful not to over-inflate this worry at the expense of moral consistency: animal and environmental art at the very least expose our own hypocrisy. Many of us are happy to eat burgers but are very ready to condemn art that kills animals. Many of us are happy to fly abroad and have an environmentally harmful diet but are quick to brand land art as ugly or destructive. So, you might conclude that cruel art is a necessary evil. It holds up a mirror to the wrongdoing of individuals and nation-states. It opens our eyes to the burning of fossil fuels, the overfishing of our oceans, and the violent subjection of the global south in the unrelenting capitalist market economy. Forcing us out of our daily malaise, it could be the electric shock we need to change the world for the better.

But artists should find ways of delivering this electric shock without causing further damage. If the creation of art is indeed the peak of our distinctly human nature, then we have a responsibility to use this power wisely: with empathy, nuance, and care.

————

Our five-headed beast is now fully in sight, both ugly and beautiful to behold. Some artworks show depravity in the form of obscenities. Some cause us to descend into depravity. Some are depraved because they oppress social groups. And some have a depraved origin – whether through their creator or the means by which they were created.

But for all its afflictions, depraved art is a complicated creature that we must treat with caution. Immorality can also reside within us as viewers – in how we talk about, curate, and react to these volatile creations. Sometimes we make mistakes, invoking faulty moral sentiments and making false allegations. Sometimes the deadliest works of art are also the most beautiful, and those we are too quick to judge as wicked are in fact brilliant forces for good.

What should we do with this Hydra? Should we imprison it, slaughter it, or simply attempt to tame it? This is our final task.

6 | ICONOCLASM

Since 7 October 2023, when the Palestinian terrorist group Hamas attacked Israel and abducted 250 hostages, Israel's bombardment of the blockaded Gaza Strip has taken the lives of at least 70,100 Palestinians (at the time of writing), mostly civilians. This mass slaughter is paired with the decimation of Palestine's cultural memory. During the last few years, at least two hundred heritage sites have reportedly been damaged or destroyed by Israeli shelling and airstrikes, including ancient mosques, churches, libraries, the Anthedon Harbour, which dates back to 800 BCE, the last remaining bathhouse of Hammam al-Sammara (a site rumoured to pre-date Islam), and contemporary art centres such as Shababeek. One Gaza resident said that he felt the loss of the 1,400-year-old mosque of Al-Masjid al-Omari al-Kabir on 8 December 2023 more deeply than the loss of his own home.[1]

Eradicating the cultural heritage of a people – which is mostly composed of civilian infrastructure – is a war crime according to international humanitarian law, and one of the several charges that South Africa recently brought against Israel at the International Court of Justice.[2] War and genocide are often characterised by this destruction of the art and architecture of an occupied territory or enemy. On 27 February 2022, during the Battle of Ivankiv in Ukraine's Kyiv region, the town's Museum of Local History was burned down by Russian forces. Among the museum's ruined collection were over twenty paintings by Ukrainian folk artist Maria Prymachenko. It is reported that some of her works – vivid paintings of fairy tales and nature in the 'naive' style, which were hugely influential for Picasso[3] – were rescued by a local man, who ran into the museum while it was still on fire.

Stories of people running into burning buildings to save art are not uncommon. When Paris's Notre Dame cathedral was engulfed in flames in 2019, firefighters and police formed a human chain to rescue priceless relics, paintings, and sculptures from the blaze. More recently, in 2024, members of the public ran into Copenhagen's historic Stock Exchange to recover centuries-old paintings before the building was ravaged by fire.

A nation's aesthetic products symbolise its identity. Past and present narratives, belief systems, and hopes for the future are embedded in a culture's artistic heritage – in its poetry, in its paint, in its carved stone. Cultural cleansing, then, 'affects the sense of identity and self-expression of the targeted group . . . it strikes closer to the heart of [their] self-determination', writes philosopher Bashshar Haydar.[4]

So how does a tyrant or a terrorist wage war on another country, or drive out entire ethnic groups from their own? As well as invading or controlling territory, they manipulate cultural worlds, eliminating traces of a people's distinct artistic expressions and thereby attacking their very way of life.

Sometimes rulers monopolise the heritage of their own citizens by not only targeting the art of persecuted groups, but driving out any cultural products which threaten their totalitarian power. The Nazi book burnings are one infamous case.

In 1933, the National Socialist German Students' Association organised nation-wide book bonfires to cleanse the country of 'degenerate' literature, further stoking Goebbels's propaganda machine. On 10 May, thousands gathered with torches in thirty-four university towns to burn 25,000 'un-German' literary works – meaning books by Jewish, liberal, pacifist, leftist, or foreign authors, or which were otherwise seen as challenging Nazi ideology. Among these were works by Erich Maria Remarque, whose raw portrait of the First World War in *All Quiet on the Western Front* (1929) was seen as a betrayal of the German soldiers who had fought in the conflict, as well as writings by the nineteenth-century German Jewish poet Heinrich Heine, who had prophetically written a century earlier, 'where they burn books, they will also ultimately burn people'.[5]

The bonfires raged, accompanied by Nazi songs, and in Berlin by the sound of Goebbels himself proclaiming, 'No to decadence and moral corruption! Yes to decency and morality in family and state! . . . commit to the flames the evil spirit of the past!'[6]

Image-smashers

Is it ever OK to destroy or censor art? Iconoclasm – derived from the Greek *eikonoklastes*, meaning 'breaker of images', and the Latin *iconoclasmus*, which described the anti-image actions of the ninth-century churchman Claudius – is a kind of censorship which physically destroys a work of art.[7] Motivations for this have historically been religious or political in nature. For instance, during the spread of Christianity under Constantine, images and sculptures of pre-Christian gods would be defaced or destroyed to remove markers of the Roman Empire's polytheist state religion.

Censorship in general stretches back to ancient Greek thought and beyond. Remember how panicked Plato was over the corrupting capacities of the arts on the souls of civilians? Because dangerous art seduces us into indulging our passions and letting these overwhelm our rationality, it was to be banned in Plato's ideal state. Censorship today is the suppression or prohibition of communication or expression which is similarly considered objectionable or threatening to the common good. It can happen to a variety of media: literature, music, film, TV, and the fine arts. It can take the form of bans, cancelling of shows, de-platforming, and outright destruction like burning and demolishing. Art can be censored for many reasons – sometimes good, sometimes bad – ranging from national security and the state's silencing of dissident views to controlling obscene material and protecting groups targeted by hate speech.

Sometimes, for instance, artworks have been considered too titillating or offensive to remain on view as they are. The forbidden pleasures of the nude – both male and female – were circumvented by the invention of the 'fig leaf' in the sixteenth century. This foliage – which was derived from the story of Adam and Eve in Genesis, who had to resort to sewing fig leaves into aprons to hide their shameful nudity after their banishment – was used to edit early Christian artworks by shielding exposed genitals in the originals. This bodily shame stretched to secular art, too. Gustave Courbet's *L'Origine du monde* (1866) – a close-up portrait of a vulva – was commissioned for the Turkish ambassador to France, Khalil Bey, who kept the painting hidden behind a green curtain and would only display it to small groups of friends. As recently as 2011, an image of the painting was removed from Facebook when the platform deactivated the account of a teacher who had posted it.[8]

But as we saw earlier in the book, we must be wary which 'obscene' artworks we censor and why – we must scrutinise the very concept of the obscene, which is plagued by double standards and prejudice. The Musée d'Orsay, which has held *L'Origine du monde* since 1995, says on its website that the work 'escapes pornographic status' all thanks to 'Courbet's great virtuosity and the refinement of his amber colour scheme'.[9] This is the attitude we must reject: that an image of a woman's vulva is automatically considered pornographic, and so therefore of lesser moral value and cultural worth. That is, unless a male painter renders the organ skilfully refined by using a splendid colour scheme, of course.

While censorship to control obscenity might sometimes rest on shaky grounds, censorship as part of state control, in its silencing of artists who challenge the dominant ideology of an authoritarian government's or ruling elites' abuses of power, is even more sinister. For instance, Ai Weiwei's *Kui Hua Zi (Sunflower Seeds)* (2008), a monumental installation consisting of millions of porcelain sunflower seeds, was removed from the 2014 Chinese Contemporary Art Award exhibition in Shanghai just before it opened, presumably due to the artist's ongoing criticism of the country's government. The artwork is a metaphor for the downtrodden Chinese populace under Mao Zedong. It invites us to see the Chinese people under Mao as sunflower seeds, emotionally conveying messages about oppression, individuality, and famine.[10] During Chairman Mao's rule of the People's Republic of China (1949–76), propaganda images showed Mao as the sun, and the people of China as sunflowers turning towards him.[11] Interviews with Weiwei also indicate personal associations with the sunflower seed: 'In China, when we grew up, we had nothing . . . But for even the poorest people, the treat or the treasure we'd have would be the sunflower seeds in everybody's pockets.'[12]

Soon after, in 2016, Nigerian artist Jelili Atiku was remanded in custody for three days after his street performance *Àràgàmàgò Will Rid This Land of Terrorism* near his home in Ejigbo. The artwork, which involved sacred Yoruba symbols and chief priests parading through the streets, was an example of Atiku's wider practice, which uses striking spectacles in densely populated public spaces to critique Nigeria's ruling class and comment on human rights violations. This piece was devised in response to a horrific incident from two years prior, where three women were sexually assaulted and tortured in a Lagos market by a 'special' security team allegedly appointed by the traditional ruler of the town, the King of Ejigbo, Oba Morufu Ojoola.[13]

The king, who is related to the artist, understood that the performance was meant to criticise him. Atiku, along with some performers and bystanders, was thrown into prison by heavily armed police, and a group of men with guns and machetes ransacked his house, destroyed his art, and terrorised his family.[14] 'I was arrested because I questioned power. I questioned the king. I questioned his actions,' the artist said.[15] While the charges were eventually dropped, Atiku has been left traumatised by the experience, and yet steadfastly continues to create his art with the aim of provoking political change.

Artistic freedom in general is being threatened across the globe. A recent report by Artists at Risk Connection (ARC), Labo Ciudadano, and Amnesty International documents the increasing restrictions on artistic expression, particularly in Latin America and the Caribbean. It shows how surveillance and repression against artists have significantly escalated. Since the 2020 pandemic, for example, the Cuban government has reportedly committed abuses against dozens of artists, including detentions, house arrests, and forced exile.[16]

Problematic censorship can also extend to museum officials and their curatorial decisions. What museums and art institutions display to the public determines our understanding of the past and our sense of the future. It is therefore imperative that these institutions tell us true, inclusive stories and offer robust education through their curatorial practices. While earlier in the book we saw supposedly obscene art being hidden away in forbidden collections (secreta), today we see attempts to purge museums of artefacts and discourses which simply don't align with the ideology of the powers that be.

President Trump's recent attack on American museums encapsulates the dangers of controlling our nations' stories. On 12 August 2025, Trump issued a directive to the Smithsonian Institution to 'replace divisive or ideologically driven language with unifying, historically accurate, and constructive descriptions'.[17] This is part of Trump's executive order called 'Restoring Truth and Sanity to American History', which criticises cultural narratives that instil 'a sense of national shame', particularly around the country's history of slavery.[18] Trump wrote on Truth Social of the Smithsonian, which comprises twenty-one history and art museums and fourteen research and education centres:

The Museums throughout Washington, but all over the Country are, essentially, the last remaining segment of 'WOKE.' The Smithsonian is OUT OF CONTROL, where everything discussed is how horrible our Country is, how bad Slavery was . . . I have instructed my attorneys to go through the Museums, and start the exact same process that

depraved

has been done with Colleges and Universities . . . WOKE IS BROKE.

This move, which has been described as 'Orwellian'[19] and a 'thinly veiled attempt to erase black history',[20] will in the coming months comprise a review of the Smithsonian's museums, with a list of objectionable artworks already having been issued by the White House. The list includes works which depict immigration and express anti-slavery and anti-racism sentiments, as well as entire exhibits dedicated to LGBTQIA+, Latinx, and disabled identities.[21] For this government, then, free speech is precious, but only insofar as they agree with what is said.

The ethics of art censorship depends on what is being censored and why. In the cases above, much of the repressed art was in fact morally *good*. The reason it was destroyed or repressed was because of its threat to authoritarian power, and we should condemn this. But what if the art itself is genuinely immoral? Our Hydra shows how artworks can be wielded as weapons to harm others. Sometimes censorship derives from a sense of justice: many statues of white supremacists and slave traders, for instance, have been subject to recent iconoclastic campaigns for this very reason. They have been removed, hidden, and destroyed. But is such censorship the right remedy for their toxicity? Must we entirely abolish this art? Must we slay our Hydra?

———

It's a human right to express our views in public without threat of punishment, a right that is preserved (but not always upheld) under the Universal Declaration of Human Rights. This includes artistic expression, despite its complexities, so how could it ever be OK to eradicate art that embodies opposing views to your own?

Well, as John Stuart Mill argued in *On Liberty* (1859), our freedom of speech isn't absolute – there are some limits. One such limit comes from the phenomenon of hate speech. Some legislators and scholars have argued for stricter regulation of hate speech because of the nature of its harm.* Recall that hate speech doesn't just have pernicious downstream consequences like breaking social peace and causing psychological damage. Hate speech can also *constitute* harm itself by altering normative reality – it amounts to an act of subordination, sustaining hierarchies, legitimising oppression, assaulting the dignity of those targeted by it.

As we've seen, hate speech can also stifle the free speech of those targeted. Returning to the issue of pornography, some philosophers like Rae Langton argue that pornography creates an environment where women's refusals of unwanted sex in real life are not taken seriously or are simply not understood due to the proliferation of rape myths. This is a case where women's right to free speech – to exercise and express their opinions, and to do things with their words like refuse or consent to sexual contact – is undermined by the free speech of pornographers. Because of this, some call for censorship or regulation of the harmful material in a bid to protect women's autonomy.

In the same way, artistic hate speech can threaten the free speech of marginalised groups. Remember how Confederate and slave-trader monuments function: they do not merely represent something, they *do* something, implicitly *ranking* people

* Legal restrictions vary. The First Amendment in the US for instance affords far more protection to some racist hate speech compared to the laws of the UK, Australia, and Canada.

of colour as inferior and legitimising their unfair treatment. As the Mayor of London Sadiq Khan said after the statue of the seventeenth-century slave trader Edward Colston was toppled in Bristol in June 2020: 'Imagine what it's like as a black person to walk past a statue of somebody who enslaved your ancestors. And we are commemorating them – celebrating them – as icons.'[22] The pervasiveness of these statues and their enduring authoritative presence in our civic spaces puts the free speech of black people at risk, especially with the recent proliferation of far-right ideology touted by some political leaders and social media communities. So, surely these oppressive artworks must be de-platformed and removed or destroyed. Should a few heads of our Hydra be sawn off?

Image-kissers

There are several issues with calling for tougher legislation around depraved art, including artistic hate speech. First, many people feel that artists and their art are near-sacred; that they should be immune from censorship and that silencing them is deplorable. But as we saw in an earlier chapter, while we often take artists to be special human beings, this doesn't mean we should allow them to transcend our moral laws.

However, this artist-worship stems from a legitimate recognition of their masterful achievements. Censoring hateful art in general would mean depriving us of things of value like positive aesthetic experiences and important genre-defining, or -defying, artworks. Museum professionals such as the former director of Tate Modern, Vicente Todolí, reiterate this sentiment: 'The person, I can totally abhor and loathe, but the work is the work . . . Once an artist creates something, it doesn't belong to the artist anymore: it belongs to the world,' he said.[23] Now, having tackled the problem of immoral artists earlier, I hope you'd disagree with Todolí here. In many cases, the artist's moral character lurks within their art; the two cannot be separated. The artwork can be immoral and oppressive in part because of who made it.

But nonetheless, Todolí stresses here that if we refused to engage with art made by bad people, or indeed immoral art in general, we'd lose the greatness of artists like Gauguin and Picasso. And *if* we were to discover something unsavoury about, say, Shakespeare, this would mean the ultimate loss to the Western art canon. Indeed, several audience members at London's National Gallery debate in 2019 proclaimed that forever locking away Gauguin's Tahitian portraits would be effectively shunning and destroying 'genius' and 'beauty'.

If we think that positive and negative aesthetic experiences are inherently as well as instrumentally valuable for human flourishing, this loss would be regrettable. In the 1950s, Simone de Beauvoir famously wrote an essay asking 'Must We Burn Sade?', to which she answered a resounding 'no'. Her stance might be surprising; as one of the most prolific feminist philosophers of all time, we'd expect Beauvoir to commit Sade's art – which bursts at the seams with extreme sexual violence towards women and girls – to the flames.

Her essay considers the ideas of authentic freedom and selfhood alongside the heartless cruelty of Sade's sexuality. She shows that the political context of Sade's writings offers a route to understanding this depraved aristocrat. In the stormy time of the French Revolution, Sade may have been trying to cling on to the feudal power of his decaying class by seeking the ultimate freedom and individuality within the arena of sex. In his fictional treatise *Philosophy in the Boudoir* (1795), Sade himself argues that the French Revolution could only be successful if citizens embrace atheism and a libertine moral system – an extreme hedonism which exalts the bodily pleasures above all other moral laws and social conventions, and rejects the Enlightenment's prioritising of reason over emotion and instinctual drives. Because of the impact Sade's art had on the then influential French existentialists – who examined what it means to be free in a godless world – Beauvoir defended its publication.

In fact, Sade's abhorrent yet transgressive pornography has offered a springboard for re-imagining the body and its relation to society through the 'Sadean imagination', in Alyce Mahon's phrase: an imagined world of sexual terror where 'our understanding of humanity is expanded through an exploration of humankind's dark, sexually explicit, violent, cruel nature'.[24] While objectively immoral, Sade's literary works nonetheless offer progressive worlds where heterosexual norms are gleefully dispensed with, and where oppressive laws of the church and state are shamelessly rejected. Women in his writings do sometimes hold positions of power, such as the procuresses in *The 120 Days of Sodom*; and in *Juliette* (1797) – where the eponymous protagonist is a nymphomaniac murderer – the libertine heroine is celebrated for her transgressive femininity.

Sade's nihilistic moral system can be used for good and has been credited with inspiring whole new movements of artistic expression. Since the twentieth century, avant-garde artists and writers have harnessed the Sadean imagination and its aesthetic language to make sense of very real terror in society in a plethora of different contexts, especially post-1945. For instance, in his film *Salò* (1975), Pier Paolo Pasolini translated the Sadean universe of *The 120 Days of Sodom* into the imagined last days of Mussolini's fascist regime. As Mahon puts it, Sade has offered artists and intellectuals after 1945 'an inexhaustible point of departure for radical thinking about the human condition . . . a powerful means . . . to interrogate systems of patriarchal, governmental, institutional, and imperial power through sexual relations in modern culture'.[25]

Some think that Sade's literature made possible the movements of dada, happenings, and surrealism by freeing the human subconscious and its libidinal drives from morality and reason. In an interview, the artist Jean-Jacques Lebel said of Sade: 'His literature is the most extreme example of somebody who dares to imagine other relationships with one's own body and the bodies of other human beings.' While we must be careful not to sanitise Sade's atrocities – both in his life and in his art – we might follow Lebel's lead in seeing Sade's work as an example to all of us to 'exert the right . . . to experiment with new ways of seeing and feeling and experiencing reality, and [our] own sexuality, as long as [we] don't oppress other human beings'.[26] So, while we should condemn Sade's eroticisation of rape, we should also be mindful of the revolutionary impact his art has had on art-making and on its capacity to be a form of political resistance.

It's important to note, though, that many of the artworks and movements inspired by Sade are re-interpretations of his creations. They take elements that are, in fact, morally laudable in his work – his subversion of gender binaries and oppressive social norms – and then run with this aesthetic imagination for the greater good. But they do this while leaving *behind* the genuine immorality within Sade's storytelling. Out of something genuinely horrific, inspired artists can mine aesthetic strategies for social and political emancipation, attempting to comprehend the depravities that have taken place in the world since Sade's time: two world wars, the Holocaust, colonial violence in Algeria, the Vietnam War, and the brutal blockade in Gaza, just to name a few.

This selective mining may explain the vehement disagreement between radical feminists such as Andrea Dworkin who deplore Sade's art for glorifying the subordination of women, and those who see within his terrorising texts glimpses of a sexual utopia, where egalitarian love and desire can be freely expressed and explored. The former see Sade's art for what it is, and the latter see Sade's art for what it could be. For Beauvoir and others, destroying such disturbing books is not a solution for feminism – rather, feminism must remain open to the vast reaches of the human condition so that we can imagine better worlds. As theorist Judith Butler ponders, perhaps 'to know oneself . . . one must undertake to know Sade'.[27]

Expedition into morally deviant worlds can be good for the enquiring mind. Many artworks may ultimately have value because they allow us to safely delve into taboo subjects, which helps us learn about ourselves and the validity of our own cultural and moral norms from the comfort of our sofas.

In fact, many of us enjoy some films and TV shows precisely *for* their immorality. Vince Gilligan's Walter White in *Breaking Bad*, for instance, is what A. W. Eaton would call a 'rough hero', a character who does terrible things but who we root for regardless – for most seasons anyway.[28] How does this work? The rough hero tugs at our 'imaginative resistance': we know they are a bad person, because they're a murdering drug lord, and we resist them.[29] And yet, because the artwork presents them to us in such a seductive and exciting way – through the character's appearance, intelligence, tragic past, and earnt power

– we have a peculiar sort of love for them. Rough heroes thereby challenge our black-and-white moral views: as philosopher Panos Paris observes, we might initially be morally averse to drug lords, but when art presents us with the complex reasons people end up in that line of work, we may develop more sympathy and compassion towards such choices in real life.[30]

The concern over losing valuable works of art explains why some commentators see censorship in general as setting a dangerous precedent for our cultural heritage. This anxiety was amplified during the 'Rhodes Must Fall' campaign, one of the defining protests of the twenty-first century so far. Ignited at the University of Cape Town in 2015 when activist Chumani Maxwele threw human faeces at a statue of British imperialist and racist Cecil Rhodes, the movement gained traction across the world, resulting in other South African universities as well as those in the UK and the US demanding a decolonisation of higher education curricula, and the removal of other Rhodes statues and apartheid symbols.

Since Rhodes Must Fall, there have been growing worries that we are at the top of a slippery slope. The Robert E. Lee Confederate monument in Richmond, Virginia, was among the many statues targeted during the Black Lives Matter (BLM) protests of 2020, which sprang up in the wake of a white police officer's murder of George Floyd. One Richmond resident lamented the widespread iconoclasm around these public sculptures: 'I cried, it's so sad. Where's it going to stop?'[31] Discussing the debate in a UK context, philosopher David Edmonds summed up this widespread view: 'If we were to denude Britain of all the statues of dead politicians and soldiers who held a few views we now find problematic, the country would be littered with unoccupied plinths.'[32]

This 'slippery slope' argument has also been made about the problem of immoral artists. In 2024, I debated the journalist Andrew Doyle on BBC Radio 4 about how to respond to the work of such artists, specifically in the wake of the sexual assault allegations against the Slovenian mosaic artist and priest Marko Rupnik. Doyle expressed the concern that removing Rupnik's mosaics and other artworks made by bad people would mean that 'you're effectively going to strip away a lot of the Western canon'.[33]

But this kind of argument risks using fallacious reasoning. It's like asserting that if we allow same-sex couples to marry, then the next thing we know we'll be allowing people to marry their parents, their cars, and even penguins, so we shouldn't concede this right in the first place. This fallacy seeks to leverage fear; in this case, that we'll lose all our cultural products. But critically rethinking our cultural landscape is not going to leave us with a barren, art-free world.

While this argument against art censorship isn't a good one, we're nonetheless left with the fact that we would still lose rather a lot of beauty and artistic greatness if we totally destroyed or locked away all depraved paintings, novels, and sculptures.

Probably the most successful argument against censoring immoral art is that it results in an erasure of history, although the spirit of this objection is often presented in the wrong way. In the UK, many commentators were concerned that the toppling of the Edward Colston statue and the pre-emptive removal of similar public artworks was tantamount to hiding and dismissing the legacies of the country's past.

Edward Colston was a born and bred Bristolian and focused his philanthropic work on the town, donating to churches and schools. Because of this, in 1893, the charity organisation The

Anchor Society, which was inspired by Colston's philanthropy, decided to commemorate the man as an expression of regional pride – 'part of a late-Victorian attempt to re-imagine the civic space around "great men" and "benign paternalism"', as Bristol historian James Watts writes.[34]

After the Colston statue came tumbling down, the UK Prime Minister at the time, Boris Johnson, commented that

> we have a complex historical legacy all around us which reflects our history and all its diversity for good or ill . . . What you can't do, is go around seeking retrospectively to change our history or to edit it . . . It's like some person trying to edit their Wikipedia entry – it's wrong.[35]

But the problem with putting the 'erasure of history' argument this way is that its central claim is categorically false. If I'm honest, I didn't know who Edward Colston was before his statue was tossed into Bristol harbour. The spectacular interventions during the 2020 BLM protests brought him into the wider public consciousness. If anything, toppling statues of these 'great men' – if done loudly enough – doesn't erase them, but can make them more visible than ever. Centring a BLM protest around the Colston statue precisely highlighted the *real* history of this man. In fact, if anyone is guilty of 'editing the Wikipedia entry' it's the then president of The Anchor Society James Arrowsmith and his committee, who commissioned the Colston statue. They conveniently left out the details about how Colston made his fortune on the statue's plaque: there was no mention, no 'hint of his trafficking in human cargo', as historian Madge Dresser points out.[36] Before 2020, many may have only known that Colston was a merchant and politician, and not that he traded in people – that his Royal African Company transported 150,000 enslaved men, women and children, who had 'RAC' branded on to their bare chests.

In the aftermath of the Colston statue's felling, the now UK Prime Minister Sir Keir Starmer wrote on Twitter/X:

> Edward Colston was responsible for 100,000 people being moved from Africa to the Caribbean as slaves. 20,000 died en route. The statue shouldn't have been taken down in the way it was. But it should have been removed from our streets a long time ago.[37]

While Starmer was right to highlight Colston's crimes against humanity, he was wrong to suggest that the statue shouldn't have been graffitied, torn down, rolled through the streets, and thrown into the water. Discretely removing statues and paintings does not adequately engage with the injustices committed, nor does it give a voice to the art's victims. Censoring depraved art, if done on the quiet, could backfire and conceal the atrocities themselves. Such erasure could lead to a widespread amnesia – at least in dominant groups – where difficult histories are forgotten or disregarded, leaving many unable to confront the reality of our past. If we didn't rage about Gauguin – if his paintings were secretly hidden away without a fuss – this would sweep his barbarity under the carpet. Removing statues and paintings without anyone noticing could even amount to dismissing the magnitude of the atrocities honoured by the monuments, or the immoral messages expressed by the paintings.

Johnson is of course correct that history is complex, but to not do *anything* in response to our civic venerations of slave traders, or to our masterpieces by immoral artists, actually risks flattening historical complexity – this do-nothing position risks undermining itself.

Even if we agreed that censoring immoral art is sometimes for the best, what would this mean in practice? Under the US's First Amendment, for example, many artworks will be protected as legal expression because it is hard to show that they incite violence; as we saw earlier in this book, it has been difficult to prove that an artwork directly causes criminal behaviour. Moreover, meaning in art is more complex than in ordinary speech: the artist could deny having certain intentions for their artwork, and so be let off the hook when it comes to legal requirements like *mens rea* for prosecution on the grounds of incitement. Art is generally more opaque than straightforward speech – there's more room for plausible deniability. It is harder to deny or disavow explicit racist speech than it is a racist artwork, where the artist could deny they had *intended* to express such a meaning. While we may condemn them for being insincere, they can still escape prosecution by exploiting legal loopholes.

If outright censorship involving the quiet formal removal, suppression, or destruction of depraved art proves problematic, public shaming offers another alternative. So-called cancel culture is the practice of withdrawing support or boycotting the work of public figures, creators, or companies after they've done or said something objectionable. While there are forms of *literal* cancellation, which consists more of the censorship we've been looking at so far (the cancellation of shows and events, removal of songs from the radio, and so on), there is also *metaphorical* cancellation. This involves refusing to consume an artist's work and encompasses an atmosphere of ostracisation and excommunication – it 'labels the artist *anathema*', as philosopher Erich Hatala Matthes puts it.[38]

Cancelling gained momentum during the #MeToo movement when figures like Harvey Weinstein and R. Kelly were 'cancelled' due to their histories of sexual violence. The idea is that instead of literally cancelling events and artworks, we cancel the *person*. This might be with an aim to change their behaviour for the better by discouraging future misdeeds, or more pressing still, to incapacitate them from acting again: fame comes with great power and freedom, which can easily facilitate serial offenders. Or quite simply, we do it because the person *deserves* punishment – we feel that such retribution balances the score.

The problem with cancel culture, though, is that it's a rather blunt instrument – it's too coarse-grained to discriminate among different cases. As Matthes points out, it 'generally fails to discriminate among different kinds of immorality, in particular, the difference between how to respond to a sexual predator versus how to respond to a morally objectionable statement'.[39] The merciless all-or-nothing nature of cancel culture can be irrevocable, and such punishment is not always fair or proportionate: people can lose their jobs and be subject to relentless abuse, which isn't always called for. Recall the PR executive Justine Sacco, who while travelling to South Africa in 2014 tweeted a tasteless racist joke. She became the target of viral internet outrage and was fired by her employer. While she did do something bad, it's a stretch to say that she should have lost her job and had her livelihood put in jeopardy as a result.[40][*]

Exacerbating this bluntness is the fact that cancel culture can contain double standards: those targeted can also be subject to

---

[*] The joke was: 'Going to Africa. Hope I don't get AIDS. Just kidding. I'm white!' While totally unacceptable, the joke itself was the last in a string of more harmless ones about travelling, and Sacco was profusely apologetic afterwards.

prejudice. When people talk about immoral artists, it's often the same culprits: R. Kelly and Michael Jackson tend to receive far more attention than white musicians like Jimmy Page or David Bowie, both of whom have faced allegations of statutory rape.[41]

Another argument against the blanket cancellation of immoral art is that abandoning certain artists entirely may compromise our deeply held personal identity. The feminist critic Michele Wallace, for instance, notes that her love and admiration for Michael Jackson's music comes partly from its commentary on black American experience – a kind of 'black modernism' – and also because of its personal significance to her and her relationship with her mother, the acclaimed artist Faith Ringgold.[42] This is important: all of us have our own 'aesthetic selves' – our favourite paintings, movies, music, and novels offer an intimate window into who we are as people. Our artistic loves and hates often express our deeply held convictions, and enable us to form relationships with others, as well as with ourselves.[43] Cancelling immoral artists and fully withdrawing from all depraved art may, then, frustrate many people's aesthetic sense of who they are.

Impasse

The iconoclast's motivations matter: the obliteration of a World Heritage Site is deeply wrong, but the censorship of depraved art might be more permissible. However, even in these more acceptable cases, there are still issues: the image-kissers are right that full-blown censorship would rob us of important cultural objects and aesthetic value, thereby closing off avenues of vital knowledge and self-discovery. It would also lead to social amnesia where some will forget or be unable to confront the truth of our collective history. Cancellation, too, is an imperfect method. So, censorship may create more problems than it solves – as Hercules learnt the hard way, cutting off one of the Hydra's heads just causes it to grow another one.

If outright censorship is ill-equipped to deal with the problem of immoral art and artists, should we just do nothing? Must we, as many passionately argue, leave be our depraved Hydra, embrace the status quo, and stop being so 'woke'?

Well, letting our Hydra loose on to the streets will cause even more damage. Continuing to uncritically engage with immoral artists, for example, can empower them by affording them financial leverage in continuing to fund their estates. It can also give them too much moral authority by signalling that their bad behaviour is still somewhat acceptable.[44] This further inflates the artist's epistemic power – by placing them on pedestals away from the moral laws demanded by the majority, we afford these people inflated credibility about matters relating to their misdeeds: we believe them over their victims. This in turn harms the victims – especially those of immoral artists who are still alive – by silencing them. Our continuing to unreflectively admire and consume this art can discourage these victims from speaking out about their trauma. And by refusing to confront those depraved artworks in our civic spaces and galleries – especially those which entrench structural injustices – society risks downplaying and sanitising the dangers they pose and failing to acknowledge how they contribute to the persecution of marginalised groups.

Doing *nothing* in response to depraved art, then, means suffering the menace of this unleashed monster. We will not learn from our mistakes, and we will fall further away from reaching a world where all of us can flourish. Where do we go from here?

7 | REPARATION

'We're not afraid of anything.'[1] Two teenage ballerinas posed on pointe in front of the Robert E. Lee Confederate monument in Richmond, Virginia, shortly after its pending removal was announced. The imposing monument was built to commemorate the Confederate Civil War General, who it depicts in bronze riding a large horse on top of a marble base standing over 60 feet tall. In black tutus with their fists raised high in the sign of Black Power, Ava Holloway and Kennedy George reclaimed this contested space at the peak of the 2020 Black Lives Matter protests.

Ava and Kennedy's intervention at the foot of the statue was an act which simultaneously expressed anger and hope. On the one hand, it echoed the subordinating force of this depraved sculpture by placing black bodies at its base, but it did so in a way that rejected its domination in celebration of black solidarity and beauty, taking up contested space. By using the art form of ballet, one which has historically been white and exclusionary, Ava and Kennedy radiated dignity and elegance as they danced around the white marble plinth. While the girls were somewhat dwarfed by the sculpture, this only served to strengthen their profound act of resistance.

The ballerinas were just one of many striking interactions

with this Confederate sculpture that took place in 2020. George Floyd's face was projected over it, with words reading 'No Justice, No Peace'. Joyous basketball games were played in front of it, a gospel band made music in its shadow, local art communities set up booths around it to help protesters create posters and cloth squares, and it was covered with a 'gorgeous, colourful blanket of graffiti' containing phrases like 'Stop White Supremacy' and 'Blood On Your Hands'.[2]

The intrusive monument was ultimately transformed to such an extent – going from a symbol of drab dominance to one of luminous communality – that it became unrecognisable, and arguably an entirely different work of art: its venom was extracted. Before it was removed it was considered one of the most influential American protest artworks since the Second World War.[3] The original, then, with its oppressive force, was permanently silenced.

This is how we must deal with depraved art. We must loudly, angrily, beautifully confront it. We must not conceal the Hydra; we must make it hyper-visible, disarm it and tame it, to the point of its effective destruction. The solution is not feeble and quiet censorship or total, literal iconoclasm. The solution is bold and defiant *metaphysical* iconoclasm.

———

In the last chapter we encountered the problems with censoring depraved art. There is an alternative. A Justice of the United States Supreme Court, Louis Brandeis, famously offered a remedy for evil speech: 'If there be time to expose through discussion the falsehood and fallacies, to avert the evil by the processes of education, the remedy to be applied is more speech, not enforced silence.'[4] The idea is that we can refute and contradict, and even undo, the harms of hate speech with more speech: counterspeech. We can offer counternarratives and counterevidence which challenge falsehoods and harmful sentiments, but we can also directly block this speech, diminishing its subordinating force by dismantling the conditions required for it to have its force in the first place. To work, oppressive speech needs authority or for certain assumptions to be accepted. Reject this authority, reject these assumptions, and the oppressive speech is undone from the inside out.

So what do we do with depraved art? The remedy is *better speech. Better art. Better curation.* We can reject and disarm an artwork's immoral content and force – we can stop its harmful moulding of social reality. The art is then transformed – by loudly rejecting it, we neutralise it and drown out its evil noise. Specifically, we can fight depraved art with aesthetic interventions and intelligent curating; a kind of curatorial activism.

Now, confronting ordinary hate speech – from oppressive legislation to racist slurs and sexist jokes – has difficulties. Philosopher Rae Langton laments:

Speakers are threatened into silence, drowned out by heckling, or by the megaphone of money, which amplifies some voices, and gags others. Tribalism walls off one group from another, in online echo-chambers that exclude dissent . . . Attempts to squash rumors can backfire, giving falsehoods more credence than they had before. Words that wound, hate speech scrawled on walls and side-walks – these are not invitations to conversation, but instructions to *get out.*[5]

Speaking back to hate can be hard, sometimes impossible.

depraved

Sometimes it is difficult to unpack what has been said before we can respond. Responding can also be unsafe for the threatened party. But engaging creatively with immoral art sidesteps the obstacles that we find in everyday linguistic interactions.

This artistic counterspeech can be broken down into roughly two connected methods: intervention and the platforming of new narratives. Both offer imaginative ways to counteract and block – and so pacify – our many-headed monster, without physically eradicating it.

Intervention

Remember the sexist football coach who shouts at a male footballer, 'even a *girl* could make that shot!' after his player misses the goal. He implies and thereby declares that girls and women are relatively poor at football, a sexist stereotype which is smuggled into the conversation as a backdoor subordinating speech act.

How might we stop this as hearers? We can try to block the speech act by challenging the presupposition that carries it: 'What do you mean, *even* a girl?!' Rae Langton shows that exposing buried content like this, perhaps with direct interjections or merely by raising an eyebrow, means that it can then be challenged or rejected. Doing this stops it being accommodated in the conversation. If this block is successful, the subordinating effect is cancelled – the sexist speech 'misfires', because its required conditions are not fulfilled: its presupposition is obstructed.[6]

When a speech act misfires, it is not performed at all; it fails.[7] In this example of counterspeech, it is not taken for granted that women are bad at football and that related sexist stereotypes are true. The social standings of women and men do not flex in the wrong direction; the illocution does not successfully shape the world in its image. The coach's credibility is also compromised – he might now be disliked by others, and perhaps his ability to be a good coach will be in doubt.

Another related way to obstruct hate speech is by rejecting the speaker's authority. If a bystander were to respond to a person spewing racist vitriol towards an Arab woman on the London Underground with 'Who do you think you are!?', the assumption of their authority is exposed and then rejected; the act's condition for subordination is unsatisfied, and the racist's speech misfires (at least, in an ideal scenario).[8] In these cases, we 'undo' the hate speech from the inside, by dismantling the conditions required for it to subordinate people.

We can do this to oppressive art, too, and perhaps with more success. Recall how the Colston statue in Bristol elevated a person responsible for colonialist violence, and celebrated the philanthropy derived from his slave-trading fortune. This statue smuggled in hateful content: that slavery was permissible. As we saw in Richmond, Virginia, there are creative ways to bring an artwork's problematic content like this to the foreground. First, we can manipulate and materially interact with the immoral art, by adding new surrounding creations. As Bristol poet Vanessa Kisuule puts it: 'I'm not necessarily for getting rid of statues . . . I want people to scribble on them, to make counteractive art with them.'[9] Vibrant interventions like those around the Robert E. Lee monument resist and push back against the presumption that the sentiment expressed by the statue is endorsed by all.[10]

In 2018, an installation appeared overnight beneath Bristol's Colston statue on Anti-Slavery Day. The artwork *Here and*

depraved

Now, by an anonymous artist, consisted of concrete figurines lying as cargo, arranged in the shape of a slave ship hull. This quiet and sombre addition to the statue underlined the real origin of Colston's philanthropy. It shone a terrible spotlight on the statue's presupposition that enslaving a race of people is somehow permissible.

Interaction with immoral art can be brilliantly simple. Glasgow's Duke of Wellington monument commemorates the imperialist military leader who led British armies to tighten the East India Company's control. The statue's friezes are at least somewhat honest – they depict the duke sacking Indian cities and slaughtering South Asians. But the overall purpose of the statue is still to honour and celebrate this military leader. For years now, though, the statue has constantly worn a traffic cone on its head. The cone forms a comical and almost elegant juxtaposition to the grandeur of the statue.

Placing traffic cones on formidable monuments of Great Men undermines their oppressive force; it dismisses the authority behind the sculpture, and what the Great Man stood for – a visual 'Who do you think you are!?'. Such simple aesthetic acts douse the art in bathos, reducing the honoured figure's power to ridiculous banality, while swiftly opening up its interrogation.

These artistic interventions are so effective precisely because of their aesthetic nature – throwing paint, ballet dancing, and toppling a statue using chains have an affective dimension which traverses across language and cultures, touching all of us. They are hard to ignore and leave a lasting impression. As one commentator described the protest art that engulfed the Robert E. Lee monument in Virginia:

the visual refashioning of the monument has afforded a display of civic and racial creativity and pride that will . . . have some legacy. In the meantime, it has lent an impact that could never be matched in the same way by a replacement object, a grassy lawn, or a moment of action and a hole in the ground.[11]

We can also curatorially interrogate depraved art in a way that presents it plainly to the world, warts and all. When the Colston statue was pulled down, it wasn't just left there. It was rolled through the streets – scraped and clanked against the concrete – and then plunged into the murky harbour to ecstatic applause. This was not an outright destruction of the piece, but a *re-curation* of it – it was reassembled and manoeuvred with magnificent sonic effect; a loud rejection and humiliation of the slave trader. Its noisy relocation echoed historic painful soundscapes of enslavement and metal restraints, and pierced the statue's poisonous force like a needle popping a balloon. Loudly lowering Colston rejected the quiet honouring that he'd enjoyed for centuries.

We can do all of this inside the gallery, too. Recall Dana Schutz's *Open Casket* (2017), a painting of the mutilated face of Emmett Till, which was accused of insensitively using black pain as its material. In response, the artist and activist Parker Bright wore a T-shirt reading 'BLACK DEATH SPECTACLE', and stood directly in front of Schutz's painting, blocking it from view. 'No one should be making money off a Black dead body,' he said during his performance.[12] Bright disrupted the gallery space in a way that exposed the objectionable painting, stating clearly that it was not OK for a white artist to aestheticise this brutal racist killing.

Curators in general have a social and moral responsibility to provide counternarratives and tell honest stories about the art they display, including where it came from and who made it. When curation is transparent, it does not hide the artwork's horrors; it does not shrink in the face of the depravity lurking there. For example, the artist Michelle Hartney placed #Me-Too-inspired wall labels next to Picasso and Gauguin paintings at the Metropolitan Museum of Art in her *Performance/Call to Action* (2018). This illuminated these artists' transgressions, which is especially important given that in some cases, their immoral acts are integral to properly understanding their art.

In 2019, the curators at the National Gallery of Canada changed the wall texts in their Gauguin exhibition before it opened to the public: texts about the artist's 'relationship with a young Tahitian woman' were altered to refer to 'his relationship with a 13- or 14-year-old Tahitian girl'.[13] Such small changes make a huge difference. Addressing these 'blind spots' in the work of immoral artists 'could make those artists more relevant', said the gallery's director, Sasha Suda. This is right – it connects these artists to present-day discourse around sexual politics and consent. But it also reminds us as viewers that these artists were real, flawed people: why hide this?

Ethical curating like this exposes the long-ignored shameful reality behind these pieces. Presenting the paintings of Titian, Gauguin, Picasso, and even Hitler in a transparent and honest way actually does greater justice to art history. Such curation will enable deeper understanding of these works and function as a warning that art can have very real consequences in the world. In the case of Hitler, it's imperative that we take his paintings seriously even if we dislike them – they form an important part of his depraved vision. In some cases, this curation will even *enhance* our experience of the art. Surely Caravaggio's dramatic paintings of death become even more incandescent when we experience them through the eyes of a killer and alcoholic brawler?[14]

We've seen how Titian's paintings being stunningly beautiful doesn't diminish their romanticised sexual violence. And just because Gauguin spearheaded post-impressionism, that doesn't mean we can avoid examining the colonialist barbarity baked into his portraits of Tahitian girls. *Correctly* framing these paintings reveals their insidious lenses on the world and on marginalised people, stopping these perspectives from being blindly accommodated into our society at large. In the same way that we can oppose the racist abuser on the Underground, or object to the sexist football coach, we can challenge depraved art and confront its terror head on. Only by doing this can we dilute the damage it does.[15]

———

In the end, the Robert E. Lee monument was placed in storage. First, the bronze sculpture was removed from the marble plinth, leaving it vacant until February 2022. The plinth was then dismantled and taken away, leaving a bare patch of grass. While documentation of this artwork will survive – capturing its wondrous transformation through ballet, music, sport, and graffiti – it's a pity, in a way, that it disappeared without a trace. I think the graffitied plinth should have remained as a remnant of something both sinister and beautiful, as a nod to our troubled history, but also as a stage where new art can be made – where forgotten tales can finally be told.

Insurrection

Sculpted figures of black patina and sparkling gold leaf are arranged along a table containing African rice, cocoa, breadfruit, catfish, frogs, and elegant birds. The imagined gathering depicts historical figures including twelve black scientists and artists, abolitionist Harriet Tubman, the US's first black congresswoman Shirley Johnson, the gay rights campaigner Marsha P. Johnson, and the first black astronaut Robert Henry Lawrence Jr. Bahamian artist Tavares Strachan's *The First Supper (Galaxy Black)* (2023) dramatically mirrors Leonardo da Vinci's *The Last Supper* (1495–98) in a decisive reckoning with our colonial past. Strachan himself is represented at the table as Judas, and the central figure is the emperor Haile Selassie of Ethiopia, who is considered by Rastafarians to be the reincarnation of Jesus Christ.[16]

This stunning spectacle was installed in the courtyard of London's Royal Academy of Arts as part of its recent exhibition *Entangled Pasts, 1768–Now: Art, Colonialism and Change*, which placed the RA's own chequered history in dialogue with contemporary pieces to challenge narratives around colonialism, race, and the legacies of empire. The artist explained:

> This work is speaking to a betrayal. It's speaking to visibility and invisibility – what is seen and unseen. Some of us have been forgotten. The rest of us reminds [*sic*] you of our haunting presence . . . This *First Supper* is a meditation on humankind's struggle for progress.[17]

As a form of counterspeech, Strachan's art practice shines a light on invisible histories, growing out of his research into the first person to reach the North Pole in 1909 – the African

American explorer Matthew Henson, whose achievement went unacknowledged and was mistakenly attributed to his white fellow explorer Robert Peary.

Art like this forces us to confront the dismal history of humanity. It also puts centre stage the lives of people who have been written out of the story of art. It makes us reassess the depraved art that excluded and othered those lives over the centuries, art which still dominates our gallery walls and civic spaces today.

Kara Walker's *Fons Americanus* (2019) similarly targeted the jaded function of our memorials head on. An enormous fountain inspired by the Victoria Memorial in front of Buckingham Palace, Walker's sculpture is a fable of the transatlantic slave trade and the interconnected histories of America, Africa, and Europe. It bursts with symbolic imagery: there is a weeping boy in a shell, a drowning figure in a broken boat, and a majestic black Venus at the very top. 'Queen Vicky' laughs vivaciously while a personification of Melancholy crouches at her feet and sharks encircle the struggling seafarer, a reference to Damien Hirst's *The Physical Impossibility of Death in the Mind of Someone Living*. Walker has played with this title, naming this part of her fountain *The Physical Impossibility of Blackness in the Mind of Someone White*. Water pours down and consumes each character, functioning as a symbol for the Middle Passage, during which around 1.8 million enslaved African men, women, and children perished and were thrown overboard.

This chilling yet beautiful work of art presents a narrative on the origins of the African diaspora, and it implores us to acknowledge forgotten tragedies. It turns the commemorative function of depraved statues on its head and interrogates how we remember history through our public monuments

– monuments which celebrate what was in fact cultural imperialism, physical violence, and egregious injustice.

Art can be used to examine its own tragic past in this way. Recall the racist bric-a-brac of the nineteenth and twentieth centuries – the popular household items and images which expressed controlling stereotypes of black people, from the happily servile Mammy to the hypersexualised Jezebel. We saw how these shameful images – ranging from ceramics and postcards to kitsch swizzle sticks and product branding – entrenched structural injustices and legitimised racial and sexual violence as a form of hate speech.

Today, many of these objects are housed in the Jim Crow Museum of Racist Memorabilia in Michigan, curated and looked after by sociologist David Pilgrim. While these educational spaces are hugely important, artists themselves can also make sense of these troubling pieces by speaking directly back to them.

Betye Saar, for instance, is known for her radical black feminist collage and assemblages, which reverse and resist stereotypes of the black female body. In her arresting *The Liberation of Aunt Jemima* (1972), the American artist took a grotesque Mammy figurine of Aunt Jemima – originally designed as a notepad and pencil holder – and armed her with a rifle and a grenade. Saar made the Mammy into a warrior, empowering her and refusing the controlling image of the happy caregiver. Saar told the *Los Angeles Times*: 'It's like they abolished slavery but they kept Black people in the kitchen as Mammy jars.'[18] Her work speaks to the pernicious banality of these domestic objects – how can a cookie jar or pencil holder showing a large, smiling black woman be so evil? This immorality has sat breeding for decades on kitchen counters and in cupboards, like snakes in the grass. Saar's art boldly shines a spotlight on it and transforms these demeaning caricatures into sites of social protest, echoing Du Bois's call to black artists to make anti-racist art during the Harlem Renaissance.

More recently, South African artist Mary Sibande has turned the figure of the servile black woman from the country's apartheid era into a literal superhero. The life-sized sculpture, named Sophie, is cast from Sibande's own body, and draws on her family history. Appearing in various installations, often dressed in a maid's uniform, Sophie is liberated in an Afrofuturist world, actualising the aspirations of Sibande's ancestors. In fantastical scenarios, Sophie dazzles in bright colours of blue, orange, and red, while she unleashes a wild gang of dogs or commands a chariot drawn by rocking horses.[19]

Counterspeech like this can be an opportunity for healing, too. The Baroque painter – and contemporary of Caravaggio – Artemisia Gentileschi used her craft to exact revenge on her rapist, a friend of her father, and process the violence done to her, but also to subvert the dominating genre of the nude itself. Rather than portraying them as passive and decorative props, Gentileschi dramatically imbued her painted women with agency and power. In her *Susanna and the Elders* (1610) – which shows the biblical story of two men blackmailing Susanna with defamation if she doesn't have sex with them – Artemisia painted the moment the elders approach Susanna while she bathes. Rather than casting this moment as charged with erotic desire, which so many male artists had done before her, Gentileschi painted Susanna as unambiguously fearful, furrowing her brow and awkwardly wrenching herself away from the clutches of the leering men. There are no rape myths here.

By presenting narratives from the victim's perspective, Gentileschi in the seventeenth century paved the way for foregrounding women's experience in the story of art. More recently, the objectifying and racialised nude genre has been challenged by artists through the lens of black femininity. Faith Ringgold's early series of thangkas (oil paintings on cotton and silk) called *Slave Rape* (1972) portray naked enslaved black women – modelled on Ringgold and her daughters – in verdant surroundings confronting their owners. In #3 of the series, called *Fight to Save Your Life*, an enslaved woman – who is pregnant – stands looking directly out at us, holding her belly with one hand and an axe in the other. In these dynamic images, which echo Saar's armoured warriors, Ringgold sought to understand the lives of the women subjected to the horrors of the slave trade: she 'metaphorically travels back in time to alter the future, arming her ancestors so that they might defend themselves against male sexual aggression', writes art historian Lisa Farrington.[20]

Immoral artists of the past have been similarly confronted by contemporary artworks. The work of Rosanna Raymond – a New Zealand-born artist of Samoan and Pākehā descent – interrogates the 'dusky maiden' stereotype enjoyed by Gauguin: the romantic colonialist image of the doe-eyed, dark-skinned, sexually available maiden or 'Eve'. Her practice draws on her experience as a catwalk model in Europe: '*Papapalagi* (foreigners) have pretty fixed ideas about women . . . no matter what people still labeled me as exotic.'[21] Raymond sought to rework this dusky maiden trope in her *Full Tusk Maiden* (1999), a digitally enhanced monochrome photograph of Raymond adorned with Polynesian symbols of strength such as boar tusks. With legs spread wide and her hands on her hips, she assumes the Māori *haka* stance, signifying defiance. She stares directly out at the viewer, her sharp angles and angry eyes challenging the ideas of gentle beauty and sweetness expressed by eighteenth-century European travellers about Polynesian girls.[22] *Full Tusk Maiden* powerfully invokes Polynesian traditions, which are replete with strong female figures, fighters, and goddesses, in the face of colonial aggression.

Returning to the responsibility of the curator, these new stories and forgotten tragedies must be given a platform. Institutions are now asking difficult and important questions about artists who have formed the cornerstones of both Western and Eastern canons, addressing issues of gender, race, and colonialism in museums, and reassessing artists' legacies. This practice of 'curatorial activism', championed by curator Maura Reilly, can counteract the unjust narratives upheld by depraved art while also addressing inequality in the artworld, which still rages today:

> Despite decades of postcolonial, feminist, anti-racist, and queer activism and theorizing, the art world continues to exclude 'Other' artists – those who are women, of color, and LGBTQ. Discrimination against these artists invades every aspect of the art world, from gallery representation, auction-price differentials, and press coverage to inclusion in permanent collections and solo exhibition programs.[23]

The curator must employ 'strategies of resistance' to the Eurocentric male canon, which has been responsible for the majority of known immoral art. Curators can address exclusion in the canon by rewriting it – by including those artists who have been prevented from defining this very canon. For instance, London's National Gallery in 2020 dedicated a major exhibition to Artemisia Gentileschi – its first to centre on a woman artist in its 196-year history.

In contrast to this revisionist approach, curators can produce new canons based on different areas like race, geography, gender, and sexual orientation. The artworld can go further and critique the notion of 'canon' itself with an upheaval of traditional curatorial techniques, such as abandoning linear historical narratives and presenting art ahistorically and multi-vocally by upending nation- and period-based categories.[24]

These strategies of resistance go hand-in-hand with art education. Through lectures and classes, young artists and curators are seeking to destabilise the canonical history of art. Curator Bolanle Tajudeen's Black Blossoms School of Art and Culture, for instance, is a UK-based curatorial platform and online school which aims to disrupt the Eurocentric artworld through creative and decolonised art education, by supporting and showcasing black women artists. An art and teaching collective I've had the privilege to contribute to – Luisa-Maria Mac-Cormack, Lucy McGeown, and Frances Stanfield's London Drawing Group – creates conversations and raises awareness of women's place in art history, particularly critiquing the historic aesthetic treatment and perception of oppressed peoples. As well as establishing much-needed communities for marginalised artists, curators, and educators, these platforms are quickly revolutionising the story of art as we know it.

This redemptive curation and fearless reckoning with depraved art and artists is part and parcel of the need for wider institutional reform. Rather than abandoning galleries and committing immoral artists to the flames, we must urge artworld institutions to take responsibility in changing their systems and suppressing the environments where predatory behaviour and bigotry thrive in the first place – to actually uphold artists' accountability.[25] Doing this well would put less pressure on approaches like public 'cancel culture' to deliver results.

Artistic counterspeech doesn't only apply to our civic spaces and galleries. To combat the dangers that we saw in depraved videogames, game designers have started to create games which generate counter-stereotypes to challenge gamers' prejudices and biases. Recent studies suggest that by employing fairer representation and storylines that debunk racist and sexist myths, designers can craft digital worlds of escapism which are nonetheless better for us in reality.[26]

There is now a plethora of feminist games which feature powerful female protagonists like the hunter Aloy in *Horizon Zero Dawn* (2017). *Tomb Raider* has now been revamped, sporting a stronger, tougher Lara Croft with a waist that could feasibly contain organs. *Treachery in Beatdown City* (2020) was heralded as the 'most relevant, antiracist videogame of 2020' by the *LA Times*. Portraying a city on the edge of chaos after the president is kidnapped, the humorous game includes entitled white people and harassing police officers, and players 'get to punch racists'.[27] *Relooted* (2025) is an upcoming Afrofuturist heist game, which allows you to repatriate African cultural artefacts by looting Western museums.

A New Iconoclasm

Aesthetic strategies that speak back to immoral art can be a way of taming our depraved Hydra, and not simply slaughtering it. But this counterspeech can do more than simply reject an artwork's depravity. We can also in some way *destroy* it.

We've learned that philosophers of art generally agree that an artwork's historical origin is essential to its meaning and identity. Recall that an artwork is more than its mere aesthetic forms: there's more to a painting than oil on a canvas, more to a novel than printed words. Artworks do not drop out of the sky – they are created by people situated within historical events, movements, and styles. These factors are built into their very identity.[28]

We've also seen how an artwork's meaning can be *disarmed* – the Robert E. Lee monument changed in meaning; it became a protest artwork. And rather than being restored to its original position or hidden from public view, the Colston statue has now been placed on its side at the public M Shed museum in Bristol, still covered in red graffiti. This horizontal placement has permanently disarmed its subordinating force.

If a work of art's original meaning is integral to its identity, then removing this meaning compromises that work's identity. We still have the same lump of bronze, but the original work of art as we knew it has ceased to exist. Like the Robert E. Lee monument, the Colston statue can now be considered a *new* protest piece: its extensive manipulation by protesters has changed it into something else entirely – something worth preserving. The original has been metaphysically destroyed without total material destruction.[29]

Artistic counterspeech, then, is not just reactive but transformative. In creating, we destroy; in destroying, we create.*

---

* Writing of the solution to the French Revolution dilemma – between preserving heritage and destroying pre-revolution era art which they saw as false – academic Stanley Idzerda observed: 'they created a public institution called a "museum"; immure a political symbol in a museum and it becomes merely art—iconoclasm is thus achieved without destruction.' (Stanley J. Idzerda, 'Iconoclasm during the French Revolution', *The American Historical Review*, 60/1 (1954), pp. 13–26, at p. 26.)

The activist counternarratives and curatorial strategies which constitute this metaphysical iconoclasm should be protected and celebrated, instead of being branded as 'violent', taken to signal civil unrest, or mocked as overly sensitive or stubbornly divisive. In a time when ethical curation is under attack, the metaphysical iconoclasts must build these vital steps towards cultural enlightenment.

Exposing depraved art is a necessary bridge towards moral and artistic progress, and it is my hope that these sites of horror will eventually be replaced by ones of joy, peace, and dignity. I envision an artworld where the subjugated are finally illuminated, where charges of obscenity derive from a robust moral system untainted by prejudice, where women can bleed and celebrate their lust free from negative judgement, and where queer love is championed. Where art can help save the planet without harming it in the process, and where we can openly confront ancient and Renaissance beauty in all its pernicious violence. Where we treat artists not as heavenly saints but as earthly people made of flesh and blood.

Depraved art forms the gruesome foundation of art history, and it should not be forgotten. We must not slaughter our Hydra, but we do have a duty to return its terrible gaze so that we can inoculate ourselves against its venom. In 1765, the French philosopher Denis Diderot warned against art (particularly religious art) that distorts or masks the truth: 'My friend, if we prefer the truth to the fine arts, let us pray God for the iconoclasts.'[30] In response, I say that to know – and love – truth, we must know and grapple with art, especially its abominations. And so, we must instead pray for the metaphysical iconoclasts.

———

Growing up, Titian was one of my favourite artists. There was something about the radiant worlds he envisioned on the canvas that spoke to me. His pastoral scenes glow, almost move, with such resplendent beauty that they'd seduce me into an enchanted realm of classical myths and divine stories, where beautiful young women inhabit verdant landscapes. But as a child, I wasn't aware that what I was looking at was in fact a poisoned chalice. Titian's paintings like *Rape of Europa* contribute to a broader system that places me lower down on a social hierarchy; one that tells me that my natural body is obscene, but that paradoxically also tells me that my role in this life is to always be pretty and quiet – to never age, to never step out of line.

This is how depraved art works. It's a pervasive toxin that we ingest, sometimes without realising; a kind of hate speech that we don't always hear or notice. As a student, I was so enraptured by painted Renaissance rape myths and ancient nudes that I ended up misunderstanding what rape was and what it could look like until well into my twenties. These beautiful artworks whispered to me that my body and sexuality were something shameful and to be subdued at all costs. They form part of a dominating historical aesthetic that told me that pale skin like mine is to be exalted and valued above the darker skin of some of my friends and loved ones.

If I'm brutally honest, I took some strange pleasure as a teenager seeing girls that looked like idealised versions of myself immortalised in paint by illustrious artists – the same misplaced pleasure I felt when grown men would cat-call me in the street when I was a child. I took pleasure in these things because I was socialised to think that this was my purpose – to be an ornament and to pander to an invisible yet pervasive white, patriarchal gaze. And so, the reason I disliked Paul Gauguin when I was a teen was simply because he'd badly upset Vincent van Gogh while they were housemates, rather than because I had any suspicion about the dark-skinned girls in his paintings. I just didn't realise – I wasn't looking closely enough.

In this book I've tried to subvert these naive sentiments, harnessing the brilliant work of some of my favourite philosophers, mentors, and colleagues – as well as my own theories – to show that depraved art is a many-headed monster that nevertheless needs to be tamed, not slain. A Hydra of five screeching heads, art can be obscene, incite and arouse criminality, constitute oppression, and have malevolent and cruel origins. But I've argued – and hopefully persuaded you – that the nature of this beast is not entirely what meets the eye. Much of the art we often jump to condemn as depraved is in fact innocent, and in such cases, we must turn our attention inwards and examine our own social mores. Sometimes it's our own accusations of obscenity or criminality that betray the true corruption.

In fact, the genuinely volatile works of art are also often the most charming – oppressive art can be alarmingly beautiful even as it conveys hatred. And while some depraved artworks can fan malignant embers in our hearts, they can still afford us knowledge about the human condition. Provenance is central to all of this: artworks don't appear out of nowhere, they are offered up to us by real, fallible people, and produced and communicated to us in imperfect ways. When we look at an artwork, we see the world through its creator's eyes; it's our choice whether we wish to share their vision.

———

When the Marquis de Sade penned that diabolical tale in his opulent prison cell, he unleashed something both hideous and mesmerising. Though it was utterly obscene, scholars and activists saw in his work – and still do – its value for humanity. A window into the most heinous psyche and a memoir of his own atrocities amid a tumultuous time, Sade's *The 120 Days of Sodom* was a radical step in the story of dangerous art. Simone de Beauvoir was right to defend it from annihilation.

But while we ride out the waves of this ancient story, we must stay grounded: depraved art is not going away, but we can learn to co-exist with it in a way that prevents its poison from being ingested. To do this, we need the metaphysical iconoclasts, as well as to draw wisdom from the humanities and social sciences. Without this activism and these academic disciplines, we will surely be blinded and defeated in the face of such adversity. Let us ensure that we are well equipped to defang our Hydra.

Titian is still one of my favourite artists, but I've now learnt to look at his work more closely – more honestly. Sade's oeuvre, including *The 120 Days of Sodom*, should, I think, continue to be mined for emancipatory material by theorists and artists, though my own copy may end up gathering dust on the shelf. And I'm afraid I still dislike Gauguin's art – the violence lurking within his portraits constitutes an ugliness which, to my mind, is not absolved by the virtues of his craft.

It was not my aim in this book to encourage you to abandon your favourite artists or burn your immoral books, but instead to confront their depravity head on – not shying away from their moral flaws but scrutinising the insights they give us into the darkest corners of the human condition. Finally, I hope to have shown how art is not simply inert decoration, something pleasant to look at or listen to as we go about our daily lives. Art shapes our very reality – it moulds minds and opens and closes doors for those who are oppressed. Aesthetics and ethics are entwined from the very beginning, for art-making itself is an ethical pursuit. The aesthetic pervades our moral and social world like air, and we must learn not to pollute it. In the words of the novelist Toni Morrison, all art, 'sensitive as a tuning fork, is an unblinking witness to the light and shade of the world we live in'.[31]

ENDNOTES

INTRODUCTION

1　Marquis de Sade, *120 Days of Sodom* [1904], in *The 120 Days of Sodom, and Other Writings* (New York: Grove Press, 1966), p. 184.

2　A. Mahon, *The Marquis de Sade and the Avant-Garde* (Princeton: Princeton University Press, 2020), p. 12.

3　Larry Wolff, 'Child Pornography and the Marquis de Sade', in *Paolina's Innocence: Child Abuse in Casanova's Venice* (Stanford: Stanford University Press, 2012), p. 186. Another translation is: 'I'm being taken for a werewolf of these parts', from: https://www.smithsonianmag.com/history/who-was-marquis-de-sade-180953980 [accessed April 2024].

4　Maurice Lever, *Sade: A Biography* (Librairie Arthème Fayard, 1993), p. 350.

5　https://www.smithsonianmag.com/history/who-was-marquis-de-sade-180953980/?all

6　Mahon 2020, pp. 6–7.

7　Iwan Bloch, *Marquis de Sade's Anthropologia Sexualis of 600 Perversions, 120 Days of Sodom or the School for Libertinage, and the Sex Life of the French Age of Debauchery, from Private Archives of the French Government* (New York: Falstaff Press, 1934), p. iii.

8　Georges Bataille, *Literature and Evil* [1957] (New York: Marion Boyars, 1997), p. 121.

9　https://www.independent.co.uk/news/world/europe/marquis-de-sade-rebel-pervert-rapist-hero-9862270.html [accessed December 2023].

10　https://www.edinburghnews.scotsman.com/whats-on/arts-and-entertainment/ben-shapiro-what-the-right-wing-commentator-said-about-cardi-bs-song-wap-and-why-hes-being-ridiculed-online-2939073 [accessed May 2023].

11 https://www.vanityfair.com/hollywood/2019/10/joker-aurora-shoot-ing-rumor [accessed February 2022].

12 For news stories on these respective events, see: https://www.theguardian.com/world/2020/sep/10/paris-museum-refuses-en-try-woman-low-cut-dress-musee-dorsay and https://www.theart-newspaper.com/2008/10/01/muslim-woman-questioned-for-wear-ing-veil-in-venetian-museum [accessed January 2022].

13 Plato, *Plato in Twelve Volumes* [370 BCE], trans. Harold N. Fowler (Cambridge, MA: Harvard University Press; London: William Heinemann Ltd, 1925), vol. 9, from: https://www.perseus.tufts.edu/hopper/text?doc=Perseus%3Atext%3A1999.01.0174%3Atext%3D-Phaedrus%3Asection%3D265e [accessed April 2023].

14 Jacobellis v. Ohio, 378 US 184 (1964).

15 Susan Wolf, 'Moral saints', *The Journal of Philosophy*, 79/8 (1982), pp. 419–39.

16 However, see Paulo Freire's *Pedagogy of the Oppressed* [1968] (New York: Penguin Classics, 2017), for the idea that severe powerlessness in the oppressed can sometimes lead to 'internalised oppression', where the oppressed become so indoctrinated by the mindsets of their oppressors that they believe their unfair or brutal treatment is permissible or even natural.

17 See A. Avramidou and D. Demetriou (eds), *Approaching the Ancient Artifact: Representation, Narrative, and Function* (Berlin and Boston: Walter de Gruyter GmbH, 2014), p. 43.

1 OBSCENITY

1 Nicholas Conard, 'Palaeolithic ivory sculptures from southwestern Germany and the origins of figurative art', *Nature*, 426 (2003) pp. 830–32, https://doi.org/10.1038/nature02186; and Nicholas J. Conard, Maria Malina and Susanne C. Münzel, 'New flutes document the earliest musical tradition in southwestern Germany', *Nature*, 460/7256 (2009), pp. 737–40.

2 Nicholas Conard, 'A female figurine from the basal Aurignacian of Hohle Fels Cave in southwestern Germany', *Nature*, 459 (2009), pp. 248–52, https://doi.org/10.1038/nature07995.

3 The Economist, 'Paleolithic Pornography Unveiled: Smut Carved from a Mammoth Tusk', *The Economist*, 14 May 2009, http://www.economist.com/node/13643965.

4 The Sun, 'The World's First Page 3 Girl', *The Sun* (2009). Reference found in April Nowell and Melanie L. Chang, 'Science, Media, and

Interpretations of Upper Paleolithic Figurines', *American Anthropologist*, 116/3 (2014), pp. 562–77, at p. 563.

5 Paul Mellars, 'Origins of the Female Image', *Nature*, 459/7244 (2009), pp. 176–7.

6 Andrew Curry, 'The Earliest Pornography?', *ScienceNow*, 13 May 2009, http://news.sciencemag.org/paleontology/2009/05/earliest-pornography [accessed March 2023].

7 Lewis Page, 'Archaeologists Unearth Oldest Known 3D Pornography', *The Register*, 15 May 2009, www.theregister.com/2009/05/15/german_stone_age_3d_smut_figurine [accessed 9 June 2023].

8 Camilla Power, 'Women in prehistoric art', in G. Berghaus (ed.), *New Perspectives on Prehistoric Art* (Westport, CT and London: Praeger, 2004), pp. 75–103.

9 Paul S. C. Taçon, Sally K. May, Ronald Lamilami et al., 'Maliwawa figures—a previously undescribed Arnhem Land rock art style', *Australian Archaeology*, 86/3 (2020), pp. 208–25.

10 See Sylvia Tamale, 'Eroticism, sensuality and "women's secrets" among the Baganda', *Feminist Africa*, 5/9–36 (2005); and Workineh Kelbessa, 'Africa and the Philosophy of Sexuality', *The Palgrave Handbook of African Philosophy* (London and New York: Palgrave Macmillan, 2017), pp. 371–89.

11 Sigmund Freud, *Civilization and Its Discontents*, Standard Edition, vol. 21 (London: Hogarth Press and the Institute of Psycho-Analysis, 1961), p. 83.

12 Z. Bahrani, *Women of Babylon: Gender and Representation in Mesopotamia* (Abingdon, Oxfordshire: Routledge, 2001), p. 45. This translation seems to have been influenced by Assyriologist Thorkild Jacobsen's *The Harps that once – : Sumerian poetry in translation* (New Haven: Yale University Press, 1987), p. 96. Bahrani appears to replace 'private parts' with 'vulva'.

13 Bahrani 2001, pp. 44–5.

14 Joan Goodnick Westenholz, 'Love lyrics from the ancient Near East', in Jack Sasson et al. (eds), *Civilisations of the Ancient Near East* (New York: Charles Scribner's Sons, 1995), pp. 2471–84.

15 https://aeon.co/essays/why-are-men-seemingly-always-naked-in-ancient-greek-art [accessed May 2023].

16 Mary Beard, *Pompeii: The Life of a Roman Town* (London: Profile Books, 2008), p. 233.

17 Fabrizio Antonelli, John Pollini, and Stefano Cancelliere, 'A short note on the archaeometric study of two sculptures in the Gabinetto Segreto of Naples National Archeological Museum: the "Pan and the

She-Goat" group and the "Bikini Venus"', *Archaeological and Anthropological Sciences*, 9 (2017), pp. 685–91, at p. 686.

18 G. R. Stone, 'Origins of obscenity', *New York University Review of Law & Social Change*, 31/4 (2007), pp. 711–32, at p. 711.

19 Stone 2007, p. 714.

20 G. E. Thiessen, 'Searching for God: theology, imagination, beauty and the arts', *Acta Theologica*, 40 (2020), Suppl. 29, pp. 28–36. For a study into the origins of this hostility towards the work, see Patrick Preston, 'The Critical Reception of Michelangelo's "The Last Judgement": The Theological Context', *Reformation & Renaissance Review*, 7/2–3 (2005), pp. 337–46.

21 Stone 2007, p. 728.

22 George Ryley Scott, *'Into Whose Hands': An Examination of Obscene Libel in Its Legal, Sociological and Literary Aspects* (London: Gerald G. Swan, 1945), p. 145 (quoted in Stone 2007, p. 729).

23 Partha Mitter, *Much Maligned Monsters: A History of European Reactions to Indian Art* (Chicago: University of Chicago Press, 1992), pp. 8–12.

24 Mitter 1992, p. 21.

25 Mitter 1992, p. 75.

26 Ibid.

27 T. S. Burt, 'Notice of an Inscription on a Slab discovered in February 1838, by Capt. T. S. Burt, Bengal Engineers, in Bundelkhund, near Chhatarpur—By the Editors', *Journal of the Asiatic Society of Bengal*, 8/87 (1839), pp. 159–84, at p. 163, https://archive.org/details/dli.calcutta.00006/page/162/mode/2up.

28 M. Kittoe, 'Account of a Journey from Calcutta via Cuttack and Pooree to Sumbulpur, and from thence to Mednipur through the Forests of Orissa', *Journal of the Asiatic Society of Bengal*, 8/89 (1839), pp. 367–84, at p. 375.

29 See Anthony Weir and James Jerman, *Images of Lust: Sexual Carvings on Medieval Churches* [1986] (Abingdon, Oxfordshire: Routledge, 2016).

30 Georgia Rhoades, 'Decoding the Sheela-Na-Gig', *Feminist Formations*, 22/2 (2010), pp. 167–94, at p. 181.

31 https://medium.com/lessons-from-history/turin-erotic-papyrus-the-worlds-first-men-playboy-850a42ab85c5 [accessed May 2023]

32 Ted Gioia, *Love Songs: The Hidden History* (Oxford: Oxford University Press, 2015), p. 20.

33 Antonelli et al. 2017, p. 686; S. De Caro, *Il gabinetto segreto del museo archeologico nazionale di napoli* (Naples: Electa Napoli, 2000), p. 12. The collection finally re-opened in 2000 after several closures. For a

critique of what they call this 'censorship myth', see Kate Fisher and Rebecca Langlands, 'The Censorship Myth and the Secret Museum', in Shelley Hales and Joanna Paul (eds), *Pompeii in the Public Imagination from Its Rediscovery to Today* (Oxford: Oxford University Press, 2011), pp. 301–15.

34 John R. Clarke, 'Before Pornography: Sexual Representation in Ancient Roman Visual Culture', in Hans Maes (ed.), *Pornographic Art and the Aesthetics of Pornography* (London and New York: Palgrave Macmillan, 2013), pp. 141–61, at p. 144.

35 Louise Boyd, 'Sex, Art and Museums: On the Changing Institutional Censorship of Shunga', in Roisin Kennedy (ed.), *Censoring Art: Silencing the Artwork* (London: Bloomsbury Publishing, 2018), pp. 71–86.

36 http://www.newschinamag.com/newschina/articleDetail.do?article_id=1391 [accessed February 2025].

37 See https://time.com/3765841/effie-gray/ [accessed December 2025].

38 Diana Souhami, *The Trials of Radclyffe Hall* (New York: Doubleday, 1999), pp. 199–200.

39 Vladimir Nabokov, 'On a Book Entitled Lolita', in *Lolita* (London: Weidenfeld & Nicolson, 1955), p. 304.

40 https://www.theguardian.com/books/2023/sep/29/graham-greene-was-ready-to-go-to-jail-for-lolita-says-vera-nabokov-diary [accessed June 2023].

41 Nabokov 1955, p. 305.

42 Claus Schatz-Jakobsen, 'The case against Lady Chatterley's Lover: The 1959 Obscene Publications Act as a New Critical subtext', in Erik Erlanson, Jon Helgason, Peter Henning, and Linnéa Lindsköld (eds), *Forbidden Literature* (Lund: Nordic Academic Press), p. 49.

43 https://www.legislation.gov.uk/ukpga/Eliz2/7-8/66/section/4 [accessed June 2023].

44 https://www.theguardian.com/books/2010/oct/22/dh-lawrence-lady-chatterley-trial [accessed June 2023].

45 Ben Yagoda, 'Trial and Eros: When Lady Chatterley's Lover Ran Afoul of Britain's 1959 Obscenity Law, the Resulting Case Had a Cast Worthy of P. G. Wodehouse', *The American Scholar*, 79/4 (2010), pp. 93–101, at p. 101.

46 http://news.bbc.co.uk/1/hi/entertainment/455902.stm [accessed August 2023].

47 https://archive.nytimes.com/www.nytimes.com/library/arts/110299brooklyn-museum.html?Partner=AOL#:~:text=O-fili%2C%20a%20Roman%20Catholic%20of,endorsement%20by%20them%20of%20religion.%22 [accessed 9 December 2025].

48 Clarke 2013, p. 141.

49 Joel Feinberg, 'Obscenity as Pornography', *The Moral Limits of the Criminal Law: Volume 2: Offense to Others* (New York, 1988; online edn, Oxford Academic, 2006), p. 127, https://doi.org/10.1093/0195052153.003.0005. As Feinberg argues, this is precisely what the US Supreme Court does.

50 https://www.everycrsreport.com/reports/95-804.html#_Toc232392755 [accessed June 2023].

51 Matthew Kieran, 'On Obscenity: The Thrill and Repulsion of the Morally Prohibited', *Philosophy and Phenomenological Research*, 64/1 (2002), pp. 31–55, at p. 35.

52 Anthony Weir and James Jerman, *Images of Lust: Sexual Carvings on Medieval Churches* [1986] (Abingdon, Oxfordshire: Routledge, 2016), p. 11.

53 Kieran 2002, p. 35.

54 Kieran 2002, pp. 41–3.

55 Kieran 2002, p. 46.

56 Berys Gaut, 'The Merited Response Argument', in *Art, Emotion and Ethics* (Oxford: Oxford University Press, 2007). Gaut does offer more arguments in support of this conclusion, which may be more convincing.

57 'Immoralists' like Eaton and Kieran reject this conclusion – they hold that an artwork's immorality can actually be an aesthetic merit. For an objection to Gaut's argument see A. W. Eaton, 'Robust Immoralism', *Journal of Aesthetics and Art Criticism*, 70/3 (2012), pp. 281–92.

58 Peter Webb, *The Erotic Arts* (London: Secker & Warburg, 1975), p. 2. See also Alyce Mahon, *Eroticism and Art* (Oxford: Oxford University Press, 2005), p. 14.

59 Steven Marcus, *The Other Victorians: A Study of Sexuality and Pornography in Mid-Nineteenth-Century England* (New York: Basic Books, 1964), p. 281.

60 See for example Christy Mag Uidhir, 'Why Pornography Can't Be Art', *Philosophy and Literature*, 33 (2009), pp. 193–203; and Jerrold Levinson, 'Erotic Art and Pornographic Pictures', *Philosophy and Literature* 29 (2005), pp. 228–40. For a persuasive critique of both of these arguments see Hans Maes, 'Drawing the line: Art versus pornography', *Philosophy Compass*, 6/6 (2011), pp. 385–97.

61 Maes 2011, p. 386.

62 Ibid. Philosopher A. W. Eaton also describes this sentiment: '[according to a] common way of thinking, pornography is by contrast dirty, low, and base: it speaks to and elicits the sexual animal in us'. From '"A Lady on the Street but a Freak in the Bed": On the Distinction between Erotic Art and Pornography', *The British Journal of Aesthetics*,

58/4 (2018), pp. 469–88, at p. 469.

63 See Maes 2011, p. 391, for alternatives.

64 See for example, Matthew Kieran, 'Pornographic Art', *Philosophy and Literature*, 25 (2001), pp. 31–45.

65 Eaton 2018, pp. 477–87.

66 Bahrani 2001, p. 43.

67 Bahrani 2001, pp. 76–9.

68 Kenneth Clark, *The Nude: A Study of Ideal Art* (London: John Murray, 1956), p. 3.

69 Bahrani 2001, p. 73. See also Edith Hall, *Inventing the Barbarian Greek Self-Definition through Tragedy* (Oxford: Oxford University Press, 1989).

70 Plato, *Epinomis*, 987*d* [n.d.], accessed at https://www.perseus.tufts.edu/hopper/text?doc=Perseus%3Atext%3A1999.01.0180%3Atext%3DEpin.%3Asection%3D987e [accessed August 2023]. See also Carol Dougherty and Leslie Kurke (eds), *The Cultures within Greek Culture: Contact, Conflict, Collaboration* (Cambridge: Cambridge University Press, 2003), p. 5.

71 Nowell and Chang 2014, p. 571.

72 Bahrani 2001, p. 86.

73 Antonelli et al. 2017, p. 686.

74 Clarke 2013, p. 145.

75 See: https://www.washingtonpost.com/archive/lifestyle/1990/05/03/the-childrens-portraits-innocence-or-pornography/34fa3716-3c0d-4a83-9c23-cc16291274d3/ [accessed December 2023].

76 From interview with filmmakers Fenton Bailey and Randy Barbado, 'Seeing Robert Mapplethorpe's idea of perfection in a new retrospective', *PBS NewsHour*, https://www.youtube.com/watch?v=XAZBdRuggno [accessed August 2025].

77 https://www.c-span.org/clip/senate-proceeding/user-clip-look-at-the-pictures/4661858 [accessed July 2024].

78 Cited in Maureen Dowd, 'Jesse Helms Takes No-Lose Position on Art', *New York Times*, 28 July 1989. Reference accessed in Richard Meyer's 'Mapplethorpe's living room: Photography and the furnishing of desire', *Art History*, 24/2 (2001), pp. 292–311.

79 https://www.washingtonpost.com/entertainment/museums/robert-mapplethorpe-was-one-of-the-most-controversial-artist-of-the-80s-now-he-looks-entirely-innocent/2019/01/24/487c1562-1f50-11e9-9145-3f74070bbdb9_story.html [accessed April 2023].

80 https://www.theguardian.com/world/2010/mar/02/south-african-minister-lesbian-exhibition [accessed July 2025].

depraved

81 https://edition.cnn.com/style/article/zanele-muholi-lgbt-photographer [accessed December 2025].

82 https://www.glamour.com/story/rokudenashiko-japanese-artist-arrested-for-vagina-art [accessed December 2025].

83 Shailini Vora, 'The realities of period poverty: how homelessness shapes women's lived experiences of menstruation', *The Palgrave Handbook of Critical Menstruation Studies* (London and New York: Palgrave Macmillan, 2020), pp. 31–4, at p. 33.

84 Samantha Ryan, Jane M. Ussher, and Alexandra Hawkey, 'Mapping the abject: Women's embodied experiences of premenstrual body dissatisfaction through body-mapping', *Feminism & Psychology*, 32/2 (2022), pp. 199–223, at p. 201.

85 https://www.businessinsider.com/menstrual-discs-better-for-heavy-periods-than-tampons-pads-study-2023-8 [accessed December 2025].

86 Bendt Alster, 'Marriage and Love in the Sumerian Love Songs', pp. 15–27, in M. E. Cohen, D. C. Snell, and D. B. Weisberg (eds), *The Tablet and the Scroll: Near Eastern Studies in Honor of William W. Hallo* (Bethesda, MD: CDL Press, 1993), p. 20 (quoted in Bahrani 2001, p. 53). Bahrani has slightly edited the Alster translation in her version, and both seem to rely partially on earlier translations; for example S. N. Kramer, 'BM 88318: The Ascension of Dumuzi to Heaven', *Recueil de travaux de l'association des études de Proche-Orient Ancient*, vol. 2, Montreal, pp. 5–9.

87 https://www.rollingstone.com/music/music-news/wet-ass-pussy-ben-shapiro-conservative-backlash-1042491/ [accessed May 2023].

88 Ibid.

89 https://www.gq-magazine.co.uk/culture/article/megan-thee-stallion-interview-2020 [accessed July 2025].

2 CRIMINALITY

1 Robert Germany, *Mimetic Contagion: Art and Artifice in Terence's Eunuch* (Oxford: Oxford University Press, 2016), p. 5.

2 Germany 2016, p. 32.

3 See for example D. Konstan, 'Love in Terence's Eunuch: The Origins of Erotic Subjectivity', *American Journal of Philosophy*, 107/3 (1986); and L. Pearson-Smith, 'Audience Response to Rape: Chaerea in Terence's Eunuchus', *Helios*, 21/1 (1994). But see Katerina Philippides, 'Terence's "Eunuchus": Elements of the Marriage Ritual in the Rape Scene', *Mnemosyne* (1995), pp. 272–84, who appears to claim that the

    rape is somewhat mitigated because it happens in the context of a marriage or engagement. Obviously I disagree with this – rape is rape, regardless of the relationship between the two people involved.

4 Augustine of Hippo, *City of God* [426 CE], ch. 7, https://catholiclibrary.org/library/view?docId=Synchronized-EN/Augustine.CityofGod.en.html&chunk.id=00000093 [accessed August 2023].

5 Germany 2016, p. 45.

6 Nigel Spivey, *Greek Sculpture* (Cambridge: Cambridge University Press, 2013), p. 208.

7 Spivey 2013, p. 209.

8 Charles FitzRoy, *The Rape of Europa: The Intriguing History of Titian's Masterpiece* (London: Bloomsbury Publishing, 2015), p. 4.

9 http://news.bbc.co.uk/1/hi/magazine/4277707.stm [accessed September 2023].

10 Plato, *Republic* (Book III: 398*e*) [*c.* 375 BCE], ed. H. D. P. Lee (London: Penguin Classics, 2003), p. 94.

11 J. Otterbeck and A. Ackfeldt, 'Music and Islam', *Contemporary Islam*, 6/3 (2012), pp. 227–33, at p. 231, https://doi.org/10.1007/s11562-012-0220-0 [accessed September 2023].

12 J. Robson, 'Tracts on Listening to Music', in *Oriental Translation Fund* (London: The Royal Asiatic Society, 1938), vol. 34, p. 27 (quoted in Otterbeck and Ackfeldt 2012, p. 231).

13 S. J. Park, 'Danger of Sound: Mozi's Criticism of Confucian Ritual Music', *The Philosophical Forum*, 51/1 (2020), pp. 49–65, at p. 58.

14 See Anna Maria Matziorinis and Stefan Koelsch, 'The promise of music therapy for Alzheimer's disease: A review.' *Annals of the New York Academy of Sciences*, 1516/1 (2022), pp. 11–17; and E. Garza-Villarreal, A. Wilson., L. Vase et al., 'Music reduces pain and increases functional mobility in fibromyalgia', *Frontiers in Psychology*, 5 (2014), https://doi.org/10.3389/fpsyg.2014.00090, retrieved from https://www.ncbi.nlm.nih.gov/pmc/articles/PMC3920463/ [accessed October 2023].

15 L. Jäncke, 'Music, memory and emotion', *Journal of Biology*, 7/6 (2008), p. 21, https://doi.org/10.1186/jbiol82, retrieved from https://www.ncbi.nlm.nih.gov/pmc/articles/PMC2776393/ [accessed September 2023].

16 See https://www.health.harvard.edu/staying-healthy/music-and-health and https://www.pfizer.com/news/articles/why_and_how_music_moves_us [accessed September 2023].

17 The subtitle here is also the name of metal band Cradle of Filth's third demo, released in 1992.

18 Neil Strauss, 'A Bogey Band to Scare Parents With', *New York Times*,

17 May 1997, https://www.nytimes.com/1997/05/17/arts/a-bogey-band-to-scare-parents-with.html [accessed October 2023].

19 S. Jones (ed.), *Pop Music and the Press* (Philadelphia: Temple University Press, 2002), p. 126.

20 James Sterngold, 'Terror in Littleton: The Culture; Rock concerts are cancelled', *New York Times*, 29 April 1999, https://www.nytimes.com/1999/04/29/us/terror-in-littleton-the-culture-rock-concerts-are-cancelled.html [accessed October 2023].

21 Jamie Crawford (dir.), *Trainwreck: Woodstock '99* [Episode 2] (Netflix, 2022).

22 Ibid.

23 Torstein Grude (dir.), *Satan rir Media* (Norwegian documentary, 1998), https://www.youtube.com/watch?v=J6q8Jwuu1a8 [accessed March 2024].

24 Michael Moynihan and Didrik Søderlind, *Lords of Chaos: The Bloody Rise of the Satanic Metal Underground* (Port Townsend, WA: Feral House, 2003), p. 141.

25 https://rateyourmusic.com/list/HelloInquisitor/black-metal-bands-and-their-politics/ [accessed June 2023]. For more on Dead's performances see Joshua Carey, 'Pure fucking art: Self-harm and performance art in Per "Dead" Ohlin's musical legacy', *Metal Music Studies*, 9/1 (2023), pp. 101–18.

26 'Nattefrost interview (full length)', *Blackhearts*, https://www.youtube.com/watch?v=JjvK-H7FdrQ&t=616s [accessed July 2025].

27 https://www.independent.co.uk/tech/rape-day-valve-statement-steam-video-game-sexual-assault-a8811771.html [accessed November 2023].

28 https://rawg.io/games/rape-day [accessed November 2023].

29 https://steamcommunity.com/games/593110/announcements/detail/1808664240304050758 [accessed November 2023].

30 https://www.polygon.com/2019/3/4/18249916/rape-day-steam-valve [accessed November 2023].

31 The belief that much pornography is fictional is supported by studies which show that this mindset is prominent among young people; see, for example, M. Coy, L. Kelly, F. Elvines et al., '"Sex without consent, I suppose that is rape": How young people in England understand sexual consent' (London: Office of the Children's Commissioner, 2013); and G. Dines, *Pornland: How Porn has Hijacked Our Sexuality* (Boston: Beacon Press, 2011). Rae Langton and Caroline West argue that fictional pornography nonetheless plays out against a background of purported fact, and some pornography can contain

false (and harmful) background presuppositions such as 'Women enjoy rape', which are misrepresented as fact ('Scorekeeping in a pornographic language game', *Australasian Journal of Philosophy*, 77/3 (1999), pp. 303–19, at p. 316).

32 G. Currie, 'The moral psychology of fiction', *Australasian Journal of Philosophy*, 73/2 (1995), pp. 250–59, at p. 250.

33 See D. Lewis, 'Truth in fiction', *American Philosophical Quarterly*, 15/1 (1978), pp. 37–46. Lewis treats this 'background' as the collection of beliefs that are overt in the author's community.

34 Artworks are especially effective sources of moral education. See, for example: M. C. Nussbaum, *Love's Knowledge: Essays on Philosophy and Literature* (Oxford: Oxford University Press, 1990); S. Friend, 'Narrating the truth (more or less)', in M. Kieran and D. M. Lopes (eds), *Knowing Art: Essays in Aesthetics and Epistemology* (Dordrecht: Springer, 2006), pp. 35–49; N. Carroll, 'Art and ethical criticism: an overview of recent directions of research', *Ethics*, 110/2 (2000), pp. 350–87; and L. D'Olimpio, P. Paris, and A. P. Thompson (eds), *Educating Character Through the Arts* (Abingdon, Oxfordshire: Routledge, 2022).

35 For more on this claim see my paper 'Novel Assertions: A Reply to Mahon', *British Journal of Aesthetics*, 62/1 (2022), pp. 115–24.

36 See Dines 2011, pp. 79–98.

37 Jeremy Waldron, *The Harm in Hate Speech* (Cambridge, MA: Harvard University Press, 2012), p. 91.

38 G. R. Stone, 'Origins of obscenity', *New York University Review of Law & Social Change*, 31/4 (2007), pp. 711–32, at p. 713. See also Germany 2016, p. 54.

39 Germany 2016, pp. 149 and 74.

40 Germany 2016, p. 77.

41 Germany 2016, p. 18.

42 Plato, *Republic* (Book X: 605*d–e*) [*c.* 375 BCE], ed. H. D. P. Lee (London: Penguin Classics, 2003), p. 349.

43 Alexander Nehamas, 'Plato and the Mass Media', *The Monist*, 71/2 (1988), pp. 214–34, at p. 219.

44 Germany 2016, p. 81.

45 See for example: S. Bailey and P. Dickinson, 'The importance of safely de-roling', *Methods: A Journal of Acting Pedagogy*, vol. 2 (2018); and D. J. Leonard and T. Thurman, 'Bleed-out on the brain: The neuroscience of character-to-player spillover in larp', *International Journal of Role-Playing*, no. 9 (2018), pp. 9–15.

46 https://www.vogue.co.uk/arts-and-lifestyle/article/lady-gaga-interview [accessed July 2025].

47 J. Robson and A. Meskin, 'Video games as self-involving interactive fictions', *The Journal of Aesthetics and Art Criticism*, 74/2 (2016), pp. 165–77.

48 Thanks to Alex Fisher for this point. See for example N. Yee, J. N. Bailenson, and N. Ducheneaut, 'The Proteus effect: Implications of transformed digital self-representation on online and offline behavior', *Communication Research*, 36/2 (2009), pp. 285–312.

49 See for example J. Harold, *Dangerous Art: On Moral Criticisms of Artwork* (Oxford: Oxford University Press, 2020); Paul Harris, *The Work of the Imagination* (Oxford: Blackwell, 2000); and T. S. Gendler, 'Imaginative Contagion', *Metaphilosophy*, 37/2 (2006), pp. 183–203.

50 Alex Fisher, 'Imaginative contagion and moral corruption', *Philosophy and Phenomenological Research*, 111/3 (2025), pp. 999–1017.

51 https://variety.com/2021/film/columns/lady-gaga-house-of-gucci-patrizia-just-for-variety-1235132676/ [accessed July 2025].

52 C. A. Anderson and K. E. Dill, 'Video games and aggressive thoughts, feelings, and behavior in the laboratory and in life', *Journal of Personality and Social Psychology*, 78/4 (2000), pp. 772–90, at p. 786.

53 Christopher Bartel, 'Ethics and Video Games', in James Harold (ed.), *Oxford Handbook of Ethics and Art* (Oxford: Oxford University Press, 2023).

54 Victoria Simpson Beck, Stephanie Boys, Christopher Rose, and Eric Beck, 'Violence against women in video games: A prequel or sequel to rape myth acceptance?', *Journal of Interpersonal Violence*, 27/15 (2012), pp. 3016–31. Other studies find that such games solidify sexist attitudes in male players (S. P. Stermer and M. Burkley, 'SeX-Box: Exposure to sexist video games predicts benevolent sexism', *Psychology of Popular Media Culture*, 4/1 (2015), pp. 47–55). Other studies did not find such a connection, however, for instance: Liam Cross, Linda K. Kaye, Juris Savostijanovs et al., 'Gendered violence and sexualized representations in video games: (Lack of) effect on gender-related attitudes', *New Media and Society* (2022), https://doi.org/10.1177/14614448221075736.

55 See Bartel 2023, p. 479; and Melinda C. R. Burgess, Karen E. Dill, S. Paul Stermer et al., 'Playing with Prejudice: The Prevalence and Consequences of Racial Stereotypes in Video Games', *Media Psychology*, 14/3 (2011), pp. 289–311, https://doi.org/10.1080/15213269.2011.596467.

56 Elizabeth Behm-Morawitz and David Ta, 'Cultivating virtual stereotypes?: The impact of video game play on racial/ethnic stereotypes', *Howard Journal of Communications*, 25/1 (2014), pp. 1–15, at p. 4.

57 Nick Robinson and Joe Whittaker, 'Playing for Hate? Extremism,

Terrorism, and Videogames', *Studies in Conflict and Terrorism* (2021), https://doi.org/10.1080/1057610X.2020.1866740.

58   Burgess et al. 2011, p. 293.

59   Behm-Morawitz and Ta 2014, p. 1.

60   Leah Sharman and Genevieve A. Dingle, 'Extreme metal music and anger processing', *Frontiers in Human Neuroscience*, vol. 9 (2015).

61   Some forums, such as the American Psychological Association, have stated that as of 2020, there is 'insufficient scientific evidence to support a causal link between violent video games and violent behavior' (https://www.apa.org/news/press/releases/2020/03/violent-video-games-behavior [accessed November 2023]). In 2018, the University of York reported that their researchers had 'found no evidence to support the theory that video games make players more violent' after a series of experiments with over 3,000 participants (https://www.york.ac.uk/news-and-events/news/2018/research/no-evidence-to-link-violence-and-video-games/#:~:text=In%20a%20series%20of%20experiments,so%20far%20provided%20mixed%20conclusions [accessed November 2023]).

62   Gail Dines, *Pornland: How Porn Hijacked Our Sexuality* (Boston: Beacon Press, 2011), p. 85.

63   A. W. Eaton, 'A Sensible Antiporn Feminism', *Ethics*, 117/4 (2007), pp. 674–715.

64   The report, which drew together research from a survey of 1,000 people aged 16–21 and focus groups with teenagers aged 13–19 in England, concluded that 'frequent users of pornography are more likely to engage in physically aggressive sex acts'. In the survey, 72 per cent of participants agreed with the statement: 'Viewing online porn affects young people's expectations around sex and relationships.' A non-binary eighteen-year-old participant, who first saw pornography at the age of seven, stated that 'it reinforces negative ideas towards young people and children that women have a place below men, they are objects of desire, and can be hurt and sexually abused as long as it results in male gratification'. The report concludes that there is 'serious cause for concern about pornography's role in priming sexual behaviour among children'. Rachel de Souza, Children's Commissioner for England, *'A lot of it is actually just abuse': Young people and pornography* (2023), https://assets.childrenscommissioner.gov.uk/wpuploads/2023/02/cc-a-lot-of-it-is-actually-just-abuse-young-people-and-pornography-updated.pdf [accessed January 2024].

65   A. W. Eaton, 'A Reply to Critics', *Symposia on Gender, Race, and Philosophy*, 4/2 (2008), p. 3.

66 For this distinction see Joseph Jaconelli, 'Incitement: A study in language crime', *Criminal Law and Philosophy*, 12/2 (2018), pp. 245–65.

67 R. E. Herzstein, *The War That Hitler Won: The Most Infamous Propaganda Campaign in History* (London: Hamish Hamilton, 1979), p. 16.

68 Randall L. Bytwerk, 'The Argument for Genocide in Nazi Propaganda', *Quarterly Journal of Speech*, 91/1 (2005), pp. 37–62, https://doi.org/10.1080/00335630500157516. See also https://research.calvin.edu/german-propaganda-archive/pudel.htm [accessed January 2024].

69 For an analysis of incitement and propaganda during the Nuremberg Trials, see G. S. Gordon, 'The Propaganda Prosecutions at Nuremberg: The Origin of Atrocity Speech Law and the Touchstone for Normative Evolution', *Loyola of Los Angeles International and Comparative Law Review*, 39/1 (2017).

70 https://www.fbi.gov/history/famous-cases/oklahoma-city-bombing#:~:text=The%20human%20toll%20was%20still,terrorism%20in%20the%20nation's%20history. [accessed March 2025].

71 https://www.theguardian.com/uk/2000/jul/01/uksecurity.jeevanvasagar [accessed April 2025].

72 https://www.nytimes.com/2021/01/12/books/turner-diaries-white-supremacists.html [accessed May 2024].

73 https://www.washingtonpost.com/archive/lifestyle/1995/04/25/the-book-of-hate/eb6d5812-0adf-4757-80f8-e5d9e8ccb5c0/ [accessed May 2024].

74 https://policyexchange.org.uk/wp-content/uploads/2021/10/Knife-Crime-in-the-Capital.pdf [accessed May 2024].

75 S. Morrison, 'London crime: Gang members "to be treated like terror suspects" under new measures to tackle violence', *Evening Standard*, 30 May 2018. Retrieved from www.standard.co.uk/news/crime/london-gang-members-to-be-treated-like-terror-suspects-under-new-measures-to-tackle-violent-crime-a3850626.html

76 A. Owusu-Bempah, 'Part of art or part of life? Rap lyrics in criminal trials', *LSE British Politics and Policy* (2020). Available at: https://blogs.lse.ac.uk/politicsandpolicy/rap-lyrics-in-criminal-trials/ [accessed May 2024].

77 See Charis E. Kubrin and Ronald Weitzer, 'Rap music's violent and misogynistic effects: Fact or fiction?', in Mathieu Deflem (ed.), *Popular Culture, Crime and Social Control* (Bingley, UK: Emerald Books, 2010), pp. 121–43. Thank you to Tareeq Jalloh for bringing this paper to my attention.

78 https://www.bbc.co.uk/news/uk-england-london-63861886 [accessed May 2024].

79 https://sociologistofcrisis.wordpress.com/2021/11/13/experts-open-letter-in-response-to-a-recent-policy-exchange-report/ [accessed May 2024].

80 https://justice.org.uk/wp-content/uploads/flipbook/46/book.html [accessed May 2024].

81 Ethan Nowak, 'Poetic Injustice', *Episteme* (2023), pp. 1–15, https://doi.org/10.1017/epi.2022.47.

82 Jonathan Ilan, 'Digital street culture decoded: Why criminalizing drill music is street illiterate and counterproductive', *The British Journal of Criminology*, 60/4 (2020), pp. 994–1013, at p. 995.

83 Tareeq Omar Jalloh, 'Does the Critical Scrutiny of Drill Constitute an Epistemic Injustice?', *British Journal of Aesthetics*, 62/4 (2022), pp. 633–51. For epistemic injustice, see M. Fricker, *Epistemic Injustice: Power and the Ethics of Knowing* (Oxford: Oxford University Press, 2007); and Kristie Dotson, 'A cautionary tale: on limiting epistemic oppression', *Frontiers: A Journal of Women Studies*, 33/1 (2012), pp. 24–47.

84 https://www.theguardian.com/commentisfree/2019/jun/13/music-banning-drill-black-british-kids-violence [accessed May 2024].

85 https://pitchfork.com/thepitch/the-moral-panic-against-uk-drill-is-deeply-misguided [accessed 7 January 2026].

86 Germany 2016, p. 48.

3 OPPRESSION

1 Charles FitzRoy, *The Rape of Europa: The Intriguing History of Titian's Masterpiece* (London: Bloomsbury Publishing, 2015), pp. 44–5. The 'rape' in the painting's name which it acquired fifty years after Titian's death is derived from the seventeenth-century term *ratto*, which referred to the abduction of women, typically with a sexual element. See A. W. Eaton, 'Where ethics and aesthetics meet: Titian's *Rape of Europa*', *Hypatia*, 18/4 (2003), pp. 159–88, at p. 161.

2 Eaton 2003, pp. 161–6.

3 Eaton 2003, p. 178.

4 FitzRoy 2015, p. 2.

5 Eaton 2003, pp. 177–8.

6 Eaton 2003, pp. 163–5.

7 Carlo Ginzburg, *Clues, Myths, and the Historical Method* (Baltimore: Johns Hopkins University Press, 1989), p. 82.

8 David Rosand, 'Ut pictor poeta: Meaning in Titian's poesie', *New Literary History*, 3/3 (1972), pp. 527–46, at p. 541.

9 FitzRoy 2015, pp. 56–8.

10 From Nochlin's essay 'Why Have There Been No Great Women Art-

ists?' (1971), reprinted in her *Women, Art, and Power and Other Essays* (New York: Harper & Row, 1988), pp. 145–78.

11 https://www.theguardian.com/world/2016/jan/18/naked-artist-deb-orah-de-robertis-decries-hypocrisy-paris-gallery-arrest [accessed December 2023].

12 Marilyn Frye, 'Oppression', in *The Politics of Reality* (Freedom, CA: Crossing Press, 1983), pp. 1–16.

13 See Alison Bailey, 'Privilege: Expanding on Marilyn Frye's "oppression"', *Journal of Social Philosophy*, 29/3 (1998), p. 106.

14 I. M. Young, *Justice and the Politics of Difference* (Princeton: Princeton University Press, 1990).

15 See https://database.ilga.org/criminalisation-consensual-same-sex-sexual-acts [accessed December 2025].

16 For more on these 'oppressive things', see Shen-yi Liao and Bryce Huebner, 'Oppressive Things', *Philosophy and Phenomenological Research*, 103/1 (2020), pp. 92–113.

17 https://www.theguardian.com/media/from-the-archive-blog/2011/may/25/newspapers-national-newspapers [accessed November 2023].

18 T. J. Clark, *Picasso and Truth: From Cubism to Guernica* (Princeton: Princeton University Press, 2013), pp. 240–42.

19 D. Walsh, 'UN conceals Picasso's "Guernica" for Powell's presentation', *World Socialist Web Site* (2003), https://www.wsws.org/en/articles/2003/02/guer-f08.html [accessed 24 July 2018].

20 Quote taken from L. G. Duggan, 'Was Art Really the "Book of the Illiterate"?', in M. Hageman and M. Mostert (eds), *Reading Images and Texts: Medieval Images and Texts as Forms of Communication* (Turnhout, Belgium: Brepols, 2005), p. 63.

21 B. Williamson, *Christian Art: A Very Short Introduction* (Oxford: Oxford University Press, 2004), p. 66.

22 A. Hayum, 'The Meaning and Function of the Isenheim Altarpiece: The Hospital Context Revisited', *The Art Bulletin*, 59/4 (1977), pp. 501–17, at p. 516.

23 For more on the nature of artwork meaning see my PhD dissertation: D. Dixon, 'Alterpieces: Artworks as Shifting Speech Acts', University of Cambridge, 2019, https://doi.org/10.17863/CAM.39458.

24 J. L. Austin, *How to Do Things with Words* (Oxford: Oxford University Press, 1962), p. 146.

25 For more on the nature of speech acts and their direction of fit, see John R. Searle's 'A classification of illocutionary acts', *Language in Society*, 5/1 (1976), pp. 1–23.

26 For support of the claim that artworks and memorials can perform

illocutionary acts, see Dixon 2019; D. Dixon, 'Artistic (Counter) Speech', *Journal of Aesthetics and Art Criticism*, 80/4 (2022), pp. 409–19; D. Friedell and S. Liao, 'How Statues Speak', *Journal of Aesthetics and Art Criticism*, 80/4 (2022), pp. 444–52; G. Scarre, 'How Memorials Speak to Us', in J. Bicknell, C. Korsmeyer, and J. Judkins (eds), *Philosophical Perspectives on Ruins, Monuments, and Memorials* (New York: Routledge, 2020), pp. 21–33; D. Novitz, *Pictures and Their Use in Communication* (The Hague: Nijhoff, 1977); and S. Kjørup, 'Pictorial Speech Acts', *Erkenntnis*, 12/1 (1978), pp. 55–71.

27 R. Langton, 'Speech Acts and Unspeakable Acts', *Philosophy and Public Affairs*, 22/4 (1993), pp. 293–330, at pp. 302–3.

28 See for example Wilson R. Huhn, 'Cross Burning as Hate Speech Under the First Amendment to the United States Constitution', *Amsterdam Law Forum*, 2/1 (2009); and Edward J. Eberle, 'Cross Burning, Hate Speech, and Free Speech in America', *Arizona State Law Journal*, vol. 36 (2004).

29 For more on this see C. MacKinnon, *Feminism Unmodified* (Cambridge, MA: Harvard University Press, 1993); and R. Langton, 'Speech Acts and Unspeakable Acts', *Philosophy and Public Affairs*, 22/4 (1993), pp. 293–330.

30 In other words, art can enact 'permissibility facts'. For this concept, see Mary Kate McGowan, 'Oppressive Speech', *Australasian Journal of Philosophy*, 87/3 (2009), pp. 389–407.

31 Martha Nussbaum, 'Objectification', *Philosophy and Public Affairs*, 24/4 (1995), pp. 249–91, at p. 257.

32 Rae Langton, *Sexual Solipsism: Philosophical Essays on Pornography and Objectification* (Oxford: Oxford University Press, 2009) pp. 228–9.

33 A. W. Eaton, 'What's Wrong with the (Female) Nude?', in H. Maes and J. Levinson (eds), *Art and Pornography: Philosophical Essays* (Oxford: Oxford University Press, 2012), p. 290.

34 Laura Mulvey, *Visual and Other Pleasures* (London: Macmillan, 1989).

35 Naomi Scheman, 'Thinking about Quality in Women's Visual Art', in *Engenderings: Constructions of Knowledge, Authority, and Privilege* (New York: Routledge, 1993), p. 159.

36 Immanuel Kant, *Anthropology from a Pragmatic Point of View* [1798], trans. Victor Lyle Dowdell (Carbondale: Southern Illinois University Press, 1978), p. 222.

37 S. Brownmiller, *Against Our Will: Men, Women, and Rape* (New York: Simon & Schuster, 1975), pp. 283–308.

38 Diane Wolfthal, *Images of Rape: The 'Heroic' Tradition and Its Alternatives* (Cambridge: Cambridge University Press, 1999), p. 9.

This compositional detail refers to the earlier version of the work, commissioned in 1633 by the French diplomat Marshal de Crequi, and which now hangs in the New York's Metropolitan Museum of Art.

39 Wolfthal 1999, pp. 10–24.

40 Wolfthal 1999, p. 25.

41 Z. Bahrani, *Women of Babylon: Gender and Representation in Mesopotamia* (Abingdon, Oxfordshire: Routledge, 2001), p. 60.

42 Bahrani 2001, p. 68.

43 Evidence for this attitude is found in ancient textual record, such as Hippocratic medical texts. See Anne Carson, 'Putting her in her place: woman, dirt, and desire', in David M. Halperin, John J. Winkler, and Froma I. Zeitlin (eds), *Before Sexuality: The Construction of Erotic Experience in the Ancient Greek World* (Princeton: Princeton University Press, 1990). pp. 135–69.

44 https://www.loebclassics.com/view/aristotle-generation_animals/1942/pb_LCL366.175.xml#:~:text=Generation%20of%20Animals%2C%20II.&text=The%20reason%20is%20that%20the,only%2C%20the%20principle%20of%20Soul [accessed May 2023], and see: https://aeon.co/essays/blame-it-on-aristotle-how-science-got-into-bed-with-sexism [accessed January 2024].

45 Bahrani 2001, p. 79.

46 C. Johns, *Sex or Symbol: Erotic Images of Greece and Rome* (London: British Museum Press, 1982), p. 72.

47 See for example S. B. Pomeroy, *Women in Hellenistic Egypt: From Alexander to Cleopatra* (Detroit: Wayne State University Press, 1990), p. 80; and M. Golden, 'Male Chauvinists and Pigs', *Echos du Monde Classique* 32/1, n.s. 7 (1988), pp. 1–12.

48 Lisa E. Farrington, 'Reinventing Herself: The Black Female Nude', *Woman's Art Journal*, 24/2 (2003), pp. 15–23, at p. 15, https://doi.org/10.2307/1358782.

49 See: https://www.bbc.com/culture/article/20190114-how-black-women-were-whitewashed-by-art [accessed September 2022].

50 E. McGrath, 'The Black Andromeda', *Journal of the Warburg and Courtauld Institutes*, 55/1 (1992), pp. 1–18, https://doi.org/10.2307/751417.

51 bell hooks, 'Oppositional Gaze: Black Female Spectators', in *Black Looks: Race and Representation* (Boston: South End Press, 1992), p. 117.

52 P. C. Taylor, *Black Is Beautiful: A Philosophy of Black Aesthetics* (Newark: John Wiley & Sons, 2016), p. 111. Also see K. Mercer, 'Black Hair/ Politics', *New Formations*, no. 3 (1987), pp. 33–54, at p. 35.

53 Charmaine Nelson, '*Coloured Nude*: Fetishization, Disguise, Dichotomy'. *RACAR: Revue d'art canadienne/Canadian Art Review*, 22/1–2

(1995), pp. 97–107, at p. 97, https://doi.org/10.7202/1072517.

54   There were some exceptions to this, however. See Paul H. D. Kaplan, 'Black women in early modern European art and culture', in *The Routledge Companion to Black Women's Cultural Histories* (Routledge, 2021), pp. 44–56.

55   See T. J. Clark, *The Painting of Modern Life: Paris in the Art of Manet and His Followers* (Princeton: Princeton University Press, 1999), p. 86; T. Dolan, 'Fringe Benefits: Manet's Olympia and Her Shawl', *The Art Bulletin*, 97/4 (2015), pp. 409–29, at p. 424, https://doi.org/10.1080/000 43079.2015.1043828.

56   This translation is from: Z. Lavallee, 'What's Wrong with the (White) Female Nude?', *Polish Journal of Aesthetics* 41.2 (2016), pp. 77-97. A slightly different translation is available at: A. Pontynen, *For the Love of Beauty: Art, History, and the Moral Foundations of Aesthetic Judgment* (New Brunswick, NJ: Transaction Publishers, 2006), p. 41.

57   hooks 1992, p. 115.

58   For more on Laure see https://pallant.org.uk/manets-olympia-laure-and-victorine/#:~:text=Laure%20appears%20in%20three%20 paintings,been%20renamed%20Portrait%20of%20Laure [accessed May 2024].

59   P. H. Collins, *Black Feminist Thought: Knowledge, Consciousness, and the Politics of Empowerment* [2000] (Abingdon, Oxfordshire: Routledge, 2014), p. 69.

60   https://jimcrowmuseum.ferris.edu/mammies/homepage.htm [accessed January 2022].

61   Robin Mitchell, 'A history of Black women in nineteenth-century France', in *The Routledge Companion to Black Women's Cultural Histories* (Routledge, 2021), pp. 159–67.

62   See for example Lorraine O'Grady, 'Olympia's Maid: Reclaiming Black Female Subjectivity', *Afterimage*, 20/1 (1992), reprinted in A. Jones (ed.), *The Feminism and Visual Culture Reader* (Hove, East Sussex: Psychology Press, 2003), pp. 174–87.

63   O'Grady 1992, p. 209.

64   Lisa E. Farrington, 'Reinventing Herself: The Black Female Nude', *Woman's Art Journal*, 24/2 (2003), pp. 15–23, at p. 16, https://doi.org/10.2307/1358782.

65   Collins 2000, p. 81.

66   See, for instance, Robert Hornback, *Racism and Early Blackface Comic Traditions: From the Old World to the New.* (Springer, 2018); and Virginia Mason Vaughan, *Performing Blackness on English Stages, 1500–1800* (Cambridge University Press, 2005).

67 R. Zheng and N. H. Stear, 'Imagining in Oppressive Contexts, or What's Wrong with Blackface?', *Ethics*, 133/3 (2023), pp. 381–414, at pp. 393–4.

68 https://www.bbc.co.uk/news/newsbeat-53192702 [accessed February 2022].

69 https://jimcrowmuseum.ferris.edu/golliwog/homepage.htm [accessed February 2022].

70 https://antisemitism.org.uk/wp-content/uploads/2020/07/Antisemit-ic-imagery-May-2020.pdf / https://www.pbs.org/wgbh/frontline/arti-cle/germanys-laws-antisemitic-hate-speech-nazi-propaganda-holo-caust-denial/ [accessed May 2022]. For more on dehumanisation in these images, see D. L. Smith, *Making Monsters: The Uncanny Power of Dehumanization* (Cambridge, MA: Harvard University Press, 2021).

71 Liudmila Alexeevna Zotova and Victoria Alexandrovna Kotova, 'The image of a disabled person in art through the ages', *Cardiovascular Diagnosis and Therapy*, 14/5 (2024), p. 982.

72 See https://www.theguardian.com/news/2023/mar/14/the-disabled-villain-why-sensitivity-reading-cant-kill-off-this-ugly-trope [accessed October 2025].

73 Colin Barnes, 'Disabling imagery and the media', *An Exploration of the Principles for Media Representations of Disabled People: The First in a Series of Reports. Halifax* (1992), https://disability-studies.leeds.ac.uk/wp-content/uploads/sites/40/library/Barnes-disabling-imagery.pdf [accessed October 2025].

74 https://www.buzzfeed.com/alexwickham/tory-councillor-anti-mus-lim-memes [accessed May 2023].

75 According to the Jim Crow Museum in Michigan: 'The pioneer study of racial and ethnic stereotyping in the United States was conducted in 1933 by Daniel Katz and Kenneth Braley, two social scientists. They questioned 100 Princeton University undergraduates regarding the prevailing stereotypes of racial and ethnic groups. Their research con-cluded that black people were consistently described as "superstitious," "happy-go-lucky," and "lazy." The respondents had these views even though they had little or no contact with black people.' https://jimcrow-museum.ferris.edu/coon/homepage.htm [accessed January 2023].

76 W. E. B. Du Bois, *The Souls of Black Folk* (Chicago: A. C. McClurg & Co., 1903), page numbers from the version edited by David W. Blight and Robert Gooding-Williams (Boston: Bedford Books, 1997), p. 38.

77 Transcribed from BBC's *David Harewood on Blackface* (2023): https://www.bbc.co.uk/iplayer/episode/m001p474/david-harewood-on-black-face [accessed July 2023].

78 https://www.salisburypost.com/2020/06/12/debate-about-fame-statue-re-location-continues-as-thousands-sign-petitions/ [accessed June 2022].

79 https://famepreservationgroup.org/about [accessed December 2023].

80 'North Carolina residents react to removal of Confederate statue', *CNN*, https://www.youtube.com/watch?v=O2bWfY8X9h0 [accessed December 2022]. The Group's website, https://famepreservationgroup.org/about [accessed December 2022].

81 R. Langton, 'Blocking as Counter-Speech', in Daniel Fogal, Daniel W. Harris, and Matt Moss (eds), *New Work on Speech Acts* (Oxford: Oxford University Press, 2018), pp. 144–64, at p. 146.

82 A. Procter, *The Whole Picture: The Colonial Story of the Art in Our Museums and Why We Need to Talk About It* (London: Octopus Books, 2020), pp. 55–9.

83 Anton Krueger, 'Gazing at Exhibit A: Interview with Brett Bailey', *Liminalities: A Journal of Performance Studies*, 9/1 (2013), pp. 1–13, at p. 7.

84 https://www.bbc.co.uk/news/magazine-35240987 [accessed August 2025]. Also see Mitchell 2021.

85 Anna Kelsey-Sugg and Marc Fennell, 'The fight for Sarah Baartman', *ABC News: Radio National, Australian Broadcasting Corporation*, 16 November 2021, https://www.abc.net.au/news/2021-11-17/stuff-the-british-stole-sarah-baartman-south-africa-london/100568276 [accessed March 2022].

86 Mitchell 2021, p. 161.

87 L. Atkin, 'Looking at the Other/Seeing the Self: Embodied Performance and Encounter in Brett Bailey's Exhibit B and Nineteenth-Century Ethnographic Displays', *Safundi*, 16/2 (2015), pp. 136–55, at p. 139.

88 https://www.theguardian.com/commentisfree/2014/sep/24/exhibit-b-challenging-work-never-sought-alienate-offend-brett-bailey [accessed April 2020].

89 https://www.heraldscotland.com/life_style/arts_ents/13174540.horrifying-exhibits-provide-bleak-education/ [accessed December 2025].

90 https://www.theguardian.com/artanddesign/2016/apr/03/andres-serrano-interview-donald-trump-piss-christ [accessed March 2023].

91 https://archive.nytimes.com/www.nytimes.com/library/arts/092899ofili-brooklyn-museum.html?module=inline [accessed May 2024].

92 Procter 2020, p. 176.

93 W. E. B. Du Bois, *Darkwater: Voices from Within the Veil* [1920] (Oxford: Oxford University Press, 2007), p. 69.

94 https://conversations.e-flux.com/t/hannah-blacks-letter-to-the-whitney-biennials-curators-dana-schutz-painting-must-go/6287 [accessed March 2022].

95 https://government.se/ quoted in http://www.jeremyriad.com/blog/art/ edible-art/swedish-performance-art-cake/ [accessed August 2022].

96 https://msafropolitan.com/2012/04/an-open-letter-from-african-women-to-the-minister-of-culture-the-venus-hottentot-cake.html [accessed August 2022].

97 P. H. Collins, *Black Feminist Thought: Knowledge, Consciousness, and the Politics of Empowerment* [2000] (Abingdon, Oxfordshire: Routledge, 2014), p. 269.

98 C. Thi Nguyen and M. Strohl, 'Cultural appropriation and the intimacy of groups', *Philosophical Studies*, 176/4 (2019), pp. 981–1002, at p. 989. Nguyen and Strohl note that this is a *pro tanto* right – one that can be overridden in some special cases if not doing so has worse consequences. For instance, reading your friend's diary after she's been kidnapped to ascertain her recent relationships in a desperate bid to find her would be overall a permissible thing to do.

4 MALEVOLENCE

1 Henri Dorra, *The Symbolism of Paul Gauguin: Erotica, Exotica, and the Great Dilemmas of Humanity* (Berkeley: University of California Press, 2007), p. 214.

2 Caroline Vercoe, 'I Am My Other, I Am My Self: Encounters with Gauguin in Polynesia', *Australian and New Zealand Journal of Art*, 13/1 (2013), pp. 104–25, at p. 108, https://doi.org/10.1080/14434318.2013.11432645.

3 Stephen F. Eisenman, *Gauguin's Skirt* (London and New York: Thames & Hudson, 1997), p. 201.

4 But see R. B. J. M. Welten, 'Paul Gauguin and the Complexity of the Primitivist Gaze', *Journal of Art Historiography* (2015), https://arthistoriography.files.wordpress.com/2015/06/welten.pdf, for a complex analysis of the types of colonialist gaze in Gauguin's paintings.

5 J. Duran, 'Education and Feminist Aesthetics: Gauguin and the Exotic', *Journal of Aesthetic Education*, 43/4 (2009), pp. 88–95, at p. 91, http://www.jstor.org/stable/25656249. But see Jehanne Teilhet, 'The Influence of Polynesian Culture and Art on the Works of Paul Gauguin: 1891–1903', PhD diss., University of California, 1975, at p. 386, who argues that Gauguin's works were authentic to their subject.

6 Bengt Danielsson, *Gauguin in the South Seas*, trans. Reginald Spink (London: George Allen and Unwin, 1965), p. 241.

7 Duran 2009, p. 90.

8 https://archive.org/details/noanoatranslated00gauguoft/page/n89/ mode/2up?view=theater [accessed November 2023].

9   Nancy Mowll Mathews, *Paul Gauguin: An Erotic Life* (London and New Haven: Yale University Press, 2001), p. 182.

10   John Rewald (ed.), *Camille Pissarro: Letters to his Son Lucien* (Abingdon, Oxfordshire: Routledge, 1980), p. 221.

11   https://www.bbc.co.uk/news/entertainment-arts-64729304 [accessed March 2025]. J. K. Rowling has denied that she is transphobic: https://www.glamourmagazine.co.uk/article/jk-rowling-transgender-comments-controversy [accessed September 2025].

12   Polanski entered a plea bargain and pleaded guilty to unlawful sexual intercourse with a minor, only to flee the US in 1978 after forty-two days in jail: https://www.theguardian.com/film/2018/jan/30/hollywood-reverence-child-rapist-roman-polanski-convicted-40-years-on-run [accessed August 2025]. Polanski then reached an out-of-court settlement with his accuser, Samantha Geimer, in 1993. As of 2009, it remains unclear whether the payment was ever made: https://abcnews.com/Business/CelebrityCafe/roman-polanski-agreed-pay-samantha-geimar-500000-unclear/story?id=8742649#:~:text=Oct.,country%20before%20he%20was%20 sentenced [accessed February 2026].

13   https://www.theguardian.com/artanddesign/2023/jun/20/shunned-boycotted-exiled-france-francoise-gilot-picasso [accessed May 2024].

14   Marina Picasso, *Picasso: My Grandfather* (London: Vintage, 2002), p. 123.

15   The Editors (2009), 'The Polanski Uproar', *Room for Debate: A New York Times Blog*, https://roomfordebate.blogs.nytimes.com/2009/09/29/the-polanski-uproar/?ref=us#gilmore [accessed September 2018].

16   S. Davies, *The Philosophy of Art* [2006] (Chichester, UK: Wiley-Blackwell, 2016), p. 127.

17   A. Danto, *The Transfiguration of the Commonplace: A Philosophy of Art* (Cambridge, MA: Harvard University Press, 1981), p. 2.

18   W. E. B. Du Bois, 'Criteria of Negro art', *The Crisis*, 32/6 (1926), pp. 290–97. Also see James Harold, *Dangerous Art: On Moral Criticisms of Artwork* (Oxford: Oxford University Press, 2020), pp. 19–21. Also see P. C. Taylor, *Black Is Beautiful: A Philosophy of Black Aesthetics* (Hoboken: John Wiley & Sons, 2016), pp. 92–9.

19   B. Gaut, *Art, Emotion and Ethics* (Oxford: Oxford University Press, 2007), p. 84.

20   Gaut 2007, p. 74.

21   Ibid.

22   https://www.bbc.co.uk/news/entertainment-arts-56563149 [accessed June 2025]. Allen has always denied these allegations and has never been criminally charged.

23 T. Nannicelli, *Artistic Creation and Ethical Criticism* (Oxford: Oxford University Press, 2020), p. 226.

24 Nannicelli 2020, p. 231.

25 E. H. Matthes, 'Immoral Artists', in James Harold (ed.), *The Oxford Handbook of Ethics and Art* (Oxford: Oxford University Press, 2023), p. 595.

26 See Johann Chapoutot, *Greeks, Romans, Germans: How the Nazis Usurped Europe's Classical Past*, trans. Richard R. Nybakken (Berkeley: University of California Press, 2016).

27 Frederic Spotts, *Hitler and the Power of Aesthetics* (London: Pimlico, 2003), pp. 134–5.

28 Henry Grosshans, *Hitler and the Artists* (New York: Holmes & Meyer, 1983), p. 86.

29 Klaus P. Fischer, *Nazi Germany: A New History* (London: Constable, 1997), p. 368.

30 https://www.npr.org/2019/02/09/692855767/opinion-paintings-by-adolf-hitler-are-unremarkable-so-why-forge-them [accessed December 2023].

31 https://www.theguardian.com/commentisfree/2009/apr/29/hitler-painting-art [accessed January 2025].

32 https://www.stereogum.com/295222/haunting-the-chapel-no-8/columns/haunting-the-chapel/ [accessed April 2025].

33 For more on this forest metaphor used by the Third Reich, see Jeffrey K. Wilson, *The German Forest: Nature, Identity, and the Contestation of a National Symbol, 1871–1914* (Toronto: University of Toronto Press, 2012). And for more on the broader ecological sentiment of the Nazis, see Anna Bramwell, *Ecology in the 20th Century: A History* (London and New Haven: Yale University Press, 1989).

34 Johannes Zechner, 'Politicized timber: The German Forest and the nature of the Nation 1800–1945', *The Brock Review*, 11/2 (2011), pp. 19–32, at pp. 22–3.

35 https://www.telegraph.co.uk/columnists/2023/06/06/picasso-misogynist-hannah-gadsby/ [accessed December 2023].

5 CRUELTY

1 https://www.schneemannfoundation.org/artworks/meat-joy [accessed April 2023].

2 https://www.phaidon.com/agenda/art/articles/2014/march/03/why-joseph-beuys-and-his-dead-hare-live-on/ [accessed March 2023].

3 Joseph Beuys, 'Interview with Willoughby Sharp, 1969', in Carin Kuoni (ed.), *Energy Plan for the Western Man: Joseph Beuys in America:*

Writings by and Interviews with the Artist (New York: Four Walls Eight Windows, 1990), pp. 77–92, at p. 82.

4 https://www.telegraph.co.uk/films/0/director-bragged-on-camera-rape-alejandro-jodorowskys-el-topo/ [accessed September 2025].

5 https://news.artnet.com/art-world/damien-whats-your-beef-916097#:~:text=SEA%20CREATURES,the%20Mind%20of%20Someone%20Living [accessed August 2025].

6 https://www.theage.com.au/national/the-shark-hunter-the-artist-and-a-nice-little-earner-20060702-ge2mtz.html [accessed September 2025].

7 C. Korsmeyer, *Gender and Aesthetics: An Introduction* (New York: Routledge, 2004), p. 145.

8 https://www.nationalgalleries.org/art-and-artists/93566 [accessed December 2023].

9 Damien Hirst and Stuart Morgan, 'An Interview with Damien Hirst' (1995), http://www.damienhirst.com/texts/1996/jan--stuart-morgan [accessed August 2024].

10 Caroline Goldstein, 'How Many Animals Have Died for Damien Hirst's Art to Live? We Counted', *Artnet News*, 13 April 2017, https://news.artnet.com/art-world/damienwhats-your-beef-916097?utm_content=buffer88639&utm_medium=social&utm_source=facebook.com&utm_campaign=socialmedia [accessed June 2025]. This same number was quoted in a piece I co-wrote for *The Conversation* in 2025. Hirst's representatives were contacted about the claims we made in this article, but they did not respond by the time of publication.

11 Martin Harries, 'Regarding the Pain of Rats: Kim Jones's "Rat Piece"', *The Drama Review*, 51/1 (2007), pp. 160–65, at p. 161.

12 Harries 2007, p. 164.

13 P. Singer, *Animal Liberation: Towards an End to Man's Inhumanity to Animals* (St Albans, Hertfordshire: Granada Publishing Ltd, 1990), p. 30.

14 http://news.bbc.co.uk/1/hi/3040891.stm [accessed May 2023].

15 Ibid.

16 T. Nannicelli, *Artistic Creation and Ethical Criticism* (Oxford: Oxford University Press, 2020). p. 125.

17 Yolandi M. Coetser, 'Cruel Art: Intersections between Art, Animals, and Morality', *de arte*, 55/1 (2020), pp. 57–75, at p. 58, https://doi.org/10.1080/00043389.2019.1643072.

18 https://beautifulbizarre.net/2019/10/01/interview-with-julia-deville/ [accessed February 2024].

19 Miranda Johnson, 'The Other Who Precedes and Possesses Me: Confronting the Maternal/Animal Divide Through the Art of Botched Taxidermy', *Feral Fem*, no. 6 (2014), pp. 68–81.

20 https://www.youtube.com/watch?v=ydWLgn2u56g [accessed December 2025].

21 Giovanni Aloi, 'Angela Singer: Animals Rights and Wrongs', *Antennae: The Journal of Nature in Visual Culture*, no. 7: *Botched Taxidermy* (2008), pp. 10–17.

22 https://www.dezeen.com/2018/12/12/ice-watch-olafur-eliasson-installation/ [accessed April 2023].

23 https://www.theguardian.com/artanddesign/2018/dec/11/icebergs-ahead-olafur-eliasson-brings-the-frozen-fjord-to-britain-ice-watch-london-climate-change [accessed April 2023].

24 Nannicelli 2020, p. 127.

25 https://transom.org/wp-content/uploads/2021/01/Herald-Harbinger-plaque-v3.pdf [accessed May 2023].

26 https://www.avenuecalgary.com/city-life/work-of-art/herald-harbinger-by-ben-rubin-and-jer-thorp/ [accessed March 2023].

27 Emily Brady, 'Aesthetic Regard for Nature in Environmental and Land Art', *Ethics Place and Environment*, 10/3 (2007), pp. 287–300, at p. 292.

28 For more on functional beauty, see Panos Paris, 'Functional Beauty, Pleasure, and Experience', *Australasian Journal of Philosophy*, 98/3 (2020), pp. 516–30.

29 https://theweek.com/articles/491115/christos-controversial-art-timeline-irritating-people-fabric [accessed March 2023].

30 According to curator Jobyl Boone, 'Small-scale trial installations revealed that manatees enjoyed loitering underneath the pink polypropylene, which in fact seemed to inspire out-of-season amorous activity.' See J. A. Boone, 'Hill to Bay, Land and Water: Christo and Jeanne-Claude and American Environmentalism', *Athanor*, vol. 27 (2009), pp. 95–103, at p. 99.

31 https://elyseemiami.com/surrounded-islands-the-art-installation-that-changed-the-trajectory-of-biscayne-bays-artistic-profile/ [accessed May 2023], and J. A. Boone, 'Hill to Bay, Land and Water: Christo and Jeanne-Claude and American Environmentalism', *Athanor*, vol. 27 (2009), pp. 95–103.

32 D. Crawford, 'Nature and art: some dialectical relationships', *Journal of Aesthetics and Art Criticism*, 42/1 (1983), pp. 49–58, at p. 57.

33 G. de Groat, 'Artists and the environment: A report from the 81st College Art Association Conference in Seattle', *Electronic Green Journal*, 1/1 (1994).

34 Brady 2007.

35 S. Boettger, *Earthworks: Art and the Landscape of the Sixties* (Berkeley: University of California Press, 2002), p. 114.

36 S. Ross, *What Gardens Mean* (Chicago: Chicago University Press, 1998), p. 210.

37 M. Andrews, *Landscape and Western Art* (Oxford: Oxford University Press, 1999), p. 213.

38 Fabio Cavallucci and Carlos Jiménez (eds), *Santiago Sierra* (Trento: Galleria Civica di Arte Contemporanea, 2005), p. 164.

39 Claire Bishop, 'Antagonism and relational aesthetics', *October*, 110 (2004), pp. 51–79.

40 Nannicelli 2020, pp. 172–4.

41 Frazer Ward, *No Innocent Bystanders: Performance Art and the Audience* (Hanover, NH: Dartmouth College Press, 2012), p. 119.

42 'Marina Abramovic on performing "Rhythm 0" (1974)', Marina Abramović Institute, https://www.youtube.com/watch?v=xTBkbseX-fOQ [accessed September 2024].

6 ICONOCLASM

1 https://www.aljazeera.com/news/2024/1/14/a-cultural-genocide-which-of-gazas-heritage-sites-have-been-destroyed [accessed February 2024].

2 https://www.icj-cij.org/sites/default/files/case-related/192/192-20231228-app-01-00-en.pdf [accessed March 2024].

3 https://oseredok.ca/ie_en_the-artistic-legacy-of-maria-prymachenko/ [accessed December 2023].

4 Bashshar Haydar, 'Killing for Culture', in W. Bülow, H. Frowe, D. Matravers, and J. L. Thomas (eds), *Heritage and War: Ethical Issues* (Oxford: Oxford University Press: 2023), pp. 51–71.

5 https://encyclopedia.ushmm.org/content/en/article/book-burning [accessed August 2025].

6 Richard Ovenden, *Burning the Books* (London: John Murray, 2020), p. 3.

7 Leslie Brubaker, *Inventing Byzantine Iconoclasm* (Bristol: Bristol Classical Press, 2012), p. 4.

8 Mahon 2016. https://www.theartnewspaper.com/2016/12/21/why-courbets-the-origin-of-the-world-is-so-popularand-its-not-what-you-think [accessed May 2023].

9 https://www.theguardian.com/technology/2018/feb/01/facebook-nude-painting-gustave-courbet [accessed May 2023].

10 See Kyle Chayka, 'Ai Weiwei Spreads a Sunflower Seed Carpet at Tate's Turbine Hall', *Hyperallergic* (2010), https://hyperallergic.com/10574/ai-weiwei-turbine-hall [accessed 9 May 2018].

11 Tate, 'Interpretation Text' (2010), www.tate.org.uk/whats-on/

tate-modern/unilever-series/unilever-series-ai-weiwei-sunflower-seeds [accessed 12 August 2019].

12 Ibid.

13 https://africanah.org/jelili-atiku-performance-artist-activist/ [accessed September 2025].

14 https://africasacountry.com/2016/01/the-trials-of-jelili-atiku [accessed September 2025].

15 https://www.cbc.ca/arts/interruptthisprogram/being-jailed-and-intimidated-for-his-lagos-street-performance-hasn-t-stopped-jelili-atiku-s-protest-1.3978375 [accessed September 2025].

16 https://artistsatriskconnection.org/story/art-in-turmoil-artistic-freedom-and-human-rights-in-latin-america-and-the-caribbean [accessed May 2023].

17 https://www.whitehouse.gov/briefings-statements/2025/08/letter-to-the-smithsonian-internal-review-of-smithsonian-exhibitions-and-materials/ [accessed September 2025].

18 https://www.whitehouse.gov/presidential-actions/2025/03/restoring-truth-and-sanity-to-american-history/#:~:text=It%20is%20the%20policy%20of,record%20of%20advancing%20liberty%2C%20prosperity%2C [accessed September 2025].

19 https://theconversation.com/the-orwellian-echoes-in-trumps-push-for-americanism-at-the-smithsonian-263304 [accessed October 2025].

20 https://www.theatlantic.com/ideas/archive/2025/08/trump-attack-smithsonian-slavery/683969/ [accessed October 2025].

21 https://www.whitehouse.gov/articles/2025/08/president-trump-is-right-about-the-smithsonian/ [accessed October 2025].

22 'Who was Edward Colston, why was his statue toppled?', *Al Jazeera English*, https://www.youtube.com/watch?v=kak-pNJyN2w [accessed May 2021].

23 https://www.nytimes.com/2019/11/18/arts/design/gauguin-national-gallery-london.html [accessed 1 October 2020].

24 A. Mahon, *The Marquis de Sade and the Avant-Garde* (Princeton: Princeton University Press, 2020), p. 1.

25 Mahon 2020, p. 19.

26 https://www.cccb.org/en/multimedia/videos/jean-jacques-lebel-sade-and-freedom-of-expression/242375 [accessed August 2025].

27 Judith Butler, 'Beauvoir on Sade: Making Sexuality into an Ethic', in *The Cambridge Companion to Simone de Beauvoir*, ed. Claudia Card (Cambridge: Cambridge University Press, 2003), pp. 168–88, at p. 187.

28 A. W. Eaton, 'Robust Immoralism', *The Journal of Aesthetics and Art Criticism*, 70/3 (2012), pp. 281–92. Eaton's concept of the rough hero

is derived from David Hume's aesthetic essay from 1757, 'Of the Standard of Taste', reprinted in *Essays: Moral and Political and Literary* (London: Longmans, Green, and Co., 1875), p. 322.

29   Tamar Szabó Gendler, 'The Puzzle of Imaginative Resistance', *The Journal of Philosophy*, 97/2 (2000), pp. 55–81.

30   For a detailed analysis of how rough heroes on TV can improve our moral character, see Panos Paris, 'Virtue and vice on TV: Television series and ethical reflection', *Educating Character Through the Arts* (Abingdon, Oxfordshire: Routledge, 2022), pp. 84–108.

31   'Supporter of Robert E. Lee statue explains his position', *WWLTV*, https://www.youtube.com/watch?v=1CX0Tkyc4DA [accessed May 2023].

32   https://www.bbc.co.uk/news/magazine-41904800 [accessed October 2025].

33   https://www.bbc.co.uk/sounds/play/m00223mx [accessed October 2025].

34   https://theconversation.com/edward-colston-statue-toppled-how-bristol-came-to-see-the-slave-trader-as-a-hero-and-philanthropist-140271#:~:text=Opponents%20to%20the%20felling%20of,170%20years%20after%20his%20death [accessed April 2024].

35   https://www.itv.com/news/westcountry/2022-01-06/pm-says-we-can-not-seek-to-change-our-history-after-colston-verdict [accessed April 2024].

36   M. Dresser, *Slavery Obscured: The Social History of the Slave Trade in an English Provincial Port* (London: Bloomsbury Publishing, 2016).

37   https://twitter.com/Keir_Starmer/status/1269949806463668224 [accessed May 2024].

38   E. H. Matthes, *Drawing the Line: What to Do with the Work of Immoral Artists from Museums to the Movies* (Oxford: Oxford University Press, 2021), p. 79.

39   Matthes 2021, p. 102.

40   https://www.theguardian.com/world/2013/dec/22/pr-exec-fired-racist-tweet-aids-africa-apology [accessed September 2025].

41   Matthes 2021, p. 110. For the Jimmy Page allegation, see https://www.independent.co.uk/arts-entertainment/music/features/led-zeppelin-there-was-a-whole-lotta-love-on-tour-763446.html [accessed September 2025].

42   M. Wallace, *Invisibility Blues: From Pop to Theory* (London: Verso, 1990), pp. 85–9. Reference found in Alfred Archer and Benjamin Matheson, *Honouring and Admiring the Immoral: An Ethical Guide* (Abingdon, Oxfordshire: Routledge, 2021), p. 74.

43 For more on the aesthetic self, see J. Fingerhut, J. Gomez-Lavin, C. Winklmayr, and J. J. Prinz, 'The Aesthetic Self: The Importance of Aesthetic Taste in Music and Art for Our Perceived Identity', *Frontiers in Psychology*, vol. 11 (2020), https://doi.org/10.3389/fpsyg.2020.577703.

44 Archer and Matheson 2021, p. 34.

7 REPARATION

1 'Black Ballet Dancers Talk About Their Powerful Protest Photo Shoot', *TODAY*, https://www.youtube.com/watch?v=_fgI8ONfs-GQ&t=27s [accessed May 2024].

2 M. Shaw, 'Refacing the Robert E. Lee Monument in Richmond', https://www.readingthepictures.org/2020/06/refacing-robert-e-lee-monument, [accessed 25 August 2023]; and https://www.washingtonpost.com/local/no-longer-untouchable-statue-of-lee-becomes-focus-of-civic-outpouring-in-richmond/2020/06/15/acf6e16e-af11-11ea-856d-5054296735e5_story.html, [accessed June 2025].

3 Thessaly La Force, Zoe Lescaze, Nancy Hass, and M. H. Miller, 'The 25 Most Influential Works of American Protest Art Since World War II', *New York Times*, 15 October 2020, https://www.nytimes.com/2020/10/15/t-magazine/most-influential-protest-art.html.

4 Louis Brandeis, Opinion in *Whitney v. California*, 274 US 357 (1927), at p. 377.

5 Rae Langton, 'Blocking as Counter-Speech', in Daniel Fogal, Daniel W. Harris, and Matt Moss (eds), *New Work on Speech Acts* (Oxford: Oxford University Press, 2018), pp. 144–64, at p. 144.

6 Langton 2018, pp. 147–58.

7 J. L. Austin, *How to Do Things with Words* (Oxford: Oxford University Press, 1962) p. 16.

8 This is a rather rosy picture of communication and social interaction. For very real obstacles to such blocking and forced misfiring, see Langton 2018; Mary Kate McGowan, 'Oppressive Speech', *Australasian Journal of Philosophy*, 87 (2009), pp. 389–407; and Robert Mark Simpson, 'Un-Ringing the Bell: McGowan on Oppressive Speech and the Asymmetric Pliability of Conversations', *Australasian Journal of Philosophy*, 91/3 (2013), pp. 555–75.

9 https://www.tate.org.uk/art/artists/kara-walker-2674/art-remembering [accessed 13 August 2020].

10 For more on this thought, see T. Lai, 'Political Vandalism as Counter-Speech: A Defence of Defacing and Destroying Tainted Monuments', *European Journal of Philosophy*, 28 (2020), pp. 602–16, at p. 608.

11 M. Shaw, 'Refacing the Robert E. Lee Monument in Richmond'
(2020), https://www.readingthepictures.org/2020/06/refacing-rob-
ert-e-lee-monument [accessed 25 August 2023].

12 A. D'Souza, *Whitewalling: Art, Race & Protest in 3 Acts* (New York: Bad-
lands Unlimited, 2018), p. 20.

13 https://www.nytimes.com/2019/11/18/arts/design/gauguin-national-
gallery-london.html [accessed 26 October 2020].

14 Christopher Bartel, 'Ordinary monsters: ethical criticism and the lives
of artists', *Contemporary Aesthetics (Journal Archive)* 17/1 (2019), p. 18.
Bartel suggests that we admire the struggles of some immoral artists,
which enhances their art by making it more authentic. Whether we
admire Caravaggio though is not clear – we don't necessarily feel
sympathy for him. And yet it seems his illicit behaviour makes his art
even better – this view would amount to an 'immoralism' about the
immoral artist.

15 Some of these ideas have been taken from my article 'Artistic (counter) speech', *The Journal of Aesthetics and Art Criticism*, 80/4 (2022),
pp. 409–19.

16 https://www.smithsonianmag.com/smart-news/monumental-sculp-
ture-reimagines-the-last-supper-with-black-historical-figures-
180983756/ [accessed May 2024].

17 https://www.royalacademy.org.uk/article/video-the-first-supper [ac-
cessed May 2024].

18 https://www.latimes.com/entertainment/arts/miranda/la-ca-cam-
betye-saar-20160501-story.html [accessed March 2024].

19 https://www.okayafrica.com/african-women-artists-art-language-resis-
tance-smithsonian/ [accessed August 2025].

20 Lisa E. Farrington, 'Reinventing Herself: The Black Female Nude',
Woman's Art Journal, 24/2 (2003), pp. 15–23, at p. 16.

21 Chloë Colchester (ed.), *Clothing the Pacific* (New York: Berg Publishers,
2003), p. 193.

22 A. Marata Tamaira, 'From full dusk to full tusk: reimagining the
"Dusky Maiden" through the visual arts', *The Contemporary Pacific*
(2010), pp. 1–35.

23 Maura Reilly and Lucy R. Lippard, *Curatorial Activism: Towards an
Ethics of Curating* (London and New York: Thames & Hudson, 2018),
p. 17.

24 Reilly and Lippard 2018, p. 33.

25 E. H. Matthes, *Drawing the Line: What to Do with the Work of Immoral
Artists from Museums to the Movies* (Oxford: Oxford University Press,
2021), p. 109.

26 See for instance G. P. Pech and E. A. Caspar, 'Can a Video Game with a Fictional Minority Group Decrease Intergroup Biases towards Non-Fictional Minorities? A Social Neuroscience Study', *International Journal of Human–Computer Interaction*, 40/2 (2024), pp. 482–96, https://doi.org/10.1080/10447318.2022.2121052; C. Yildirim and D. F. Harrell, 'On the Plane: A Roleplaying Game for Simulating Ingroup-Outgroup Biases in Virtual Reality,' *IEEE International Conference on Artificial Intelligence and Virtual Reality (AIVR)*, California, 2022, pp. 207–9; and the MIT initiative on antiracism and games: https://idss.mit.edu/research/collaborations/icsr/icsr-project-teams/antiracism-games-and-immersive-media/ [accessed August 2025].

27 https://www.latimes.com/entertainment-arts/story/2020-06-09/anti-racist-video-game-treachery-in-breakdown-city [accessed July 2025].

28 This philosophical position is called 'ontological contextualism': 'an artwork's identity and contents are generated in part by relations it holds to aspects of the socio-historical setting in which it was created' from: Stephen Davies, *The Philosophy of Art* [2006] (Chichester: Wiley-Blackwell, 2016), p. 81. Arthur Danto argued for this position with his red canvas thought experiment.

29 I outline this concept in more detail in Dixon 2022, pp. 409–19.

30 From Diderot's critique of the Salon of 1765. This translated quote is taken from R. Loyalty Cru, *Diderot as a Disciple of English Thought* (New York: Columbia University Press, 1913), p. 418.

31 Toni Morrison, 'The Future of Time: Literature and Diminished Expectations', 25th Jefferson Lecture in the Humanities, John F. Kennedy Center for the Performing Arts, Washington, DC, 1996.

ACKNOWLEDGEMENTS

This book has been at least fifteen years in the making, ever since I discovered philosophy as a seventeen-year-old art student at sixth-form college. I therefore won't be able to do justice to all the brilliant people along the way who have made this book possible.

First, my deepest thanks to my editors at Faber & Faber and Viking Books – Walter Donohue, Alex Eccles, Phoebe Colley, and Terezia Cicel – for their passion and patience in transforming this work of analytic philosophy into an enjoyable read! I have learned so much from all of you.

Huge thanks to my agent, Georgina Capel, and her team for believing in me and in the book's premise. Endless thanks are due to my mentor and friend, Dan Jones, who discovered me in the depths of Twitter during the pandemic – if it weren't for you and your unwavering support, *Depraved* would never have happened.

I am indebted to the distinguished philosophers, artists, and teachers who have shaped my philosophical career in ways I am still discovering, and who opened up university as a possible pathway for me: Jenny Alexander, Emma Borg, Susanne Clausen, A. W. Eaton, Nat Hansen, Drew Hewett, Lauren Jones, Pil & Galia Kollectiv, Rae Langton, the late D. H. Mellor, Alun Rowlands, John Russell, and Alan Thomas.

depraved

I owe thanks to audiences at the London School of Economics, Prague Institute of Philosophy, Scottish Aesthetics Forum, London Aesthetics Forum, American Society for Aesthetics, British Society of Aesthetics, Open University, Queen's University Belfast, and Central European University for their insightful feedback on material that formed the basis of parts of *Depraved*. I also express my gratitude to the University of Cambridge and its School of Arts and Humanities Doctoral Award and Gunn Studentship, and particularly to Peterhouse for being my beautiful home for almost a decade. My thanks also to the Addenbrooke's Pain Clinic for their excellent treatment, which made writing a book physically possible. Thanks as well to my colleagues at Cardiff University, who always provide a friendly and inspiring working environment, and to Sophie Grace Chappell, Louise Hanson, Derek Matravers, Panos Paris, Vid Simoniti, and Heather Widdows, for reading *Depraved* drafts or examining earlier versions of the material.

On a more personal note, I owe so much to my brilliant friends who have kept me sane, loved, and supported: Ian Grant Armstrong, Rachel Bedder, Alix Beeston, Jan-Jonathan Bock, Emma Burchett, Alexandra Cracknell, Naomi Davies, Emma Greensmith, Anna Klieber, Lucy Osler, Alexa & Colin Richardson, Louise Richardson-Self, Claire Martin-Quirk, Mat Simpson, Shyane Siriwardena, Rachel & Roy Sunderland, Christina Thatcher, May Walker-Wallis, Hannah Rose Woods, and The Famous Five. Love always to Heather and the boys, Jenny and my beloved late Uncle Glen, Jess & Naomi, Tink, Lynne & Paul.

I am forever grateful to my wonderful brother, Will, and sister-in-law, Ermelinda, and of course the Bärchen – you always keep me laughing and feeling safe, no matter what happens. You are my rock.

Finally, to my mum and dad – the biggest champions anyone could ever wish for. You are my North, my South, my East, and my West: my best friends. You taught me to reach for the stars, and this book (and hopefully the next few) are testament to your resilience, wisdom, and boundless love.

PICTURE CREDITS

Section 1

1 *The 120 Days of Sodom*. Fine Art Images / Heritage Images via Getty Images
2 Portrait of the Marquis de Sade. The Trustees of the British Museum. All rights reserved
3 Venus of Hohle Fels figurine. Wikimedia Commons / Ramessos
4 Sculpture at the Temple of Khajuraho. Wikimedia Commons / Sankara Subramanian
5 *Red Flag, Artist Proof 4*, 1971, Judy Chicago. © 2024 Judy Chicago / Artists Rights Society (ARS), New York / DACS, London. Photo: Tate
6 Boeotian bell krater. RMN-Grand Palais / Hervé Lewandowski / RMN-GP / Dist. Foto SCALA, Florence
7 Mayhem. Øyvind Ihlen, courtesy of Mayhem
8 *Meat Joy* © 2026 Carolee Schneemann Foundation / DACS. Courtesy Lisson Gallery and P•P•O•W, New York

Section 2

1 *The Rape of Europa*. Wikimedia Commons / Isabella Stewart Gardner Museum
2 *The East Offering its Riches to Britannia*. Wikimedia Commons / British Library
3 *Painful Cake*. Makode Linde / © 2026 DACS
4 *Manaò tupapaú* (*Spirit of the Dead Watching*). Wikimedia Commons / A. Conger Goodyear Collection, 1965 / C1cada
5 *Schloss Neuschwanstein*. Wikimedia Commons / YitzhakNat
6 *Judith Beheading Holofernes*. Wikimedia Commons / Google Cultural Institute
7 *#3 Fight to Save Your Life* © 2026 Anyone Can Fly Foundation / DACS
8 Black Lives Matter protest: Kennedy George and Ava Holloway. Reuters / Julia Rendleman

INDEX